SQL Clearly Explained

Second Edition

Related Titles by Jan L. Harrington

Relational Database Design Clearly Explained, second edition

Object-Oriented C++ Data Structures for Real Programmers

Object-Oriented Database Design Clearly Explained

Ethernet Networking Clearly Explained

SQL Clearly Explained
Second Edition

Jan L. Harrington

Morgan Kaufmann Publishers
An Imprint of Elsevier Science

Amsterdam   London   New York   Oxford   Paris   Tokyo
Boston   San Diego   San Francisco   Singapore   Sydney

Senior Editor: Lothlórien Homet
Publishing Services Manager: Simon Crump
Senior Project Manager: Angela G. Dooley
Design, illustration, and composition: Black Gryphon Ltd.
Editorial Coordinator: Corina Derman
Cover Design: Hannus Design
Copyeditor: Adrienne Rebello
Proofreader: Phyllis Coyne et al.
Printer: Maple-Vail
Cover image: Creatas

Designations used by companies to distinguish their products are often claimed as trademarks or registered trademarks. In all instances in which Morgan Kaufmann Publishers is aware of a claim, the product names appear in initial capital or all capital letters. Readers, however, should contact the appropriate companies for more complete information regarding trademarks and registration.

Morgan Kaufmann Publishers
An imprint of Elsevier Science
340 Pine Street, Sixth Floor
San Francisco, CA 94104-3205
www.mkp.com

2007   2006   2005   2004   2003   5   4   3   2   1

Library of Congress Control Number: 2003101672
ISBN: 1-55860-876-1

This book is printed on acid-free paper.

Contents

Part 1: Getting Started

Chapter 7: Calculations and Grouping Queries 119

Chapter 8: Data Modification 147

Part 3: Managing Database Structure

Part 4: Program-Based Data Manipulation

Chapter 11: Users, Sessions, and Transaction Control 203

Chapter 12: Embedded SQL 217

Preface to the Second Edition

If you have had any contact with a relational database, then it is very likely that you have seen the letters "SQL." SQL (Structured Query Language) is a computer language designed to manipulate relational databases. You can use it to define a database's structure, to modify data, and to retrieve data.

This book has been written to give you an in-depth introduction to using SQL. You will learn not only SQL syntax, but also how SQL works. Understanding the "how" as well as the "what" will help you to create SQL statements that execute as quickly as possible. It provides a gentle but complete approach to learning SQL.

The elements of the SQL language covered in the first four parts of this book are based on those parts of the SQL standard that are available with current database software. Rather than frustrating you by giving you syntax from the standard that you cannot use because it is not supported by any current products, this book focuses on what is really out there. This means that you get practical, usable knowledge up front, rather than documentation of features that are not completely implemented.

Nonetheless, there have been some substantial enhancements to the SQL standard since the first edition of this book was published. Most of the enhancements haven't been implemented as yet, but to keep you up-to-date with what has been accepted for the SQL language, this edition does contain two chapters that focus on unimplemented, advanced features.

The Organization of This Book

If you look at the table of contents of this book, you might think that its organization is backwards: It starts by talking about data retrieval, follows with data modification, and then finally turns to managing database structure. There is actually a very good reason for this.

SQL presents someone trying to learn the language with a bit of a catch-22. You need to know how to retrieve data before you can modify it, because modifying data means finding the data you want to change. On the other hand, you need to be able to create a database and enter some data before you have some data on which you can perform retrievals. Like Yosarian trying to meet with Major Major, it does not seem that you can win!

The best alternative is to assume that someone else has created a sample database and loaded it with data for you. Then you can learn to query that database and carry those techniques over to modifying data. At that point, you'll have an understanding of SQL basics and will be ready to learn to create databases.

The CD and the Sample Database

New to this edition is a CD containing a full-featured SQL DMBS: MySQL. MySQL is an open source DBMS that runs runs under Windows and a variety of UNIX implementations, including Linux and Mac OS X. The first two chapters of the book contain enough information to get you up and running with the DBMS so you can follow along with the code in the book.

> *Note: If there is no MySQL distribution for your OS on the CD, visit www.mysql.com to see if a distribution is available.*

Although MySQL is available for many different OSs, the databases created by each OS aren't necessarily compatible. The sample database used throughout this book is therefore supplied as a set of text files. The first contains SQL commands for creating the database structure; the remainder load data. You can find details on how to use them in Chapter 2.

> *Note: You can use the sample database with other SQL DBMSs. However, you should examine the statements that create the database tables to be sure that they are compatible with what is available with your software.*

Acknowledgments

It takes a lot of help to put together a book, and I would like to thank the following people who were part of the team:

- Lothlórien Homet, Editor, who took over the project midstream and handled it with great expertise.
- Angela Dooley, the best production manager in the world. I love working with her.
- Adrienne Rebello, a terrific copy editor who I'm thrilled to have on our team again.
- Robert Standefer, industry consultant, the technical reviewer.

- Carole McClendon, my agent, who hooked me up with AP Professional/Morgan Kaufmann in the first place.

And above all, to my very active three-year-old son, Sean, who slept long enough for me to finish this book.

JLH

Part One

Getting Started

1

Installing and Running MySQL

MySQL is a open-source database management system (DBMS) that runs under Windows and many versions of UNIX. It can be distributed free under the General Public License (GPL), as long as the distributor makes the program's source code available along with the binary versions.

The CD accompanying this book contains a number of binary versions of MySQL (and the source code). At the time of this printing, the current stable release is 3.23. However, betas for 4.0.3 are also available, so you will find both 3.23 and 4.0.3 releases on the disc. The only new feature in the beta that is relevant to this book is support for the UNION operator.

> *Note: Many important new features, including foreign key support and nested subqueries, will appear in release 4.1, which was under development when this book went to press. Check*

http://www.mysql.com/downloads to find the most recent release.

MySQL is a combination of a database server and a command-line client. Once the server is running in the background (no associated window), you use the client software to type SQL commands and send them to the server. There are some third-party graphic user interfaces (GUIs) available as front ends to MySQL, but generally they are commercial products that must be purchased separately.

> *Note: The complete documentation for MySQL can be found at http://www.mysql.com/doc/en/index.html.*

The way in which you install MySQL depends on the operating system (OS) under which you will be running it. The remainder of this chapter looks at installation and software launching on three of the major platforms: Linux, Windows, and Mac OS X. For details on other platforms, consult the MySQL documentation.

> *Note: This chapter and Chapter 2 aren't intended to be a complete installation manual. However, they should give you enough information to get up and running and to install the sample database used in this book so you can follow along with the examples.*

Linux

The Linux distribution consists of a set of Red Hat Package Managers (RPMs), two of which will be of most interest as you are learning SQL:

- ◆ MySQL-VERSION.i386.rpm: This RPM contains the MySQL server. If you don't have access to a MySQL server somewhere on your network, then you will need to install the server.
- ◆ MySQL-client-VERSION.i386.rpm: This RPM contains the MySQL client. You will need this software on your

local machine to access the MySQL server, regardless of whether it is running on your local machine or on a machine somewhere else on your network.

Note: At least one user has reported problems with the MySQL distribution on the Red Hat Linux 7.3 disc. The distribution on the CD accompanying this book came from the MySQL.com site and doesn't exhibit the problems encountered by the Red Hat distribution.

Installing Under Linux

To create a minimal installation with both the server and client, get to a shell prompt and type

```
shell> rpm -i MySQL-VERSION.i386.rpm MySQL-client-VERSION.i386.rpm
```

If you need just the client, type

```
shell> rpm -i MySQL-client-VERSION.i386.rpm
```

The installation of the server should also launch the server. However, before you can work with MySQL, you need to initialize the GRANT tables and install the TEST database. To do so, run the following script:

```
shell> scripts/mysql_install_db
```

The script creates six tables (USER, DB, HOST, TABLES_PRIV, COLUMNS_PRIV, and FUNC) and gives the ROOT user rights to perform all administrative activities.

Note: Depending on your system configuration, you may need to be logged on as root to install/configure/launch MySQL.

Launching the Server Under Linux

If you have installed the server, the RPM software will have modified */etc/rc.d/* so that the server daemon starts automatically when you boot Linux. If for some reason you have removed the autostart commands, you can start the server manually with

```
shell> cd mysql_installation_directory
shell> bin/safe_mysqld --user=mysql &
```

Windows

The MySQL distribution for Windows contains several versions of the server. If you are using Windows 95, 98, or Me, use MYSQLD or MYSQLD-MAX. For Windows NT, 2000, or XP, use MYSQLD-MAX-NT.

> *Note: Windows NT 4.0 installations require at least service pack 3 to be compatible with MySQL.*

Installing a Windows Distribution

To install MySQL under any version of Windows, do the following:

1. Unzip the MySQL archive to a temporary folder.
2. Launch SETUP.EXE and proceed with the installation.

By default, the installer uses the C:\MYSQL directory to store the installed file. If you want to use an alternate directory, use the installer's BROWSE button to choose the directory you want. Note, however, that if you do use an alternate directory, you will need to create an option file (MY.INI, which should be stored in the Windows system directory) for MySQL to use when it launches. You can edit the file using the program WINMYSQLADMIN.

> *Note: For details on MySQL's ini files, see Section 2.1.2.2 of the online MySQL documentation.*

Starting the Server Under Windows

There is a fundamental difference between the way in which you run the MySQL server under the older versions of Windows (95, 98, or Me) and how you run it under Windows NT, 2000, or XP.

Starting the Server Under Windows 95, 98, or Me

The first time you start the MySQL server, you should start it from a DOS prompt so you can see if any error messages appear. The command to do so is

```
C:\mysql\bin> mysqld-max --standalone
```

After that, you can start the server with

```
C:\> C:\mysql\bin\mysqld-max
```

Starting the Server Under Windows NT, 2000, or XP

Typically, you will install and run MySQL as a service under newer versions of Windows. After installing the binaries, install the new service with

```
C:\mysql\bin> mysqld-max-nt --install
```

You can then start the server from the SERVER utility or with the following command from a DOS prompt:

```
NET START MySQL
```

Windows will shut down the server automatically when you shut down the computer.

Mac OS X

Because Mac OS X is a Macintosh GUI blended with BSD UNIX, installation and server startup are very similar to Linux. The archive is a zipped tar package. Therefore, you need to decompress it before installation. (Just double-click on the distribution file.)

Note: There are different versions of MySQL for Jaguar (version 2) and earlier versions of Mac OS X. Only the Jaguar version is on the CD.

Once you've completed the decompression, the installation process is as follows:

1. Create a new user named MYSQL USER with a short name of MYSQL. Assign any password you like.
2. Open a terminal window.
3. Change to the MySQL directory.

   ```
   cd /usr/local/mysql
   ```

4. Set the superuser password by typing

   ```
   su -v
   ```

   and entering the superuser password when asked.
5. Install the software and run the server for the first time with

   ```
   sudo ./scripts/mysql_install_db
   sudo chown -R mysql /usr/local/mysql/*
   sudo ./bin/safe_mysqld --user=mysql &
   ```

2

Creating and Loading Databases

A new installation of MySQL leaves you with a single database (TEST), stored in a single file by the same name. This database allows you access to the DBMS so that you can create new databases for your own use. In this chapter you will learn to create new databases and to use SQL stored in text files to create database structure (the tables) and to load that structure with data.

> Note: The irony of many SQL-based DBMSs is that you must
> be able to connect to a database to create a new database. There-
> fore, you have no choice but to install the sample database that
> accompanies the DBMS.

There are no software restrictions on the logical scope of the data that you can store in one database. However, in most cases you will want to use each physical file for a single logical database, or *schema*. For example, the sample database used in this book has been designed to handle the inventory and ordering operations of an on-line bookstore. The company's human resources database would almost certainly be stored in a separate file. This strategy has several advantages:

♦ The database files are smaller than they would be if multiple business functions were stored together in the same file. Smaller files are faster to back up and therefore increase the likelihood that regular backups will occur.

♦ The separation of business functions reduces exposure to security violations. If one database is compromised by unauthorized access, the data in the other remain untouched.

♦ Separate databases are less vulnerable to failure. If one database goes down, the company can continue to use the other.

♦ Separate databases are less logically complex, and are therefore easier to understand and maintain.

The bottom line is that generally you will want a separate database for each functional area within an organization.

Note: The concept of a schema as the overall logical plan of a database is discussed in Chapter 3.

Creating a New Database

To create a new database, you must first start the MySQL daemon and then log on to an existing database using the client software. At that point you can use SQL to create the new database.

Starting the MySQL Daemon

You must be running as the ROOT (or as an administrator) to start the MySQL daemon/server. For UNIX systems (include Mac OS X), it is more secure to use the SUDO command (superuser do) than to actually log on as ROOT. Therefore, you first want to set the superuser password. Type

```
sudo -v
```

The computer responds with the password prompt:

```
password:
```

Enter the password, press ENTER and you will have set the superuser password for about five minutes. (The exact period depends on your OS.)

> *Note: You can theoretically get away without the preceding step, but in my experimentations with this, the command that actually launches the MySQL daemon asks for the password but doesn't accept it.*

Then you can launch the MySQL daemon with

```
cd /usr/local/mysql
sudo ./bin/safe_mysqld --user=mysql &
```

Windows 95, 98, or Me users can start the server from an MS-DOS window with

```
C:\> C:\mysql\bin\mysqld
```

To start the server using Windows NT, 2000, or XP, you must first start the server service with

```
C:\mysql\bin> mysqld-max-nt --install
```

The service will be named MySQL. You can start it from the Services utility or manually with the command

```
NET START MySQL
```

Running the Client

When you run the client for the first time, you will connect to the sample database (TEST). Once you have created a database that you actually intend to use, you can connect to that alternative database directly.

To launch the client for the first time, type the following from a command prompt:

```
mysql -h host -u user -p password database
```

The command will typically look like

```
mysql --user=root test
```

As you can see, not all of the parameters are required:

◆ The -H parameter is followed by the name of the host computer on which the MySQL server is running. However, if you are running the client on the same machine as the server, then you can omit this parameter.
◆ The -U parameter is followed by the user name. After a default installation, you will need to log on as ROOT. Once logged on, you can create other users with fewer privileges that can be used regularly.
◆ The -P parameter indicates that a password will be supplied. Putting the actual password on the command line is optional. If you omit it, the MySQL client will respond with

```
Enter password:
```

and wait for the password.
◆ If you want to connect to a database other than MySQL's default database, include the name of the database on the command line. (See the section on creating a database for details on how to change databases if you are signed on already.)

When you have logged on successfully, the command line prompt will change to

```
mysql>
```

To exit the client, either type QUIT at the MYSQL> prompt or press CTRL-D.

Creating New Users

You need to maintain the ROOT user as a database administrator account that has all access to all databases. However, you generally don't want to use this account for daily processing. You will therefore want to create at least one new user.

To create a new user, first log on as the root:

```
mysql -user=root
```

Then, create a user that can "use" the database but has no specific access privileges:

```
GRANT USAGE ON *.* TO user_name@localhost IDENTIFIED BY 'password';
```

You will then need to grant the user access to elements within a specific database. (See Chapter 10 for details.)

Creating and Using the Database

Once you have logged on to the sample database, you can create a new database, generating a new directory in which the new database's files will be stored.

To create the bookstore database used for the examples throughout this book, type

```
create database bookstore;
```

MySQL creates the new directory as a subdirectory of the MySQL data directory.

> *Note: In UNIX implementations, including Mac OS X, database names are case sensitive. In Windows, they are not.*

To set the database with which you are working without leaving the client, type

```
USE bookstore;
```

Creating the Tables

A newly created database is empty. To do anything useful with it, you must create tables in which you will store data. The complete syntax for creating tables is covered in Chapter 9. However, you will need to have a functioning database to practice queries long before then. The CD accompanying this book therefore contains a text file (*creates.txt*) that contains all the commands you need.

There are two methods for using this file to install the tables you need:

- ◆ You can cut each command from the text file and paste it into a MySQL client. Press Enter after each command and it will run. Since there are so few tables, this is a quick and easy method.
- ◆ Use the MySQL batch processing facility, which reads commands from a text file and executes them.

To use the batch processing method:

1. Make sure that the MySQL server is running.
2. From the command line, type

```
mysql < batch-file
```

where BATCH-FILE is the path name of the file containing the commands to be executed.

At this point, you have created empty data table structures, and have populated the system tables that contain information about the data tables.

Populating the Tables

The data for the sample tables can be found in a set of text files, each of which contains a set of SQL INSERT commands (one for each row of data to be loaded). You can use either of the methods described in the preceding section to use these commands: either copy and paste them at the client's prompt or use them as batch files.

3

Introduction to SQL

SQL is a database manipulation language that has been implemented by virtually every relational database management system (DBMS) intended for multiple users, partly because it has been accepted by ANSI (the American National Standards Institute) and the ISO (International Standards Organization) as a standard query language for relational databases.

This chapter presents an overview of the environment in which SQL exists. The text begins with a bit of SQL history, so you will know where it came from and where it is heading. Next, you will be introduced to the database that is used for sample queries throughout this book, along with an overview of relational database terminology. Finally, you will read about the way in which SQL commands are processed and the software environments in which they function.

A Bit of SQL History

SQL was developed by IBM at its San Jose Research Laboratory in the early 1970s. Presented at an ACM conference in 1974, the language was originally named SEQUEL (Structured English Query Language) and pronounced "sequel." The language's name was later shortened to SQL.

> *Note: Today, people pronounce SQL as either "sequel" or "es-que-el." I use "sequel" because I have been in this business so long that when I first learned SQL, there was no other pronunciation. That is why you will see "a SQL" ("a sequel") rather than "an SQL" ("an es-que-el") throughout this book. Old habits die hard! However, many people do prefer the acronym.*

Although IBM authored SQL, the first SQL implementation was provided by Oracle Corporation (then called Relational Software, Inc.). Early commercial implementations were concentrated on midsized UNIX-based DBMSs, such as Oracle, Ingres, and Informix. IBM followed in 1981 with SQL/DS, the forerunner to DB/2, which debuted in 1983.

ANSI published the first SQL standard (SQL-86) in 1986. An international version of the standard issued by ISO appeared in 1987. A significant update to SQL-86 was released in 1989 (SQL-89). Virtually all relational DBMSs that you encounter today support at least some level of the 1989 standard.

In 1992, the standard was revised again (SQL-92), adding more capabilities to the language. Because SQL-92 is a superset of SQL-89, older database application programs ran under the new standard with minimal modifications. In fact, until October 1996, DBMS vendors could submit their products to NIST (National Institute for Standards and Technology) for verification of SQL standard compliance. This testing and certification process provided significant motivation for DBMS vendors to adhere to the SQL standard. Although discontinuing standard compliance testing will save the vendors money, it is too soon to tell if it will also result in a divergence from this level of the standard.

The SQL-92 standard has been superseded by SQL:1999, which is once again a superset of the preceding standard. The primary new features of SQL:1999 support the object-relational data model. Users can create user-defined data types, including classes, and use those types as column domains. SQL:1999 also supports *typed tables*, tables in which each row of the table represents a single object of a specific type. In other words, the table's structure is defined by a class and the table itself is a repository for objects created from that class.

The language also adds extensions to SQL to allow methods/functions/procedures to be written in SQL or to be written in another programming language such as C++ or Java and then invoked from within a SQL statement. As a result, SQL becomes less "relational," a trend decried by some relational purists.

> *Note: SQL:1999 has also been called SQL-99 and SQL3. The latter was the working title of the standard before its adoption. The correct name of the standard is SQL:1999.*

> *Note: Regardless of where you come down on the relational theory argument, you will need to live with the fact that the major commercial DBMSs, such as Oracle and DB2, have provided support of classes as domains for several years now. The object-relational data model is a fact of life, although there certainly is no rule that says that you must use those features should you choose not to do so.*

Even the full SQL:1999 standard does not turn SQL into a complete, stand-alone programming language. In particular, SQL lacks I/O statements. This makes perfect sense, since SQL should be implementation and operating system independent. However, the full SQL:1999 standard does include operations such as selection and iteration that make it *computationally complete*.

Conformance Levels

This book is based on SQL:1999, the most recent version of the SQL standard. However, keep in mind that SQL:1999 is simply a standard, not a mandate. Various DBMSs exhibit different levels of conformance to the standard.

For previous standards (SQL-92 and earlier) conformance was measured by how many SQL features were supported by a DBMS. Each feature was ranked on the basis of the conformance level at which it needed to be implemented:

♦ Intermediate SQL-92 conformance: The feature is required for full conformance, but not for intermediate level conformance.
♦ Entry SQL-92 conformance: The feature is required for intermediate level conformance, but not for entry level conformance.
♦ SQL-89: The feature is required for SQL-92 entry level conformance, but not for SQL-89 conformance.
♦ SQL-86: The feature is required for SQL-86 conformance.
♦ Nonconformance: The feature does not appear in any SQL standard, but is commonly implemented.

At the time this book was written, most DBMSs were generally entry level SQL-92 compliant. Many also supported some of the features required for intermediate level conformance. However, no DBMS was in full conformance with the SQL-92 standard.

Given that the purpose of this book is to explain SQL that you can use, the main body of the book does not attempt to document every SQL:1999 feature but instead focuses on those that are actually available for use. Nonetheless, you can find coverage of the major unimplemented features that were introduced in the SQL-92 standard in Chapter 14.

SQL:1999 defines two levels of conformance: core and full. At the time this book was written, there were no DBMSs that were even core compliant with the SQL:1999 standard. In particular, Core SQL:1999 requires support for SQL embedded in a number of high-level programming languages, including Pascal and PL/1, languages which are seldom used today for business programming. By the same token, the full standard includes provisions for inheritance and polymorphism. The two major object-relational DBMSs—Oracle and DB2—do not support either. Because many of the new features of SQL:1999 have not been implemented fully, they are covered in Chapter 15.

> *Note: It's somewhat ironic that Oracle, which provides significant support for classes as well as extending SQL into a complete programming language, fails to support parts of the SQL-92 standard. For example, Oracle still does not support the new* JOIN *operator.*

Throughout this book you will see notes that indicate whether a SQL feature is part of the Core SQL:1999 standard; you may also find indications of when it entered the standard and how it rates in the SQL-92 standard. A complete listing of Core SQL:1999 features can be found in Appendix D.

Relational Database Terminology and the Sample Database

You don't need to know a great deal about designing relational databases to work with SQL. However, you do need to be familiar with the terminology used to describe the components of a relational database. This section therefore introduces you to basic relational concepts and then focuses on the sample database used for examples in this book to show you how the terminology is applied. You will learn about the features of a relational database throughout this book as we discuss the aspects of SQL that manipulate them.

> *Note: If you are familiar with relational database concepts, you may wish to glance at the design of the example database and then skip to the next major section of this chapter.*

Basic Relational Database Concepts

A relational database is a collection of two-dimensional tables (*relations*) made up of columns (*attributes*) and rows (*tuples*). The design of the tables is stored in a *data dictionary*, a set of tables (often known as *system tables*) that contain descriptive information about the database.

Although a table in a relational database looks a lot like a range on a spreadsheet or simple data file, it has some very specific characteristics that set it apart:

♦ A table can contain zero, one, or more rows of data. Strictly speaking, a relation is only the definition of the structure of a table (the columns it contains). When you include rows of data, you have an *instance* of the relation.

♦ In any single data row, each column contains only one value. More formally, we say that there are no multivalued attributes.

♦ The data placed in a column are taken from the column's *domain*, an expression of the permissible values for the column. In most cases, a column's domain corresponds to the data type you specify when you create a table. A DBMS validates this *constraint* (or rule) whenever data are modified.

♦ A relation has a *primary key*, one or more columns whose values uniquely identify each row. When there is no single column in which values don't duplicate, you can combine two or more columns into a *concatenated primary key* to create a unique identifier.

♦ Because primary keys must be unique, their values cannot be *null*, a database value meaning "unknown." A relational DBMS should validate that primary keys are unique and nonnull.

The relationships between tables in a relational database are expressed by including matching columns in two or more tables. When a table contains a column or combination of columns that is the same as the primary key of another table, then a logical relationship exists between the two tables. The table containing the matching column is said to contain a *foreign key*. Every foreign key that has a value (in other words, is not null) must match an existing primary key value. This is known as *referential integrity* and is another of the constraints that you expect a DBMS to enforce for you.

Base Tables, Virtual Tables, and Views

The tables that are physically stored in a database are known as *base tables*. They are permanent parts of the database. In contrast, when someone issues a data retrieval request, the DBMS creates a table containing the result of the query in main memory. Because this type of table exists only in main memory and not in the database it is known as a *virtual table*. Virtual query tables are temporary, and in most cases are destroyed each time a user issues another data retrieval request.

A relational database may also contain *views*. A view is stored in the data dictionary as a named query expression. When a user includes the name of a view in a data manipulation statement, the DBMS executes the query and creates a virtual table containing the query's result in main memory. This view table can then be queried just like a table whose rows are stored in the database. You will read a great deal more about views in Chapter 10.

The Online Bookstore Database

The examples in this book are drawn from a portion of a database that supports an online (web-based) bookstore. Throughout the book, a table is expressed using the following notation:

```
table_name (primary key, column, column, …)
```

A table begins with its name. It is followed by its columns, which are surrounded by parentheses. The primary key column or columns come first and are underlined. The online bookstore database contains the following seven tables:

```
Customers (customer_numb, customer_first_name,
    customer_last_name,customer_street, customer_city,
    customer_city, customer_state, customer_zip, customer_phone,
    customer_email)
Books (isbn, author_name, title, publisher_name, publication_year,
    binding, sosource_numb, retail_price)
Authors (author_name)
Publishers (publisher_name)
Sources (source_numb, source_name, source_street, source_city,
    source_state, source_zip, source_phone)
Orders (order_numb, customer_numb, order_date, credit_card_numb,
    card_exp_date, order_filled)
Order_lines (order_numb, isbn, quantity, cost_each, cost_line,
    shipped)
```

A number of characteristics of these relations are typical of relational databases:

- ◆ It is often difficult to find a primary key for entities such as people whose identifiers are names, because names duplicate. Although you might try concatenating a name with an address or phone number, the resulting primary key is long and unwieldy. More important, it can create data consistency problems when values in that primary key change. We therefore usually assign arbitrary unique identifiers such as customer numbers to entities that don't have practical primary keys. In the bookstore database, the CUSTOMER, SOURCE, and ORDERS tables have primary keys of this type.
- ◆ The BOOKS table has a practical, built-in primary key, a book's ISBN (International Standard Book Number). The ISBN is unique throughout the world and will never change.
- ◆ The ORDER_LINES table has a concatenated primary key. Its purpose is to indicate which books appear on which specific order.
- ◆ The AUTHORS and PUBLISHERS tables are reference tables that will be used to verify that author and publisher names are always entered consistently in the BOOKS relation. The AUTHOR_NAME and PUBLISHER_NAME columns in the BOOKS relation are foreign keys that reference the primary keys of the AUTHOR and PUBLISHER relations, respec-

tively. Whenever a row is modified in the BOOKS relation, a DBMS verifies that the values in the AUTHOR_NAME and PUBLISHER_NAME columns match values in the relations where they are primary keys.

♦ The BOOKS relation contains one additional foreign key (SOURCE_NUMB, which references the primary key of the SOURCE table). This relates a book to the source from which it can be ordered.

♦ The ORDERS relation contains one foreign key, the CUSTOMER_NUMB. This relates an order to the customer.

♦ The ORDER_LINES table contains two foreign keys (ISBN and ORDER_NUMB). These relate an order line to both an order and a book.

The relationships between the tables in the online bookstore database are diagrammed in Figure 3-1. Each icon with a P in it —

represents a primary key; each icon with an F in it—

represents a foreign key. The lines between the foreign keys and primary keys indicate where the primary key–foreign key relationships occur.

Keep in mind, however, that this is only a visual representation of data relationships. Inside the database, there is nothing like the "lines" that you see connecting the tables. The relationships are indicated merely by the presence of matching data between the tables. In fact, one of the major principles of the relational data model is that there are no data structures other than the two-dimensional tables (the relations).

Note: The data with which the sample database has been loaded can be found in Appendix A.

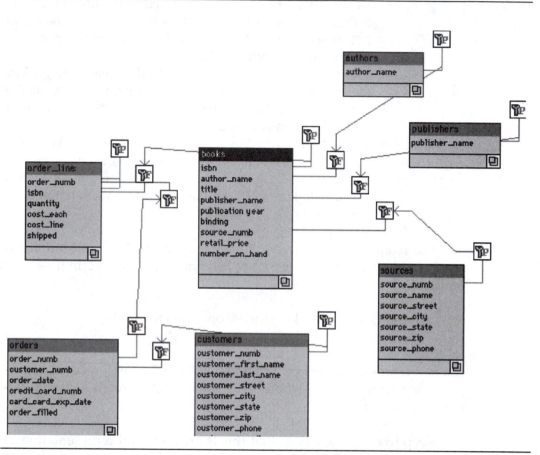

Figure 3-1: The tables in the online bookstore database

Manipulating Relations

The manipulation of relations within a relational database has its basis in mathematical set theory. To obtain a portion or a relation or to combine two relations, you use operations from the *relational algebra*. At its lowest level, a DBMS uses sequences of these operations to perform database queries. We therefore say that relational algebra is *procedural*, because it constitutes a step-by-step procedure for obtaining data.

SQL, however, is *nonprocedural*. When you develop a SQL query, you specify *what* you want from the database, but not *how* the DBMS should do its work. SQL is therefore based on the *relational calculus*, allowing you to request multiple relational algebra operations in a single statement.

> *Note: Although you have been reading about an algebra and a calculus, rest assured that you will not need to perform any mathematics when working with a relational database. The underlying math is hidden by the DBMS.*

When you send a SQL query to a DBMS, a *query optimizer* examines the query and determines the most efficient way to retrieve the requested data. Query optimization is a complex topic and in most cases application programmers and end users don't worry about it. However, there are often several ways to write a SQL query that will produce the same results; some syntaxes will perform better than others. If you know something about relational algebra as well as the general distribution of data in your database, you can make some intelligent guesses about what the query optimizer will do and therefore make a determination as to which syntax is more efficient.

For the most part, SQL syntax doesn't reflect the underlying relational algebra used to process a query. However, there are a few relational algebra operations that are actually part of SQL (in particular, UNION and JOIN). You will therefore learn about relational algebra throughout this book. Knowing how a query is likely to be processed can help you create more efficient SQL queries.

SQL Environments

There are two general ways in which you can issue a SQL command to a database:

- ◆ Interactive SQL, in which a user types a single command and sends it immediately to the database. The result of an interactive query is a table in main memory (a *virtual table*). In mainframe environments, each user has one result table at a time, which is replaced each time a new retrieval query is executed; PC environments often allow several. Result tables may not be legal relations—because of nulls they may have no primary key—but that is not a problem because they are not part of the database but exist only in main memory.

♦ Embedded SQL, in which SQL statements are placed in an application program. Embedded SQL may be *static*, in which case the entire command is specified at the time the program is written. Alternatively, it may be *dynamic*, in which case the program builds the statement using user input and then submits it to the database.

The basic syntaxes of interactive SQL and static embedded SQL are very similar. We will therefore spend the first portion of this book looking at interactive syntax and then turn to adapting and extending that syntax for embedding it in a program. Once you understand static embedded SQL syntax, you will be ready to look at preparing dynamic SQL statements for execution.

Interactive SQL Command Processors

At the most general level, we can describe working with an interactive SQL command processor in the following way:

♦ Type the SQL command.
♦ Send the command to the database and wait for the result.

Exactly how it works is very implementation dependent. As an example, let's look at two extremes: a mainframe and a desktop PC.

SQL on a Mainframe

If you are working with IBM's DB/2 or SQL/DS on a mainframe, then you will probably use QMF (Query Management Facility) to perform interactive SQL commands. As you can see in Figure 3-2,

QMF presents a blank screen for typing a command. You can use the keyboard's arrow keys for navigating around the screen, but your mouse and keys such as Page Up and Page Down are useless. Commands can be issued using function keys—the mappings are at the bottom of the screen—or you can type commands directly at the COMMAND==> prompt.

```
SQL QUERY                                                     LINE    1

SELECT *
FROM CAB_




*** END ***


1=Help        2=Run        3=End        4=Print    5=Chart    6=Draw
7=Backward    8=Forward    9=Form       10=Insert  11=Delete  12=Report
OK, cursor positioned.
COMMAND ===>                                            SCROLL ===> PAGE
```

Figure 3-2: A SQL query using IBM's QMF

QMF waits until the user presses F2 to execute the query. The query then goes to the DBMS, which returns data to QMF. The result table appears on the report screen (for example, Figure 3-3). Notice that there are no scroll bars; scrolling up and down, left and right, is performed with function keys.

SQL on a PC

There is a wide variety of desktop interactive SQL command processors. PowerBuilder, a database application development tool that communicates with many different DBMSs, provides a simple interface. As you can see in Figure 3-4, PowerBuilder's Database Administration painter provides a text editor for entering a SQL statement. Because this is a graphic user interface (GUI) environment, all of the standard text editing tools (for example, cut/copy/paste and scrolling) are available. The only requirement is that you end the statement with a semicolon.

```
REPORT                                          LINE 1     POS 1      79


    CABNUM   MAKE            MODEL          YEAR   PURDATE   LICNUM   CONDITN
    ------   -------         --------       ----   -------   ------   --------
    002      Checker         4-DOOR SEDAN   73     03/15/84  345 YAO  NEW ENGINE
    006      Checker         4-door sedan   72     07/18/72  997 IUP  Needs new
    045      Ford            LTD            89     07/12/89  867 POP  Excellent;
    104      Checker         4-door sedan   63     05/15/67  365 QLT  Needs new
    105      Checker         4-door sedan   63     05/15/67  111 ABC  Excellent
    108      Ford            LTD            89     07/12/89  760 PLP  Excellent;
    144      Ford            LTD            88     12/06/88  290 AAQ  Needs majo
    215      Ford            LTD            88     12/06/88  776 IKL  Excellent;
    238      Ford            LTD            89     12/12/89  980 JAM  Excellent
    378      Checker         4-door sedan   68     02/02/68  771 TOW  Should be
    404      Checker         4-door sedan   68     02/02/68  206 TTL  Excellent

*** END ***
1=Help         2=             3=End        4=Print        5=Chart      6=Query
7=Backward     8=Forward      9=Form      10=Left        11=Right     12=
OK, this is the REPORT from your RUN command.
COMMAND ===> _                                           SCROLL ===> PAGE
```

Figure 3-3: The result of a SQL query using IBM's QMF

Note: Whether you need a semicolon at the end of a SQL statement is implementation dependent. Check your product documentation to be sure.

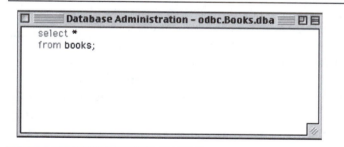

Figure 3-4: A SQL query in PowerBuilder's Database Administration painter

To execute a SQL command, you click the Run button. The result, a portion of which can be seen in Figure 3-5, appears in an independent window that can be moved, scrolled, printed, and so on. As you can see, the major difference between the two environments is the user interface of the interactive SQL command processor. Because most PC DBMSs work within a GUI, they support multiple windows, allowing you to have multiple queries, each with its own result table, at one time. In the mainframe environment, however, users typically are limited to only one result table.

Isbn	Author Name	
0-123-1233-0	Dumas, Alexandre	Three Musketeers, The
0-124-5544-X	Dumas, Alexandre	Titans, The
0-126-3367-2	Dumas, Alexandre	Count of Monte Cristo, The
0-125-3344-1	Dumas, Alexandre	Black Tulip, The
0-127-3948-2	Dumas, Alexandre	Corsican Brothers, The
0-128-4321-1	Clavell, James	Tai-Pan
0-129-9876-5	Clavell, James	Shogun
0-128-3939-X	Clavell, James	Noble House
0-128-3939-2	Clavell, James	Gai-Jin
0-129-4567-1	McCaffrey, Anne	Dragonsong
0-129-4912-0	McCaffrey, Anne	Dragonsinger
0-130-2939-4	McCaffrey, Anne	White Dragon, The
0-130-2943-2	McCaffrey, Anne	Dragonflight

Figure 3-5: The result of a SQL query using PowerBuilder's Database Administration painter

The Embedded SQL Dilemma

Embedding SQL in a general-purpose programming language presents an interesting challenge. The host languages (for example, COBOL, Ada, C, PL/1) have compilers that don't recognize SQL. The solution is to provide SQL support through an application library that can be linked to a program. Program source code is passed through a precompiler that changes SQL into calls to library routines. The modified source code will then be acceptable to a host language compiler.

Some of today's database application development tools have languages that recognize SQL without resorting to a precompiler. PowerBuilder's PowerScript language, for example, recognizes SQL syntax. As mentioned earlier, the only special requirement is that SQL statements end with a semicolon.

Part Two

Performing Interactive Data Manipulation

4

Simple SQL Retrieval

It may seem a bit backwards to talk about retrieval before creating a database or entering data, but much of SQL's data modification syntax relies on finding data to be changed. You will therefore find it easier to work with modification statements if you are first familiar with retrieving data. We are therefore going to assume that someone else has created a database and loaded it with data for our use.

SQL has one command for retrieving data: SELECT. This is nowhere as restrictive as it might seem. SELECT contains syntax for choosing columns, choosing rows, combining tables, grouping data, and performing some simple calculations. In fact, a single SELECT statement can result in a DBMS performing any or all of the relational algebra operations.

The basic syntax of the SELECT statement has the following general structure:

```
SELECT column1, column2, …
FROM
table1, table2, …
WHERE selection_criteria
```

The SELECT clause specifies the columns you want to see. You specify the tables used in the query in the FROM clause. The optional WHERE clause can contain a wide variety of criteria that identify which rows you want to retrieve.

> *Note: Most SQL command processors are not case sensitive when it comes to parts of a SQL statement. SQL keywords, table names, column names, and so on can be in any case you choose. However, most DBMSs are case sensitive when it comes to matching data values. Therefore whenever you place a value in quotes for SQL to match, you must match the case of the stored data. In this book, SQL keywords will appear in uppercase letters; database components such as columns and table names will appear in lowercase letters.*

In addition to these basic clauses, SELECT has many other syntax options. Rather than attempt to summarize them all in a single general statement, you will learn to build the parts of a SELECT gradually throughout the first few chapters of this book.

Choosing Columns

One of the characteristics of a relation is that you can view any of the columns in any order you choose. SQL therefore lets you specify the columns you want to see and the order in which you want to see them.

Retrieving All Columns

To retrieve all the columns in a table, viewing the columns in the order in which they were defined when the table was created, you can use an asterisk (*) rather than listing each column. For example, to see all the distributors from which the online bookstore orders its books, you would use

```
SELECT *
FROM sources
```

Because this query is requesting all rows in the table, there is no WHERE clause. As you can see in Figure 4-1, the result table labels each column with its name.

source _numb	source _name	source_street	source_city	source _state	source _zip	source _phone
1	Ingram	123 West 99th	Philadelphia	PA	19112	555-555-1111
2	Baker and Taylor	99 256th Ave.	Minneapolis	MN	68112	555-551-2222
3	Jostens	19594 Highway 28	Seattle	WA	98333	555-552-3333
4	Brodart	1944 Bayview Blvd.	Los Angeles	CA	96111	555-553-4444

Figure 4-1: Viewing all columns in a table

Note: The layout of the printed output of many SQL queries has been adjusted so that it will fit across the width of the pages of this book. When you actually view listings on the screen, each row will be in a single horizontal line. If a listing is too wide to fit on the screen, you will need to scroll it.

Using the * operator to view all columns is a convenient shorthand for interactive SQL when you want a quick overview of data. However, it can be troublesome when used in embedded SQL if the columns in the table are changed. In particular, if a column is added to the table and the application is not modified to handle the new column, then the application may not work properly.

Retrieving Selected Columns

In most SQL queries, you will want to specify exactly which column or columns you want retrieved. To specify columns, you list them following SELECT in the order in which you want to see them. For example, a query to view the phone numbers and names of the online bookstore's sources is written

```
SELECT source_phone, source_name
FROM sources
```

The result (see Figure 4-2) shows all rows in the table for just the two columns specified in the query. The order of the columns in the result table matches the order in which the columns appeared after the SELECT keyword.

source_phone	source_name
555-555-1111	Ingram
551-555-2222	Baker and Taylor
552-555-3333	Jostens
553-555-4444	Brodart

Figure 4-2: Choosing specific columns

Removing Duplicates

Unique primary keys ensure that relations have no duplicate rows. However, when you view only a portion of the columns in a table, you may end up with duplicates. For example, executing the following query produces the result in Figure 4-3:

```
SELECT customer_numb, credit_card_numb
FROM orders;
```

Duplicates appear because the same customer uses the same credit card number for more than one order. Keep in mind that although this table with duplicate rows is not a legal relation, that doesn't present a problem for the database because it is not stored in the database. To remove duplicates from a result table, you insert the keyword DISTINCT following SELECT:

customer_numb	credit_card_numb
1	123 123 123 123
1	123 123 123 123
2	234 234 234 234
2	234 234 234 234
2	234 234 234 234
3	345 345 345 345
3	345 345 345 345
4	456 456 456 456
4	456 456 456 456
5	567 567 567 567
6	678 678 678 678
6	678 678 678 678
6	678 678 678 678
7	789 789 789 789
7	789 789 789 789
8	890 890 890 890
8	890 890 890 890
8	890 890 890 890
9	901 901 901 901
10	1000 1000 1000
10	1000 1000 1000
11	1100 1100 1100
11	1100 1100 1100
11	1100 1100 1100
12	1200 1200 1200

Figure 4-3: A result table with duplicate rows

```
SELECT DISTINCT customer_numb, credit_card_numb
FROM orders;
```

The result is a table without the duplicate rows (see Figure 4-4). Although a legal relation has no duplicate rows, most DBMS vendors have implemented SQL so that it leaves the duplicates. The primary reason is performance. To remove duplicates, a DBMS must sort the result table by every column in the table. It must then scan the table from top to bottom, looking at every "next" row to identify duplicate rows that are next to one another. If a result table is large, the sorting and scanning can significantly slow down the query. It is therefore up to the user to decide whether to request unique rows.

customer_numb	credit_card_numb
1	123 123 123 123
2	234 234 234 234
3	345 345 345 345
4	456 456 456 456
5	567 567 567 567
6	678 678 678 678
7	789 789 789 789
8	890 890 890 890
9	901 901 901 901
10	1000 1000 1000
11	1100 1100 1100
11	1100 1100 1100
12	1200 1200 1200

Figure 4-4: The result table with duplicate rows removed

The Relational Algebra Project Operation

When you choose columns from a table, you are asking the DBMS to perform a relational algebra project operation. Project extracts all rows from specified columns in a table. Because the DBMS does not need to evaluate any of the data in the table, project is a very fast operation.

There is one issue with project with which you need to be concerned. A DBMS will project any columns that you request. It makes no judgment as to whether the selected columns produce a meaningful result. For example, consider the following query:

```
SELECT order_numb, cost_line
FROM order_lines
```

A portion of the result can be found in Figure 4-5. Why is this table meaningless? Because it implies an association between an order number and a price, something that is not really the case. In fact, the relationship is between a book and a price, both of which happen to be part of an order. It is therefore up to you to determine which combinations of columns are meaningful.

```
order_numb   cost_line

1            23.95
1            19.95
1            15.95
4            27.95
3            23.95
3            23.95
3            39.90
3            19.95
2            39.95
2            24.95
8            15.95
8            17.95
8            21.95
8            24.95
8            22.95
7            23.95
7            109.75
7            124.75
6            21.95
6            31.90
6            21.95
6            23.95
6            21.95
5            21.95
5            18.95
5            27.95
```

Figure 4-5: A meaningless projection

Ordering the Result Table

Unless you specify otherwise, the rows in a result table appear in the order in which they are physically stored in the table. If you want to change that order, you add an ORDER BY clause to your SE-LECT statement.

> *Note: In most cases, new rows are added to the bottom of a table and the default display order of the table is the order in which the rows were entered. However, in very large, active, old databases, this may not be true. If the DBMS has run out of unique internal row identifiers for a table, it will reuse those for rows*

that have been deleted, causing new rows to be inserted at seemingly random places throughout the table.

For example, if you issue the query

```
SELECT *
FROM publishers
```

you will see the unordered listing in Figure 4-6. Adding the ORDER BY clause sorts the results in alphabetical order (see Figure 4-7):

```
SELECT *
FROM publishers
ORDER BY publisher_name
```

The keywords ORDER BY are followed by the column or columns on which you want to sort the result table. When you include more than one column, the first column represents the outer sort, the next column a sort within it. For example, assume you issue the query

```
SELECT customer_last_name, customer_zip
FROM customers
ORDER BY customer_last_name, customer_zip
```

The result (see Figure 4-8) first orders by the customer's last name and then sorts by zip code within each last name. If we reverse the order of the columns on which the output is to be sorted, as in

```
SELECT customer_last_name, customer_zip
FROM customers
ORDER BY customer_zip, customer_last_name
```

the output (see Figure 4-9) then sorts first by zip code and then alphabetically by customer within each zip code.

Choosing Rows

As well as viewing any columns from a relation, you can also view any rows you want. We specify row selection criteria in a SELECT statement's WHERE clause.

```
publisher_name

Grosset & Dunlap
World Pub. Co.
Harper
Platt & Munk
P. F. Collier & Son
Methuen
Atheneum
Delacorte
Knopf
Ballantine Books
James R. Osgood and Co.
American Publishing Co.
Scribner
J. W. Lovell Co.
University of Nebraska Press
Dodd, Mead
Clarendon Press
D. Appleton & Co.
Hart Publishing Co.
St. Martin's Press
Columbia University Press
Random House
E. R. Burroughs, Inc.
Tandem
New English Library
Gregg Press
R. Marek Publishers
Dial Press
Putnam
Franklin Library
Deutsch
Anchor Press
Doubleday
Macmillan
Overlook Press
Warner Books
```

Figure 4-6: An unordered output table

In its simplest form, a WHERE clause contains a logical expression against which each row in a table is evaluated. If a row meets the criteria in the expression, then it becomes a part of the result table. If the row does not meet the criteria, then it is omitted. The trick to writing row selection criteria is therefore knowing how to create logical expressions against which data can be evaluated.

```
publisher_name

American Publishing Co.
Anchor Press
Atheneum
Ballantine Books
Clarendon Press
Columbia University Press
D. Appleton & Co.
Delacorte
Deutsch
Dial Press
Dodd, Mead
Doubleday
E. R. Burroughs, Inc.
Franklin Library
Gregg Press
Grosset & Dunlap
Harper
Hart Publishing Co.
J. W. Lovell Co.
James R. Osgood and Co.
Knopf
Macmillan
Methuen
New English Library
Overlook Press
P. F. Collier & Son
Platt & Munk
Putnam
R. Marek Publishers
Random House
Scribner
St. Martin's Press
Tandem
University of Nebraska Press
Warner Books
```

Figure 4-7: The result table from Figure 4-6 sorted in alphabetical order

Predicates

A logical expression that follows WHERE is known as a *predicate*. It uses a variety of operators to represent row selection criteria. If a row meets the criteria in a predicate (in other words, the criteria evaluate as true), then the row is included in the result table. If the

```
customer_last_name  customer_zip

Collins              23456
Collins              45678
Hayes                23456
Hayes                23458
Johnson              12345
Johnson              23456
Jones                01011
Jones                12344
Smith                01011
Smith                01011
Smith                12345
Smith                45678
```

Figure 4-8: Sorting output by two columns

```
customer_last_name  customer_zip

Jones                01011
Smith                01011
Smith                01011
Jones                12344
Johnson              12345
Smith                12345
Collins              23456
Hayes                23456
Johnson              23456
Hayes                23458
Collins              45678
Smith                45678
```

Figure 4-9: Reversing the sort order in a query

row doesn't meet the criteria (the criteria evaluate as false), then the row is excluded.

Relationship Operators

In Table 4-1 you can see the six operators used to express data relationships. To write an expression using one of the operators, you surround it with two values. In database queries, such expressions have either a column name on one side and a literal value on the other, as in

```
cost > 1.95
```

Operator	Meaning	Examples
=	Equal to	cost = 1.95 numb_in_stock = reorder_point
<	Less than	cost < 1.95 numb_in_stock < reorder_point
<=	Less than or equal to	cost <= 1.95 numb_in_stock <= reorder_point
>	Greater than	cost > 1.95 numb_in_stock > reorder_point
>=	Greater than or equal to	cost >= 1.95 numb_in_stock >= reorder_point
!= or <>[a]	Not equal to	cost != 1.95 numb_in_stock != reorder point

Table 4-1: The relationship operators

a. Check the documentation that accompanies your DBMS to determine whether the not equal to operator is != or <>.

or column names on both sides:

```
numb_on_hand <= reorder_point
```

The first expression asks the question "Is the cost of the item greater than 50?" The second asks "Is the number of items in stock less than or equal to the reorder point?" The way in which you enter literal values into a logical expression depends on the data type of the column to which you are comparing the value:

- ◆ Numbers: Type numbers without any formatting. In other words, leave out dollar signs, commas, and so on. You should, however, put decimal points in the appropriate place in a number with a fractional portion.
- ◆ Characters: Type characters surrounded by quotation marks. Most DBMSs accept pairs of either single or double quotes. If your characters include an apostrophe (a

single quote), then you should use double quotes. Otherwise, use single quotes.

♦ Dates: Type dates in the format used to store them in the database. This will vary from one DBMS to another.

♦ Times: Type times in the format used to store them in the database. This will vary from one DBMS to another.

When you are using two column names, keep in mind that the predicate is applied to each row in the table individually. The DBMS substitutes the values stored in the columns in the same row when making its evaluation of the criteria. You can therefore use two column names when you need to examine data that are stored in the same row but in different columns. However, you cannot use a simple logical expression to compare the same column in two or more rows.

The DBMS also bases the way it evaluates data on the type of data:

♦ Comparisons involving numeric data are based on numerical order.

♦ Comparisons involving character data are based on alphabetical order.

♦ Comparisons involving dates and times are based on chronological order.

Logical Operators

Sometimes a simple logical expression is not enough to identify the rows you want to retrieve; you need more than one criterion. In that case, you can chain criteria together with logical operators. For example, assume that you want to retrieve items that you sell that cost more than $50 each and have a stock level less than the reorder point. The predicate you need is therefore made up of two simple expressions:

```
cost > 50
numb_in_stock < reorder_point
```

A row must meet both of these criteria to be included in the result table. You therefore connect the two expressions with the logical operator AND into a single complex expression:

```
cost > 50 AND numb_in_stock < reorder_point
```

Whenever you connect two simple expressions with AND, a row must meet *all* of the conditions to be included in the result.

You can use the AND operator to create a predicate that includes a range of dates. For example, if you want to find all orders that were placed between 10/10/2004 and 10/10/2005, the predicate would be written

```
order_date >= 10/10/04 AND order_date <= 10/10/05
```

To be within the interval, an order date must meet *both* individual criteria.

> *Important note: The precise format for dates in SQL queries varies considerably from one DBMS to another. For example, the DBMS that accompanies this book, MySQL, defaults to the format YYYY-MM-DD for input, but also accepts numbers (no quotes, no delimiters) or strings with slashes (/) or periods as delimiters. You should consult the documentation that accompanies your DBMS to determine the acceptable date format. Also pay close attention to the way in which it handles dates beginning in the year 2000 and beyond.*

You will find a summary of the action of the AND operator in Table 4-2. The labels in the columns and rows represent the result of evaluating the simple expressions on either side of the AND. As you can see, the only way to get a true result for the entire expression is for both simple expressions to be true.

If you want to create an expression from which a row needs to meet only one condition, then you connect simple expressions with the logical operator OR. For example, if you want to retrieve merchandise items that cost more than $100 or less than $10, you would use the predicate

AND	True	False
True	True	False
False	False	False

Table 4-2: AND **truth table**

```
cost > 100 OR cost < 10
```

Whenever you connect two simple expressions with OR, a row needs to meet only one of the conditions to be included in the result of the query. When you want to create a predicate that looks for dates outside an interval, you use the OR operator. For example, to find all orders that were placed prior to 10/10/2004 or after 10/10/2005, the predicate is written

```
order_date < 10/10/04 OR order_date > 10/10/05
```

You can find a summary of the OR operator in Table 4-3. Notice that the only way to get a false result is for both simple expressions surrounding OR to be false.

OR	True	False
True	True	True
False	True	False

Table 4-3: OR **truth table**

There is no limit to the number of simple expressions you can connect with AND and OR. For example, the following expression is legal

```
binding = 'leather' AND cost < 150 AND numb_in_stock < reorder_point
```

Negation

The logical operator NOT (or !) inverts the result of a logical expression. If a row meets the criteria in a predicate, then placing NOT in front of the criteria *excludes* the row from the result. By the same token, if a row does not meet the criteria in a predicate, then placing

NOT in front of the expression *includes* the row in the result. For example, the expression

```
NOT (cost <= 50)
```

retrieves all rows where the cost is not less than or equal to $50 (in other words, greater than $50). First the DBMS evaluates the value in the cost column against the expression COST <= 50. If the row meets the criteria, then the DBMS does nothing. If the row does not meet the criteria, it includes the row in the result.

The parentheses in the preceding example group the expression to which NOT is to be applied. In the following example, the NOT operator applies only to the expression COST <= 50

```
NOT (cost <= 50) AND numb_in_stock <= reorder_point
```

NOT can be a bit tricky when it is applied to complex expressions. As an example, consider this expression

```
NOT (cost <= 50 AND numb_in_stock <= reorder_point)
```

Rows that have both a cost of less than or equal to $50 and a stock level less than or equal to their reorder point will meet the criteria within parentheses. However, the NOT operator excludes them from the result. Those rows that have either a cost of more than $50 or a stock level greater than their reorder point will fail the criteria within parentheses, but will be included in the result by the NOT. This means that the expression is actually the same as

```
cost > 50 OR numb_in_stock > reorder_point
```

or

```
NOT (cost <= 50) OR NOT (numb_in_stock <= reorder_point)
```

Precedence and Parentheses

When you create an expression with more than one logical operator, the DBMS must decide on the order in which it will process the simple expressions. Unless you tell it otherwise, a DBMS uses a set of default *rules of precedence*. In general, a DBMS evaluates simple expressions first, followed by the logical operators. When there is more than one operator of the same type, evaluation proceeds from left to right.

As a first example, consider this expression:

```
cost < 50 OR binding = 'pbk' AND numb_in_stock <= reorder_point
```

If the cost of a book is $25, its binding is leather, there are 45 in stock, and the reorder point is 30, the DBMS will exclude the row from the result. The first simple expression is true; the second is false. An OR between the two produces a true result because at least one of the criteria is true. Then the DBMS performs an AND between the true result of the first portion and the result of the third simple expression (false). Because we are combining a true result and a false result with AND, the overall result is false. The row is therefore excluded from the result.

We can change the order in which the DBMS evaluates the logical operators and, coincidentally, the result of the expression, by using parentheses to group the expressions that are to have higher precedence:

```
cost < 50 OR (binding = 'pbk' AND numb_in_stock <= reorder_point)
```

A DBMS gives highest precedence to the parts of the expression within parentheses. In this case, the expression within parentheses is false (both simple expressions are false). However, the OR with the first simple expression produces true, because the first simple expression is true. Therefore, the row is included in the result.

Special Operators

SQL predicates can include a number of special operators that make writing logical criteria easier. These include BETWEEN, LIKE, IN, and IS NULL.

> *Note: There are additional operators that are used primarily with subqueries, SELECT statements in which you embed one*

complete SELECT within another. You will be introduced to
them in Chapter 5.

BETWEEN

The BETWEEN operator simplifies writing predicates that look for values that lie within an interval. Remember the example you saw earlier in this chapter using AND to generate a date interval? Using the BETWEEN operator, you could rewrite that predicate as

```
order_date BETWEEN 10/10/04 AND 10/10/05
```

Any row with an order date of 10/10/04 through 10/10/05 will be included in the result.

If you negate the BETWEEN operator, the DBMS returns all rows that are outside the interval. For example,

```
order_date NOT BETWEEN 10/10/04 AND 10/10/05
```

retrieves all rows with dates *prior* to 10/10/04 and *after* 10/10/05. It does not include the 10/10/04 or 10/10/05. NOT BETWEEN is therefore a shorthand for the two simple expressions linked by OR that you saw earlier in this chapter.

LIKE

The LIKE operator provides a measure of character string pattern matching by allowing you to use placeholders (wildcards) for one or more characters. Although you may find that the wildcards are different in your particular DBMS, in most cases, % stands for zero, one, or more characters and _ stands for zero or one character.

The way in which the LIKE operator works is summarized in Table 4-4. As you can see, you can combine the two wildcards to produce a variety of begins with, ends with, and contains expressions. As with BETWEEN, you can negate the LIKE operator:

```
last_name NOT LIKE 'Sm%'
```

Expression	Meaning
LIKE 'Sm%'	Begins with Sm
LIKE '%ith'	Ends with ith
LIKE '%ith%'	Contains ith
LIKE 'Sm_'	Begins with Sm and is followed by at most one character
LIKE '_ith'	Ends with ith and is preceded by at most one character
LIKE '_ith_'	Contains ith and begins and ends with at most one additional character
LIKE '%ith_'	Contains ith, begins with any number of characters, and ends with at most one additional character
LIKE '_ith%'	Contains ith, begins with at most one additional character, and ends with any number of characters

Table 4-4: Using LIKE

Rows that are like the pattern are therefore excluded from the result.

One of the problems you may run into when using LIKE is that you need to include the wildcard characters as part of your data. For example, what can you do if you want to search for rows that contain 'nd_by'? The expression you want is

```
column_name LIKE '%nd_by%'
```

The problem is that the DBMS will see the _ as a wildcard, rather than as a character in your search string. The solution was introduced in the SQL-92 standard, providing you with the ability to designate an *escape character*.

An escape character removes the special meaning of the character that follows. Because many programming languages use \ as the escape character, it is a logical choice for pattern matching, although it can be any character that is not part of your data. To establish the escape character, you add the keyword ESCAPE, followed by the escape character, to your expression:

```
column_name LIKE '%nd\_by%' ESCAPE '\'
```

Notice that the escape character has also been placed in front of the _ within the search string. A query using this expression will now interpret the _ as a part of the string rather than as a placeholder for a single character.

IN

The IN operator compares the value in a column against a set of values. It returns true if the value is within the set. For example, assume that you are checking the price of an item and want to know if it is either $18.95, $19.95, or $20.95. Using the IN operator, the expression would be written:

```
retail_price IN (18.95, 19.95, 20.95)
```

This is shorthand for

```
retail_price = 18.95 OR retail_price = 19.95 OR retail_price = 20.95
```

Therefore, any row whose price is one of those three values will be included in the result. Conversely, if you write the predicate

```
retail_price NOT IN (18.95, 19.95, 20.95)
```

the DBMS will return the rows with prices other than those in the set of values. The preceding expression is therefore the same as

```
retail_price != 18.95 AND retail_price != 19.95
AND retail_price != 20.95
```

or

```
NOT (retail_price = 18.95 OR retail_price = 19.95
OR retail_price = 20.95)
```

> *Note: The most common use of IN and NOT IN is with a subquery, where the set of values to which data are compared are generated by an embedded SELECT. You will learn about this in Chapter 5.*

IS NULL

Null is a specific database value. Although columns that contain nulls appear empty when you view them, the database actually stores a value that represents null so that an unknown value can be distinguished from, for example, a string value containing a blank. As a user, however, you will rarely know exactly what a DBMS is using internally for null. This means that you need some special way to identify null in a predicate so you can retrieve rows containing nulls. That is where the IS NULL operator comes in.

For example, an expression to identify all rows where the telephone number is null is written as

```
customer_phone IS NULL
```

Conversely, to identify all rows that contain a telephone number, you would use

```
customer_phone IS NOT NULL
```

> *Note: You will find more information about the impact of nulls on database queries in the last section of this chapter.*

Performing Row Selection Queries

To perform SQL queries that select specific rows, you place a predicate after the SQL keyword WHERE. Depending on the nature of the predicate, the intention of the query may be to retrieve one or more rows. In this section you will therefore see some SELECT examples that combine a variety of row selection criteria. You will also see how those criteria are combined in queries with column selection and with sorting of the output.

Using a Primary Key Expression to Retrieve One Row

A common type of SQL retrieval query uses a primary key expression in its predicate to retrieve exactly one row. For example, if

someone at the online bookstore wants to see the name and telephone number of customer number 6, then the query is written

```
SELECT customer_first_name, customer_last_name, customer_phone
FROM customers
WHERE customer_numb = 6
```

The result is the single row requested by the predicate

```
customer_last_name      customer_first_name  customer_phone
Johnson                 Peter                555-555-3456
```

If a table has a concatenated primary key, such as the online bookstore's ORDER_LINES table, then a primary key expression needs to
include a complex predicate in which each column of the primary
key appears in its own simple logical expression. For example, if
you wanted to find out how many copies of a book with an ISBN of
0-127-3948-2 appear on order number 8, you would use the following query:

```
select quantity
from order_lines
where order_numb = 8 and isbn = '0-127-3948-2'
```

In this case, the result is simply

```
quantity
1
```

> Note: The ISBN is surrounded by quotes because it is stored as
> characters. ISBNs include hyphens and letters and therefore
> don't constitute legal numbers.

Retrieving Multiple Rows

Although queries with primary key expressions are written with
the intention of retrieving only one row, more commonly SQL queries are designed to retrieve multiple rows.

Using Simple Predicates

When you want to retrieve data based on a value in a single column, you construct a predicate that includes just a simple logical

expression. For example, to see all the books ordered on order number 8, someone at the online bookstore would use

```
select isbn
from order_lines
where order_numb = 8
```

The output (see Figure 4-10) displays a single column for rows
where the order number is 8.

order_numb	isbn
8	0-180-4712-X
8	0-131-4912-X
8	0-130-2939-4
8	0-127-3948-2
8	0-133-5935-2
8	0-161-0123-9
8	0-167-1945-1
8	0-190-3967-5

**Figure 4-10: Retrieving selected columns from multiple rows using a simple
predicate**

Using Complex Predicates

When you want to see rows that meet two or more simple conditions, you use a complex predicate in which the simple conditions
are connected by AND or OR. For example, if someone wanted to see
all the orders that included more than one copy of a book priced less
than $20, the query would be written

```
SELECT order_numb, isbn, quantity, cost_each
FROM orders
WHERE quantity > 1 AND cost_each < 20
```

As you can see in Figure 4-11, five rows in the ORDERS table meet
these criteria.

By the same token, if you wanted to see all the orders placed prior
to 2/1/2005 that have not been filled, the query would be written

```
SELECT order_numb, customer_numb, order_date
FROM orders
WHERE order_date < '2005-2-1' AND order_filled = 'N'
```

order_numb	isbn	quantity	cost_each
3	0-180-4712-X	2	19.95
2	0-159-3845-3	2	19.95
6	0-132-3949-2	2	15.95
16	0-132-9876-4	2	19.95
22	0-130-2943-2	2	15.95

Figure 4-11: Retrieving selected columns from multiple rows using a complex predicate

It produces the result in Figure 4-12.

order_numb	customer_numb	order_date
9	4	1/6/05
15	7	1/9/05

Figure 4-12: Retrieving rows using a complex predicate including a date

> *Note: Don't forget that the date format required by your DBMS may be different from the one used in examples in this book.*

Alternatively, if you needed information about all orders that were placed prior to 10/1/2004 and have *not* been filled as well as orders that were placed after 10/1/2004 and *have* been filled, you would write the query

```
SELECT order_numb, customer_numb, order_date
FROM orders
WHERE (order_date < '2004-10-1' AND order_filled = 'N') OR
    (order_date >= '2004-10-1' AND order_filled = 'Y')
```

Notice that although the AND operator has precedence over OR and therefore parentheses are not strictly necessary, the predicate in this query includes parentheses for clarity. Extra parentheses are never a problem—as long as you balance every opening parenthesis with a closing parenthesis—and you should feel free to use them whenever they help make it easier to understand the meaning of a complex predicate. The result of this query can be found in Figure 4-13.

order_numb	customer_numb	order_date
1	1	12/5/04
3	2	11/12/04
7	3	12/2/04
8	4	11/22/04
14	7	12/13/04
16	8	10/12/04
20	10	11/15/04
25	12	10/10/04

Figure 4-13: Using a complex predicate that includes multiple logical operators

Using Between and Not Between

As an example of using one of the special predicate operators, consider a query where someone wants to see all orders placed between 10/1/2004 and 1/1/2005. The query would be written

```
SELECT order_numb, customer_numb, order_date
FROM orders
WHERE order_date BETWEEN '2004-10-1' AND '2005-1-1'
```

It produces the output in Figure 4-14.

order_numb	customer_numb	order_date
1	1	12/5/04
3	2	11/12/04
7	3	12/2/04
8	4	11/22/04
14	7	12/13/04
16	8	10/12/04
20	10	11/15/04
25	12	10/10/04

Figure 4-14: Using BETWEEN to retrieve rows in a date range

The inverse query to retrieve all orders not placed between 10/1/2004 and 1/1/2005 is written

```
SELECT order_numb, customer_numb, order_date
FROM orders
WHERE order_date NOT BETWEEN '2004-10-1' AND '2005-1-1'
```

and produces the output in Figure 4-15.

```
order_numb    customer_num    order_date
2             1               2005-07-06
4             2               2005-03-18
5             2               2005-07-06
6             3               2004-08-15
9             4               2005-01-06
10            5               2005-03-12
11            6               2004-09-19
12            6               2005-03-12
13            6               2005-07-21
15            7               2005-01-09
17            8               2005-02-22
18            8               2005-05-13
19            9               2004-07-15
```

Figure 4-15: Using NOT BETWEEN to retrieve rows outside a date range

If we want output that is easier to read, we might ask the DBMS to sort the result table by date,

```
SELECT order_numb, customer_numb, order_date
FROM orders
WHERE order_date NOT BETWEEN '2004-10-1' AND '2005-1-1'
ORDER BY order_date
```

producing the result in Figure 4-16.

```
order_numb    customer_numb    order_date
19            9                7/15/99
6             3                8/15/99
11            6                9/19/99
22            11               9/19/99
9             4                1/6/00
15            7                1/9/00
23            11               2/21/00
17            8                2/22/00
21            10               3/4/00
10            5                3/12/00
12            6                3/12/00
4             2                3/18/00
18            8                5/13/00
```

Figure 4-16: Sorted output by date

The Relational Algebra Restrict Operation

Row selection criteria ask a DBMS to perform a relational algebra restrict operation, which creates a horizontal subset of a table by comparing rows to logical criteria. The most important thing to keep in mind about restrict is that it cannot be used to specify columns. Therefore, a query that asks for specific columns and specific rows requires a restrict and a project.

> *Note: The restrict operation is more commonly known as select. However, because that word is the same as SQL's retrieval command, it is easy to confuse the two. Therefore, many database people have substituted the word restrict for the relational algebra operation to alleviate the confusion.*

Assume that you have a query such as

```
SELECT customer_first_name, customer_last_name
FROM customers
WHERE customer_zip = '01234'
```

Which will the DBMS perform first, the restrict or the project? Although it is often hard to tell, in this case we can be sure that the restrict will occur first. Why? Because the project removes the column needed for the restrict and doing the project first would therefore make the restrict impossible.

In general, a DBMS tries to speed up query operations by cutting down on the amount of data it must manipulate. A query optimizer therefore usually performs the most "discriminatory" operation first. Used in this way, "discriminatory" refers to being able to discriminate, or distinguish between, parts of a table. Therefore, a discriminatory operation is one that retrieves only a small portion of the data. As you have just seen in the preceding example, however, there are cases in which the DBMS must perform one operation before another because doing them in any other order would make completing the query impossible, regardless of performance considerations.

Nulls and Retrieval: Three-Valued Logic

The predicates you have seen to this point omit one important thing: the presence of nulls. What should a DBMS do when it encounters a row that contains null rather than a value? For example, assume that you have an employee table with a column for salary. Some of the rows have no value in the salary column. What should a DBMS do with those rows when you issue the following query?

```
SELECT emp_name
WHERE salary > 75000
FROM employees
```

If the salary column contains null, then the DBMS is not able to decide whether the predicate in the WHERE clause is true or false. The answer is "maybe." This means that as far as database queries are concerned, logical expressions really have three possible results, rather than just two—true, false, and maybe. A DBMS therefore works with *three-valued logic*.

Most DBMSs will exclude rows with null in the salary column from the result of the preceding query. That seems pretty straightforward. But what happens when you have a complex logical expression of which one portion returns a maybe? The operation of AND, OR, and NOT must be expanded to take into account that they may be operating on a maybe.

The three-valued logical table for AND can be found in Table 4-5. Notice that something important hasn't changed: The only way to get a true result is for both simple expressions linked by AND to be true. Given that most DBMSs exclude rows where the predicate evaluates to maybe, the presence of nulls in the data will not change what an end user sees.

The same is true when you look at the three-valued truth table for OR (see Table 4-6). As long as one simple expression is true, it does not matter whether the second returns true, false, or maybe. The result will always be true.

AND	True	False	Maybe
True	True	False	Maybe
False	False	False	False
Maybe	Maybe	False	Maybe

Table 4-5: Three-valued AND truth table

OR	True	False	Maybe
True	True	True	True
False	True	False	Maybe
Maybe	True	Maybe	Maybe

Table 4-6: Three-valued OR truth table

If you negate an expression that returns maybe, the NOT operator has no effect. In other words, NOT (MAYBE) is still maybe.

To see the rows that return maybe, you need to add an expression to your query that uses the IS NULL operator. For example, to include rows with null for the salary in a query on the employees table used as an example earlier in this section, the query would be

```
SELECT emp_name, salary
FROM employees
WHERE salary > 75000 OR salary IS NULL
```

Note that we need to display the salary column to determine which rows actually have values for salary and which are null.

> Conformance note: All of the syntax you have seen in this chapter is required for conformance to the SQL-86 standard. It should therefore be available on virtually any DBMS that supports SQL. In addition, it is all part of the Core SQL:1999 syntax.

5

Retrieving Data from More Than One Table: Joins

As you read in Chapter 3, logical relationships between entities in a relational database are represented by matching primary and foreign key values. Given that there are no permanent connections between tables stored in the database, a DBMS must provide some way for users to match primary and foreign key values when needed. This capability is provided by the relational algebra join operation, which combines two tables based on a specified relationship between data they contain.

In this chapter you will first learn about how joins work. Then you will be introduced to the syntax for including a join in a SQL query. Throughout this chapter you will read about the impact joins have on database performance. At the end you will see how subqueries (SELECTs within SELECTs) can be used to avoid joins, and in some cases, significantly decrease the time it takes for a DBMS to complete a query.

The Relational Algebra Join Operation

The relational algebra join creates one result table from two source tables by pasting a row from one source table onto the end of a row from the other source table. A DBMS uses a relationship between data in the two source tables to determine which rows should be combined.

A Non-Database Example

To help you understand how a join works, we will begin with an example that has absolutely nothing to do with relations. Assume that you have been given the task of creating manufacturing part assemblies by connecting two individual parts. The parts are classified as either A parts or B parts.

There are many types of A parts (A1 through An, where n is the total number of types of A parts) and many types of B parts (B1 through Bn). Each B is to be matched to the A part with the same number; conversely, an A part is to be matched to a B part with the same number.

The assembly process requires four bins. One contains the A parts, one contains the B parts, and one will hold the completed assemblies. The remaining bin will hold parts that cannot be matched. (The unmatched parts bin is not strictly necessary; it is simply for your convenience.)

You begin by extracting a part from the B bin. You look at the part to determine the A part to which it should be connected. Then, you search the A bin for the correct part. If you can find a matching A part, you connect the two pieces and toss them into the completed assemblies bin. If you cannot find a matching A part, then you toss the unmatched B part into the bin that holds unmatched B parts. You repeat this process until the B bin is empty. Any unmatched A parts will be left in their original location.

> *Note: You could just as easily have started with the bin containing the A parts. The contents of the bin holding the completed assemblies will be the same.*

As you might guess, the A parts and B parts are analogous to tables with primary and foreign key relationships. This matching of part numbers is very much like the matching of data that occurs when you perform a join. The completed assemblies bin corresponds to the result table of the operation. As you read about the operation of a join, keep in mind that parts that could not be matched were left out of the completed assemblies bin.

Equi-Joins

In its most common form, a join forms new rows when data in the two source tables match. Because we are looking for rows with equal values, this type of join is known as an *equi-join* (or a *natural equi-join*). As an example, consider the two tables in Figure 5-1.

Notice that the ID_NUMB column is the primary key of the CUSTOMERS table and that the same column is a foreign key in the ORDERS table. The ID_NUMB column in ORDERS therefore serves to relate orders to the customers to which they belong.

Assume that you want to see the names of the customers who placed each order. To do so, you must join the two tables, creating combined rows wherever there is a matching ID_NUMB. In database terminology, we are joining the two tables *over* ID_NUMB. The result table can be found in Figure 5-2.

An equi-join can begin with either source table. (The result should be the same regardless of the direction in which the join is performed.) The join compares each row in one source table with the rows in the second. For each row in the first source table that matches data in the second source table in the column or columns over which the join is being performed, a new row is placed in the result table.

```
Customers

id_numb      first_name      last_name

001          Jane            Doe
002          John            Doe
003          Jane            Smith
004          John            Smith
005          Jane            Jones
006          John            Jones


Orders

order_numb   id_numb         order_date      order_total

001          002             10/10/04            250.65
002          002             2/21/05             125.89
003          003             11/15/04           1567.99
004          004             11/22/04            180.92
005          004             12/15/04            565.00
006          006             10/8/04              25.00
007          006             11/12/04             85.00
008          006             12/29/04            109.12
```

Figure 5-1: Two tables with a primary key–foreign key relationship

```
Result_table

id_numb   first_name   last_name   order_numb   order_date   order_total

002       John         Doe         001          10/10/04        250.65
002       John         Doe         002          2/21/05         125.89
003       Jane         Smith       003          11/15/04       1597.99
004       John         Smith       004          11/22/04        180.92
004       John         Smith       005          12/15/04        565.00
006       John         Jones       006          10/8/04          25.00
006       John         Jones       007          11/12/04         85.00
006       John         Jones       008          12/29/04        109.12
```

Figure 5-2: The joined table

Assuming that we are using the CUSTOMERS table as the first source table, producing the result table in Figure 5-2 might therefore proceed conceptually as follows:

1. Search ORDERS for rows with ID_NUMB of 001. Because there are no matching rows in ORDERS, do not place a row in the result table.

2. Search ORDERS for rows with ID_NUMB of 002. There are two matching rows in ORDERS. Create two new rows in the result table, placing the same customer information at the end of each row in ORDERS.

3. Search ORDERS for rows with ID_NUMB of 003. There is one matching row in ORDERS. Place one new row in the result table.

4. Search ORDERS for rows with ID_NUMB of 004. There are two matching rows in ORDERS. Place two rows in the result table.

5. Search ORDERS for rows with ID_NUMB of 005. There are no matching rows in ORDERS. Therefore do not place a row in the result table.

6. Search ORDERS for rows with ID_NUMB of 006. There are three matching rows in ORDERS. Place three rows in the result table.

Notice that if an ID number does not appear in both tables, then no row is placed in the result table. This behavior categorizes this type of join as an *inner join*. (Yes, there is such a thing as an *outer join*. You will read about it later in this chapter.)

What's Really Going On: Product and Restrict

From a relational algebra point of view, a join can be implemented using two other operations: product and restrict. As you will see, this sequence of operations requires the manipulation of a great deal of data and, if implemented by a DBMS, can result in slow query performance. Nonetheless, it underlies the SQL-89 join syntax.

The product operation (the mathematical Cartesian product) makes every possible pairing of rows from two source tables. In Figure 5-3, for example, the product of the CUSTOMERS and ORDERS tables produces a result table with 48 rows (the 6 customers times the 8 orders). The ID_NUMB column appears twice because it is a part of both source tables.

> *Note: Although 48 rows may not seem like a lot, consider the size of a product table created from tables with 100 and 1000 rows! The manipulation of a table of this size can tie up a lot of disk I/O and CPU time.*

```
Product_table
```

id_numb (Customers)	first_name	last_name	id_numb (Orders)	order_numb	order_date	order_total
001	Jane	Doe	002	001	10/10/04	250.65
001	Jane	Doe	002	002	2/21/05	125.89
001	Jane	Doe	003	003	11/15/04	1597.99
001	Jane	Doe	004	004	11/22/04	180.92
001	Jane	Doe	004	005	12/15/04	565.00
001	Jane	Doe	006	006	10/8/04	25.00
001	Jane	Doe	006	007	11/12/04	85.00
001	Jane	Doe	006	008	12/29/04	109.12
002	John	Doe	002	001	10/10/04	250.65
002	John	Doe	002	002	2/21/05	125.89
002	John	Doe	003	003	11/15/04	1597.99
002	John	Doe	004	004	11/22/04	180.92
002	John	Doe	004	005	12/15/04	565.00
002	John	Doe	006	006	10/8/04	25.00
002	John	Doe	006	007	11/12/04	85.00
002	John	Doe	006	008	12/29/04	109.12
003	Jane	Smith	002	001	10/10/04	250.65
003	Jane	Smith	002	002	2/21/05	125.89
003	Jane	Smith	003	003	11/15/04	1597.99
003	Jane	Smith	004	004	11/22/04	180.92
003	Jane	Smith	004	005	12/15/04	565.00
003	Jane	Smith	006	006	10/8/04	25.00
003	Jane	Smith	006	007	11/12/04	85.00
003	Jane	Smith	006	008	12/29/04	109.12
004	John	Smith	002	001	10/10/04	250.65
004	John	Smith	002	002	2/21/05	125.89
004	John	Smith	003	003	11/15/04	1597.99
004	John	Smith	004	004	11/22/04	180.92
004	John	Smith	004	005	12/15/04	565.00
004	John	Smith	006	006	10/8/04	25.00
004	John	Smith	006	006	10/8/04	25.00
004	John	Smith	006	008	12/29/04	109.12
006	John	Jones	002	001	10/10/04	250.65
006	John	Jones	002	002	2/21/05	125.89
006	John	Jones	003	003	11/15/04	1597.99
006	John	Jones	004	004	11/22/04	180.92
006	John	Jones	004	005	12/15/04	565.00
006	John	Jones	006	006	10/8/04	25.00
006	John	Jones	006	006	10/8/04	25.00
006	John	Jones	006	008	12/29/04	109.12

Figure 5-3: The product of the Customers and Orders tables

In some rows, the `ID_NUMB` is the same. These are the rows that would have been included in a join. We can therefore apply a restrict predicate to the product table to end up with the same table provided by the join you saw earlier. The predicate can be written:

```
customers.id_numb = orders.id_numb
```

The rows that are selected by this predicate appear in black in Figure 5-4; those eliminated by the predicate are in gray. Notice that the black rows are exactly the same as those in the result table of the join (Figure 5-2).

It is important that you keep in mind the implication of this sequence of two relational algebra operations when you are writing SQL joins. If you are using the traditional SQL syntax for a join and forget the predicate for the restrict portion, you will end up with a product. The product table contains bad information; it implies facts that are not actually stored in the database. It is therefore potentially harmful, in that a user who does not understand how the result table came to be might assume that it is correct and make business decisions based on the bad data.

SQL Syntax for Inner Joins

There are two types of syntax you can use for requesting the join of two tables. The first, which we have been calling the "traditional" join syntax, is the only way to write a join in the SQL standards through SQL-89. SQL-92 added some join syntax that is both more flexible and easier to use.

Traditional SQL Joins

The traditional SQL join syntax is based on the combination of the product and restrict operations about which you just read. It has the following general form:

```
SELECT columns
FROM table1, table2
WHERE table1.primary_key = table2.foreign_key
```

Joined_table

id_numb (Customers)	first_name	last_name	id_numb (Orders)	order_numb	order_date	order_total
001	Jane	Doe	002	001	10/10/04	250.65
001	Jane	Doe	002	002	2/21/05	125.89
001	Jane	Doe	003	003	11/15/04	1597.99
001	Jane	Doe	004	004	11/22/04	180.92
001	Jane	Doe	004	005	12/15/04	565.00
001	Jane	Doe	006	006	10/8/04	25.00
001	Jane	Doe	006	007	11/12/04	85.00
001	Jane	Doe	006	008	12/29/04	109.12
002	**John**	**Doe**	**002**	**001**	**10/10/04**	**250.65**
002	**John**	**Doe**	**002**	**002**	**2/21/05**	**125.89**
002	John	Doe	003	003	11/15/04	1597.99
002	John	Doe	004	004	11/22/04	180.92
002	John	Doe	004	005	12/15/04	565.00
002	John	Doe	006	006	10/8/04	25.00
002	John	Doe	006	007	11/12/04	85.00
002	John	Doe	006	008	12/29/04	109.12
003	Jane	Smith	002	001	10/10/04	250.65
003	Jane	Smith	002	002	2/21/05	125.89
003	**Jane**	**Smith**	**003**	**003**	**11/15/04**	**1597.99**
003	Jane	Smith	004	004	11/22/04	180.92
003	Jane	Smith	004	005	12/15/04	565.00
003	Jane	Smith	006	006	10/8/04	25.00
003	Jane	Smith	006	007	11/12/04	85.00
003	Jane	Smith	006	008	12/29/04	109.12
004	John	Smith	002	001	10/10/04	250.65
004	John	Smith	002	002	2/21/05	125.89
004	John	Smith	003	003	11/15/04	1597.99
004	**John**	**Smith**	**004**	**004**	**11/22/04**	**180.92**
004	**John**	**Smith**	**004**	**005**	**12/15/04**	**565.00**
004	John	Smith	006	006	10/8/04	25.00
004	John	Smith	006	006	10/8/04	25.00
004	John	Smith	006	008	12/29/04	109.12
006	John	Jones	002	001	10/10/04	250.65
006	John	Jones	002	002	2/21/05	125.89
006	John	Jones	003	003	11/15/04	1597.99
006	John	Jones	004	004	11/22/04	180.92
006	John	Jones	004	005	12/15/04	565.00
006	**John**	**Jones**	**006**	**006**	**10/8/04**	**25.00**
006	**John**	**Jones**	**006**	**006**	**10/8/04**	**25.00**
006	**John**	**Jones**	**006**	**008**	**12/29/04**	**109.12**

Figure 5-4: The product of the Customers and Orders tables after applying a restrict predicate

Listing the tables to be joined after FROM requests the product. The join condition in the WHERE clause's predicate requests the restrict that identifies the rows that are part of the joined tables. If you leave off the join condition in the predicate, then the presence of the two tables after FROM simply generates a product table.

For example, assume you wanted to see all the orders placed by a customer whose phone number is 555-555-4321. The phone number is part of the CUSTOMERS table; the order information is in ORDERS. The two relations are related by the presence of the customer number in both (primary key of the CUSTOMERS table; foreign key in ORDERS). The query to satisfy the information request therefore requires an equi-join of the two tables over the customer number, the result of which can be seen in Figure 5-5:

```
SELECT customer_first_name, customer_last_name, order_numb,
    order_date
FROM customers, orders
WHERE customer_phone = '555-555-4321'
    and customers.customer_numb = orders.customer_numb
```

customer_ first_name	customer_ last_name	order_numb	order_date
Tom	Smith	3	11/12/99
Tom	Smith	4	3/18/00
Tom	Smith	5	7/6/00

Figure 5-5: Output from a query containing an equi-join between a primary key and a foreign key

There are two important things to notice about the preceding query:

- ◆ The join is between a primary key in one table and a foreign key in another. Equi-joins that don't meet this pattern are frequently invalid. You will read more about this issue later in this chapter.
- ◆ Because the CUSTOMER_NUMB column appears in more than one table in the query, it must be qualified by the name of the table from which it should be taken. To add a qualifier, precede the name of a column by its table name, separating the two with a period.

Note: With some large DBMSs, you must also qualify the names of tables you did not create with the user ID of the account that did create the table. For example, if user ID DBA created the Customers table, then the full name of the customer number column would be DBA.customers.customer_numb. Check your product documentation to determine whether your DBMS is one of those that require the user ID qualifier.

How might a SQL query optimizer choose to process this query? Although we cannot be certain because there is more than one order of operations that will work, it is likely that the restrict operation to choose the customer with a telephone number of 555-555-4321 will be performed first. This cuts down on the amount of data that needs to be manipulated for the join. The second step probably will be the join operation, because doing the project would eliminate the columns needed for the join.

Conformance note: The traditional join syntax is required for SQL-86 conformance; it is also required for SQL:1999 Core compliance. It should therefore be available with any DBMS that supports SQL.

SQL-92 Join Syntax

The SQL-92 adds syntax for joins that is both simpler and more flexible than the traditional join syntax. If you are performing a natural equi-join, there are three variations of the syntax you can use, depending on whether the column or columns over which you are joining have the same name and whether you want to use all matching columns in the join.

Joins over All Columns with the Same Names

When the primary key and foreign key columns you are joining have the same name and you want to use all matching columns in the join condition, all you need to do is indicate that you want to join the tables, using the following general syntax:

```
SELECT column(s)
FROM table1 NATURAL JOIN table2
```

The query we used as an example in the preceding section could therefore be written as

```
SELECT customer_first_name, customer_last_name, order_numb,
    order_date
FROM customers NATURAL JOIN orders
WHERE customer_phone = '555-555-4321'
```

> *Note: Because the default is a natural equi-join, you will obtain the same result if you simply use* JOIN *instead of* NATURAL JOIN.

> *Note: As ironic as it may seem, Oracle, which provided the first commercial SQL implementation, does not support the SQL-92 join syntax. In contrast, MySQL does support it.*

The SQL command processor identifies all columns in the two tables that have the same name and automatically performs the join over those columns.

> *Note: If you are determined to obtain a product rather than a natural join, you can do it by using the SQL-92* CROSS JOIN *operator.*

Joins over Selected Columns

If you don't want to use all matching columns in a join condition but the columns still have the same name, you specify the names of the columns over which the join is to be made by adding a USING clause:

```
SELECT column(s)
FROM table1 JOIN table2 USING (column)
```

Using this syntax, the sample query would be written

```
SELECT customer_first_name, customer_last_name, order_numb,
    order_date
FROM customers JOIN orders USING (customer_numb)
WHERE customer_phone = '555-555-4321'
```

Joins over Columns with Different Names

When the columns over which you are joining tables don't have the same name, then you must use a join condition similar to that used in the traditional SQL join syntax:

```
SELECT column(s)
FROM table1 JOIN table2 ON join_condition
```

In this case, the sample query will appear as

```
SELECT customer_first_name, customer_last_name, order_numb,
    order_date
FROM customers JOIN orders
ON customers.customer_numb = orders.customer_numb
WHERE customer_phone = '555-555-4321'
```

Joining Using Concatenated Keys

All of the joins you have seen to this point have been performed using a single matching column. However, on occasion you may run tables where you are dealing with concatenated primary and foreign keys. As an example, we will modify the designs of the ORDERS and ORDER_LINES tables so that there is no order number:

```
Orders (id_numb, order_date, order_total)
Order_lines (id_numb, order_date, isbn, quantity, cost_each)
```

Notice that we now have a concatenated primary key for ORDERS, which becomes a concatenated foreign key in ORDER_LINES.

> Note: This redesign assumes that a customer never places more than one order per day. Given that this is not a very realistic assumption, using the order number is a much better design. However, the redesign will suffice for purposes of this example.

To see all the books ordered by customer number 006, a query requires the following join condition:

```
orders.id_numb || orders.order_date =
    order_lines.id_numb || order_lines.order_date
```

The | | operator represents concatenation in most SQL implementations. It instructs the SQL command processor to view the two columns as if they were one and to base its comparison on that concatenation rather than individual column values.

Note: MySQL uses the | | operator to represent the logical operation OR. *Therefore, to perform concatenation you must use the* CONCAT( ) *function, which takes any number of strings (literal or column names) as arguments. For example,* CONCAT (CUSTOMER_FIRST_NAME ,' ', CUSTOMER_LAST_NAME) *produces the first name followed by a space and the last name. Although the name of the function is not case sensitive, you must put the opening parenthesis of the argument list right next to the function name; be sure not to leave a space.*

The following join condition produces the same result because it pulls rows from a produc⊤ table where *both* the customer ID numbers and the order dates are the same:

```
orders.id_numb = order_lines.id_numb AND
    orders.order_date = order_lines.order_date
```

You can therefore write a query using the traditional SQL join syntax in two ways:

```
SELECT isbn
FROM orders, order_lines
WHERE orders.id_numb || orders.order_date = order_lines.id_numb ||
    order_lines.order_date AND id_numb = '006'
```

or

```
SELECT isbn
FROM orders, order_lines
WHERE orders.id_numb = order_lines.id_numb AND orders.order_date =
    order_lines.order_date AND id_numb = '006'
```

Note: With MySQL, you would use

```
SELECT isbn
FROM orders, order_lines
WHERE CONCAT(orders.id_numb, orders.order_date) =
    CONCAT(order_lines.id_numb, order_lines.order_date)
    AND id_numb = '006';
```

If the columns have the same names in both tables and are the only matching columns, then the SQL-92 syntax

```
SELECT isbn
FROM orders JOIN order_lines
WHERE id_numb = '006'
```

has the same effect as the preceding two queries.

When the columns have the same names but aren't the only matching columns, then you can specify both columns in a USING clause:

```
SELECT isbn
FROM orders JOIN order_lines USING (id_numb, order_date)
WHERE id_numb = '006'
```

Alternatively, if the columns don't have the same names, you can use the complete join condition, just as you would if you were using the traditional join syntax:

```
SELECT isbn
FROM orders JOIN order_lines ON orders.id_numb || orders.order_date
    = order_lines.id_numb || order_lines.order_date
WHERE id_numb = '006'
```

or

```
SELECT isbn
FROM orders JOIN order_lines ON orders.id_numb = order_lines.id_numb
    AND orders.order_date = order_lines.order_date
WHERE id_numb = '006'
```

Joining More Than Two Tables

What if you need to join more than two tables in the same query? For example, someone at the online bookstore might want to see the names of all the people who have ordered the book with the ISBN of 0-131-4966-9. The query that retrieves that information must join ORDER_LINES to ORDERS to find all the order numbers on which the desired ISBN appears. Then the result of the first join must be joined again to CUSTOMERS to gain access to the names.

Using the traditional join syntax, the query is written

```
SELECT customer_last_name, customer_first_name
FROM order_lines, orders, customers
WHERE isbn = '0-131-4966-9'
    AND order_lines.order_numb = orders.order_numb
    AND orders.customer_numb = customers.customer_numb
```

With the simplest form of the SQL-92 syntax, the query becomes

```
SELECT customer_last_name, customer_first_name
FROM order_lines JOIN orders JOIN customers
WHERE isbn = '0-131-4966-9';
```

Both syntaxes produce the results in Figure 5-6.

customer_last_name	customer_first_name
Smith	Anne
Collins	Peter
Smith	Anne
Smith	Tom

Figure 5-6: **The result of a query that joins three tables**

Keep in mind that the join operation can work on only two tables at a time. If you need to join more than two tables, you must join them in pairs. Therefore, a join of three tables requires two joins, a join of four tables requires three joins, and so on.

SQL-92 Syntax and Multiple-Table Join Performance

Although the SQL-92 syntax is certainly simpler than the traditional join syntax, it has another major benefit: It gives you control over the order in which the joins are performed. With the traditional join syntax, the query optimizer is in complete control of the order of the joins. However, in SQL-92, the joins are performed from left to right, following the order in which the joins are placed in the FROM clause.

This means that you sometimes can affect the performance of a query by varying the order in which the joins are performed. Remember that the less data the DBMS has to manipulate, the faster a query will execute. Therefore, you want to perform the most discriminatory joins first.

As an example, consider the sample query used in the previous section. The ORDER_LINES table has the most rows, followed by ORDERS and then CUSTOMERS. However, the query also contains a highly discriminatory restrict predicate that limits the rows from that table. Therefore, it is highly likely that the DBMS will perform the restrict on ORDER_LINES first. This means that the query is likely to execute faster if you write it so that ORDER_LINES is joined with ORDERS first, given that this join will significantly limit the rows from ORDERS that need to be joined with CUSTOMERS.

In contrast, what would happen if there was no restrict predicate in the query, and you wanted to retrieve the name of the customer for every book ordered in the database? The query would appear as

```
SELECT customer_first_name, customer_last_name
FROM customers JOIN orders JOIN order_lines
```

First, keep in mind that this type of query, which is asking for large amounts of data, will rarely execute as quickly as one that contains predicates to limit the number of rows. Nonetheless, it will execute a bit faster if CUSTOMERS is joined to ORDERS before joining to ORDER_LINES. Why? Because the joins manipulate fewer rows in that order.

Assume that there are 20 customers, 100 orders, and 300 order lines Every row in ORDER_LINES must have a matching row in ORDERS. Therefore, the result table from that join will be 300 rows long. Those 300 rows must be joined to the 20 rows in CUSTOMERS. However, if we reverse the order, then the 20 rows in CUSTOMERS are joined to 100 rows in ORDERS, producing a table of 100 rows, which can then be joined to ORDER_LINES. In either case, we are stuck with a join of 100 rows to 300 rows, but when the CUSTOMERS table is handled first, the other join is 20 to 100 rows, rather than 20 to 300 rows.

> Note: The example query you just saw will include a lot of duplicate rows. It you add DISTINCT to the query, that will remove the duplicates but also slow down performance even further.

Conformance note: Support for the JOIN keyword is not required for entry level SQL-92 conformance. It is required, however, for intermediate level conformance. The JOIN keyword is required for Core SQL:1999 conformance, as is support for the INNER keyword. The use of either JOIN by itself or INNER JOIN must produce the equi-join about which you have been reading.

Finding Multiple Rows in One Table: Joining a Table to Itself

One of the limitations of a restrict operation is that its predicate is applied to only one row in a table at a time. This means that a predicate such as

```
isbn = '0-131-4966-9' AND isbn = '0-191-4934-8'
```

and the query

```
SELECT customer_first_name, customer_last_name
FROM customers JOIN orders JOIN order_lines
WHERE isbn = '0-131-4966-9' AND isbn = '0-191-4934-8'
```

will always return 0 rows. No row can have more than one value in the ISBN column!

What the preceding query is actually trying to do is locate customers who have ordered two specific books. This means that there must be at least two rows for a customer in the ORDER_LINES table, one for each of the books in question.

Given that you cannot do this type of query with a simple restrict predicate, how can you retrieve the data? The technique is to join the ORDER_LINES table to itself over the order number. The result table will have two columns for the book's ISBN, one from each copy of the original table. Those rows that have both the ISBNs that we want will finally be joined to the ORDERS (over order number) and CUSTOMERS (over customer number) tables so that the query can project the customer's name.

Before looking at the SQL syntax, however, let us examine the relational algebra of the joins so you can see exactly what is happening. Assume that we are working with the subset of the ORDER_LINES table in Figure 5-7. (The order number and the ISBN are the only columns that affect the relational algebra; the rest have been left off for simplicity.) Notice first that the result of our sample query should display the first and last names of the customer who placed order number 3. (It is the only order that contains both of the books in question.)

order_numb	isbn
1	0-136-3966-7
1	0-129-4912-0
1	0-123-1233-0
4	0-140-3877-0
3	0-131-4966-9
3	0-191-4934-8
3	0-180-4712-X
3	0-150-5948-9
2	0-159-3845-3
2	0-131-4912-X

Figure 5-7: A subset of the ORDER_LINES table

The first step in the query is to join the table in Figure 5-7 to itself over the order number, producing the result table in Figure 5-8. The columns that come from the first copy have been labeled T1; those that come from the second copy are labeled T2.

The two rows in black are those that have the two ISBNs for which we are searching. Therefore, we need to follow the join with a restrict that says something like

```
WHERE isbn (from table 1) = '0-131-4966-9'
   AND isbn (from table 2) = '0-191-4934-8'
```

The result will be a table with one row in it (the second of the two black rows in Figure 5-8).

At this point, the query can join the table to ORDERS over the order number to provide access to the customer number of the person who placed the order. The result of that second join can then be

order_numb (T1)	isbn (T1)	order_numb (T2)	isbn (T2)
1	0-136-3966-7	1	0-136-3966-7
1	0-129-4912-0	1	0-136-3966-7
1	0-123-1233-0	1	0-136-3966-7
1	0-136-3966-7	1	0-129-4912-0
1	0-129-4912-0	1	0-129-4912-0
1	0-123-1233-0	1	0-129-4912-0
1	0-136-3966-7	1	0-123-1233-0
1	0-129-4912-0	1	0-123-1233-0
1	0-123-1233-0	1	0-123-1233-0
4	0-140-3877-0	4	0-140-3877-0
3	0-131-4966-9	3	0-131-4966-9
3	**0-191-4934-8**	**3**	**0-131-4966-9**
3	0-180-4712-X	3	0-131-4966-9
3	0-150-5948-9	3	0-131-4966-9
3	**0-131-4966-9**	**3**	**0-191-4934-8**
3	0-191-4934-8	3	0-191-4934-8
3	0-180-4712-X	3	0-191-4934-8
3	0-150-5948-9	3	0-191-4934-8
3	0-131-4966-9	3	0-180-4712-X
3	0-191-4934-8	3	0-180-4712-X
3	0-180-4712-X	3	0-180-4712-X
3	0-150-5948-9	3	0-180-4712-X
3	0-131-4966-9	3	0-150-5948-9
3	0-191-4934-8	3	0-150-5948-9
3	0-180-4712-X	3	0-150-5948-9
3	0-150-5948-9	3	0-150-5948-9
2	0-159-3845-3	2	0-159-3845-3
2	0-131-4912-X	2	0-159-3845-3
2	0-159-3845-3	2	0-131-4912-X
2	0-131-4912-X	2	0-131-4912-X

Figure 5-8: The result of joining the table in Figure 5-7 to itself

joined to CUSTOMERS to obtain the customer's name (Tom Smith). Finally, the query projects the columns the user wants to see.

Correlation Names

The challenge facing a query that needs to work with multiple copies of a single table is to tell the SQL command processor to make the copies of the table. We do this by placing the name of the table more than once on the FROM line, associating each instance of the name with a different alias. Such aliases for table names are known as *correlation names* and take the syntax

```
FROM table_name AS correlation_name
```

For example, to instruct SQL to use two copies of the ORDER_LINES table, you might use

```
FROM order_lines AS T1, order_lines AS T2
```

The AS is optional. Therefore, the following syntax is also legal:

```
FROM order_lines T1, order_lines T2
```

In the rest of the query, you refer to the two copies using the correlation names rather than the original table name.

> *Note: You can give any table a correlation name; its use is not restricted to queries that work with multiple copies of a single table. In fact, if a table name is difficult to type and appears several times in a query, you can save yourself some typing and avoid problems with typing errors by giving the table a short correlation name.*
>
> *Conformance note: Correlation names are part of the SQL-86 standard and should therefore be available with all SQL DBMSs. They are required on the FROM line as part of the Core SQL:1999 standard.*

Performing the Same-Table Join

The query that performs the same-table join needs to specify all of the relational algebra operations you read about in the preceding section. It can be written using the traditional join syntax as follows:

```
SELECT customer_last_name, customer_first_name
FROM order_lines t1, order_lines t2, customers, orders
WHERE t1.isbn = '0-131-4966-9' AND t2.isbn = '0-191-4934-8'
   AND t1.order_numb = t2.order_numb
   AND t1.order_numb = orders.order_numb
   AND orders.customer_numb = customers.customer_numb;
```

There is one very important thing to notice about this query. Although our earlier discussion of the relational algebra indicated that the same-table join would be performed first, followed by a restrict and the other two joins, there is no way using the traditional syntax to indicate the joining of an intermediate result table (in this case, the same-table join). Therefore, the query syntax must join OR-DERS to either T1 or T2. Nonetheless, it is likely that the query optimizer will determine that performing the same-table join, followed by the restrict, is a more efficient way to process the query than joining ORDERS to T1 first.

If you use the SQL-92 join syntax, then you have some control over the order in which the joins are performed:

```
SELECT customer_last_name, customer_first_name
FROM order_lines t1 join order_lines t2 ON
    (t1.order_numb = t2.order_numb) JOIN orders JOIN customers
WHERE t1.isbn = '0-131-4966-9' AND t2.isbn = '0-191-4934-8';
```

The SQL command processor will process the multiple joins in the FROM clause from left to right, ensuring that the same-table join is performed first.

> Note: You can extend the technique you have just read about to
> find as many rows in a table as you need. Create a copy of the
> table with a correlation name for each row predicate and include
> it in the joins. Place the predicate in the WHERE clause. For ex-
> ample, to retrieve data that have four specified rows in a table
> you need four copies of the table, three joins, and four restrict
> predicates.

Outer Joins

An *outer join* (as opposed to the inner joins we have been considering so far) is a join that includes rows in a result table even though there may not be a match between rows in the two tables being joined. Wherever the DBMS can't match rows, it places nulls in the columns for which no data exist. The result may therefore not be a legal relation, since it may not have a primary key. However, because a query's result table is a virtual table that is never stored in the database, having no primary key does not present a data integrity problem.

Why might someone want to perform an outer join? An employee of the online bookstore, for example, might want to see the names of all customers along with the books ordered in the last week. An inner join of CUSTOMERS to ORDERS would eliminate those customers who have not placed an order during the previous week. However, an outer join will include all customers, placing nulls in the order data columns for the customers who have not ordered. An outer join therefore not only shows you matching data but also tells you about where matching data *do not* exist.

> Note: Although the outer join operation has been supported by individual SQL implementations for many years, it became a part of the language standard only in SQL-92. Both left and right outer joins are required for Core SQL:1999 conformance.

The Relational Algebra Outer Join

There are really three types of outer joins, which vary depending on the table or tables from which you want to include rows that have no matches. All three types are supported in the SQL-92 standard.

The Left Outer Join

The left outer join includes all rows from the first table in the join expression

```
table1 LEFT OUTER JOIN table2
```

For example, if we use the data from the tables in Figure 5-1 and perform the left outer join as

```
customers LEFT OUTER JOIN orders
```

then the result will appear as in Figure 5-9. Notice the difference between this table and that in Figure 5-2: There is a row for every row in CUSTOMERS. For the rows that don't have orders (customers 1 and 5), the columns that come from ORDERS have been filled with nulls.

```
Result_table

id_numb  first_name  last_name  order_numb  order_date  order_total

001      Jane        Doe        null        null        null
002      John        Doe        001         10/10/04     250.65
002      John        Doe        002         2/21/05      125.89
003      Jane        Smith      003         11/15/04     1597.99
004      John        Smith      004         11/22/04     180.92
004      John        Smith      005         12/15/04     565.00
005      Jane        Jones      null        null        null
006      John        Jones      006         10/8/04      25.00
006      John        Jones      007         11/12/04     85.00
006      John        Jones      008         12/29/04     109.12
```

Figure 5-9: The result of a left outer join

The Right Outer Join

The right outer join is the precise opposite of the left outer join. It includes all rows from the table on the right of the OUTER JOIN operator. If you perform

```
customers RIGHT OUTER JOIN orders
```

using the data from Figure 5-1, the result will be the same as an inner join of the two tables. This occurs because there are no rows in ORDERS that don't appear in CUSTOMERS. However, if you reverse the order of the tables, as in

```
orders RIGHT OUTER JOIN customers
```

you end up with the same data as in Figure 5-9.

Choosing a Right versus Left Outer Join

If you are performing an outer join on two tables that have a primary key–foreign key relationship, then the result of left and right outer joins on those tables is summarized in Table 5-1. Referential integrity ensures that no rows from a table containing a foreign key will ever be omitted from a join with the table that contains the referenced primary key. Therefore, a left outer join where the foreign key table is on the left of the operator and a right outer join where the foreign key table is on the right of the operator are no different from an inner join.

Outer Join Format	Outer Join Result
`primary_key_table LEFT OUTER JOIN foreign_key_table`	All rows from primary key table retained
`foreign_key_table LEFT OUTER JOIN primary_key_table`	Same as inner join
`primary_key_table RIGHT OUTER JOIN foreign_key_table`	Same as inner join
`foreign_key_table RIGHT OUTER JOIN primary_key_table`	All rows from primary key table retained

Table 5-1: The effect of left and right outer joins on tables with a primary key–foreign key relationship

When choosing between a left and a right outer join, you therefore need to pay attention to which table will appear on which side of the operator. If the outer join is to produce a result different from that of an inner join, then the table containing the primary key must appear on the side that matches the name of the operator.

The Full Outer Join

A full outer join includes all rows from both tables, filling in rows with nulls where necessary. If the two tables have a primary key–foreign key relationship, then the result will be the same as that of either a left outer join when the primary key table is on the left of the operator or a right outer join when the primary key table is on the right of the operator. In the case of the full outer join, it does not matter on which side of the operator the primary key table appears; all rows from the primary key table will be retained.

> Note: The outer join defaults to a full outer join. Therefore, if you don't specify `RIGHT`, `LEFT`, or `FULL`, you will get a full outer join.

SQL Syntax for Outer Joins

To perform an outer join using the SQL-92 syntax, you indicate the type of join in the FROM clause. For example, to perform a left outer join between the CUSTOMERS and ORDERS tables you could write

```
SELECT customer_first_name, customer_last_name, order_numb,
    order_date
FROM customers LEFT OUTER JOIN orders
```

The result appears in Figure 5-10. Notice that the last two rows appear to be empty in the ORDER_NUMB and ORDER_DATE columns. These two customers haven't placed any orders. Therefore, the columns in question are actually null. However, most DBMSs have no visible indicator for null; it looks as if the values are blank. It is the responsibility of the person viewing the result table to realize that the empty spaces represent nulls rather than blanks.

The SQL-92 outer join syntax for joins has the same options as the inner join syntax:

♦ If you use the syntax in the preceding example, the DBMS will automatically perform the outer join on all matching columns between the two tables.

♦ If you want to specify the columns over which the outer join will be performed and the columns have the same names in both tables, add a USING clause:

```
SELECT customer_first_name, customer_last_name,
    order_numb, order_date
FROM customers LEFT OUTER JOIN orders USING
    (customer_numb)
```

♦ If the columns over which you want to perform the outer join do not have the same name, then append an ON clause that contains the join condition:

```
SELECT customer_first_name, customer_last_name,
    order_date, order_numb
FROM customers T1 LEFT OUTER JOIN orders T2 ON
    (T1.customer_numb = T2.customer_numb)
```

customer_first_name	customer_last_name	order_numb	order_date
Jane	Jones	1	12/5/04
Jane	Jones	2	7/6/05
Tom	Smith	3	11/12/04
Tom	Smith	4	3/18/05
Tom	Smith	5	7/6/05
Mary	Johnson	6	8/15/04
Mary	Johnson	7	12/2/04
John	Smith	8	11/22/04
John	Smith	9	1/6/05
Emily	Jones	10	3/12/05
Peter	Johnson	11	9/19/04
Peter	Johnson	12	3/12/05
Peter	Johnson	13	7/21/05
Edna	Hayes	14	12/13/04
Edna	Hayes	15	1/9/05
Franklin	Hayes	16	10/12/04
Franklin	Hayes	17	2/22/05
Franklin	Hayes	18	5/13/05
Mary	Collins	19	7/15/04
Peter	Collins	20	11/15/04
Peter	Collins	21	3/4/05
Anne	Smith	22	9/19/04
Anne	Smith	24	5/14/05
Anne	Smith	23	2/21/05
Peter	Smith	25	10/10/04
Jerry Brown			
Helen Brown			

Figure 5-10: The result of an outer join

Conformance note: Outer joins are required for intermediate level SQL-92 conformance but not for entry level.

Valid versus Invalid Joins

To this point, all of the joins you have seen have involved tables with a primary key–foreign key relationship. These are the most typical types of joins and always produce valid result tables. In contrast, in most cases joins between tables that do not have a primary key–foreign key relationship are invalid. This means that the result tables contain information that is not represented in the database, conveying misinformation to the user. Invalid joins are therefore far more dangerous than meaningless projections.

As an example, let us change the business rules of the online bookstore slightly: Instead of restricting a book to only one source, assume that the same book can come from many suppliers. In that case, the database must include another table:

```
Book_sources (isbn, source_numb)
```

Someone looking at this table and the ORDERS table might conclude that because the two tables have a matching column (ISBN) it makes sense to join the tables to find out the source of every book on order. Unfortunately, this is not the information that the result table will contain.

To keep the result table relatively short, we will work with the two source tables in Figure 5-11. Assume that only one copy of a book appears on each order. The result of an inner join on the two tables over the ISBN can be found in Figure 5-12.

If a book comes from only one source, then there is no problem with that book in the result table (for example, ISBN 0-124-5544-X). However, look carefully at what appears in the result table for the rest of the books, each of which comes from more than one source. There are multiple rows for each book on each order. The implication is that the same book on the same order came from more than one source. Clearly, the same item cannot come from more than one place; it is physically impossible! This invalid join therefore implies facts that simply cannot be true.

The reason this join is invalid is that the two columns over which the join is performed are not in a primary key–foreign key relationship. In fact, in both tables the ISBN column is a foreign key that references the primary key of the BOOKS table.

Are joins between tables that do not have a primary key–foreign key relationship ever valid? On occasion, they are, in particular if you are joining two tables with the same primary key. You saw one

```
Orders

order_numb        isbn

205               0-123-1233-0
206               0-124-5544-X
207               0-124-5544-X
208               0-126-3367-2
209               0-125-3344-1
210               0-123-1233-0
211               0-126-3367-2
212               0-125-3344-1


Book_sources

isbn              source_numb

0-123-1233-0      1
0-123-1233-0      2
0-124-5544-X      1
0-126-3367-2      2
0-126-3367-2      4
0-125-3344-1      3
0-125-3344-1      4
```

Figure 5-11: Two tables that share a column but do not have a foreign key–primary key relationship

```
Invalid_result_table

order_numb   isbn              source_numb

205          0-123-1233-0      1
205          0-123-1233-0      2
206          0-124-5544-X      1
207          0-124-5544-X      1
208          0-126-3367-2      2
208          0-126-3367-2      4
209          0-125-3344-1      3
209          0-125-3344-1      4
210          0-123-1233-0      1
210          0-123-1233-0      2
211          0-126-3367-2      2
211          0-126-3367-2      4
212          0-125-3344-1      3
212          0-125-3344-1      4
```

Figure 5-12: The result of an invalid join

example of this type of join earlier in this chapter during the discussion of retrievals that found multiple rows in the same table by joining the table to itself.

For another example, assume that you want to create a table to store data about your employees:

```
Employees (ID_numb, first_name, last_name, department, job_title,
    salary, hire_date)
```

Some of the employees are managers. For those individuals, you also want to store data about the project they are currently managing and the date they began managing that project. You could add the columns to the EMPLOYEES table and let them contain nulls for employees who are not managers. An alternative is to create a second table just for the managers:

```
Managers (ID_numb, current_project, project_start_date)
```

When you want to see all the information about a manager, you must join the two tables over the ID_NUMB column. The result table will contain rows only for the managers because employees without rows in the MANAGERS table will be left out of the join. There will be no spurious rows such as those we got when we joined the ORDERS and BOOK_SOURCES tables. This join is therefore valid.

> *Note: Although the **ID_NUMB** column in the* MANAGERS *table technically is not a foreign key referencing* EMPLOYEES, *many DBMSs would nonetheless include a constraint that forced the presence of a matching row in* EMPLOYEES *for every manager.*

The bottom line is that you need to be very careful when performing joins between tables that do not have a primary key–foreign key relationship. Although such joins are not always invalid, in most cases they will be.

Avoiding Joins with Uncorrelated Subqueries

As you have read, you can control the order in which joins are performed by using the SQL-92 syntax and being careful with the order in which you place joins in the FROM clause. However, there is a type of SQL syntax—a subquery—that you can use to obtain the same result but avoid performing a join altogether.

A *subquery* (or *subselect*) is a complete SELECT statement embedded within another SELECT. The result of the inner SELECT becomes data used by the outer.

> *Note: Subqueries have other uses besides avoiding joins, which you will see throughout the rest of this book.*

> *Note: One of the major limitations of versions of MySQL prior to 4.1 (which had not been released at the time the second edition of this book was prepared) is that they do not support subqueries. If you happen to need a type of query that can be best performed using a subquery, then this is a significant problem. As we discuss subqueries, you will encounter both text and notes that show alternative syntaxes that you can use with MySQL until the 4.1 release is available.*

A query containing a subquery has the following general form:

```
SELECT column(s)
FROM table
WHERE operator (SELECT column(s))
                FROM table
                WHERE … )
```

There are two general types of subqueries. In an *uncorrelated subquery*, the SQL command processor is able to complete the processing of the inner SELECT before moving to the outer. However, in a *correlated subquery*, the SQL command processor cannot complete the inner query without information from the outer. Correlated subqueries usually require that the inner SELECT be performed more than once and therefore can execute relatively slowly. The same is not true for uncorrelated subqueries, which can be used to replace join syntax and therefore may produce faster performance.

> *Note: You will see examples of correlated subqueries beginning in Chapter 6.*

> *Conformance note: Subqueries are part of the SQL-86 standard and therefore are supported by most SQL DBMSs. They are required for conformance to the Core SQL:1999 standard.*

Using the IN Operator

As a first example, consider the following query containing a join that produces the result in Figure 5-13:

```
SELECT order_date, customer_numb
FROM orders JOIN order_lines
WHERE isbn = '0-131-4966-9'
```

order_date	customer_number
2/21/05	1
3/4/05	0
5/14/05	11
11/12/05	2

Figure 5-13: Output of the query containing a join

We can rewrite the query using subquery syntax as

```
SELECT order_date, customer_numb
FROM orders
WHERE order_numb IN (SELECT order_numb
                     FROM order_lines
                     WHERE isbn = '0-131-4966-9')
```

The inner SELECT retrieves data from the ORDER_LINES table and produces a set of order numbers. The outer SELECT then retrieves data from ORDERS where the order number is the set of values retrieved by the subquery.

This use of the IN operator is actually exactly the same as the use you read about in Chapter 4. The only difference is that rather than placing the set of values in parentheses as literals, the set is generated by a SELECT.

When processing this query, the DBMS never joins the two tables. It performs the inner SELECT first and then uses the result table from that query when processing the outer SELECT. In the case in which the two tables are very large, this can significantly speed up processing of the query.

Note: You can also use NOT IN with subqueries. This is a very powerful syntax that you will read about in Chapter 6.

Conformance note: The IN operator is part of the SQL-86 standard and is available with all SQL DBMSs. It must be supported for lists and subqueries for Core SQL:1999 conformance.

Using the ANY Operator

Like IN, the ANY operator searches a set of values. In its simplest form, ANY is equivalent to IN:

```
SELECT order_date, customer_numb
FROM orders
WHERE order_numb = ANY (SELECT order_numb
                        FROM order_lines
                        WHERE isbn = '0-131-4966-9')
```

This syntax tells the DBMS to retrieve rows from ORDERS where the order number is "equal to any" of those retrieved by the SELECT in the subquery.

What sets ANY apart from IN is that the = can be replaced with any other relationship operator (for example, < and >). For example, you could use it to create a query that asked for all customers who had purchased a book with a price greater than the average cost of a book. Because queries of this type require the use of SQL summary functions, we will leave their discussion until Chapter 7.

Conformance note: The ANY *keyword is part of the SQL-86 standard and is available with all SQL DBMSs. In the Core SQL:1999 standard,* ANY *is specified as required as part of set functions, along with* EVERY *and* SOME.

Nesting Subqueries

The SELECT that you use as a subquery can have a subquery. In fact, if you want to rewrite a query that joins more than two tables, you will need to nest subqueries in this way. As an example, consider the following query that you saw earlier in this chapter:

```
SELECT customer_last_name, customer_first_name
FROM order_lines JOIN orders JOIN customers
WHERE isbn = '0-131-4966-9';
```

It can be rewritten as

```
SELECT customer_last_name, customer_first_name
FROM customers
WHERE customer_numb IN
              (SELECT customer_numb
              FROM orders
              WHERE order_numb = ANY
                            (SELECT order_numb
                            FROM order_lines
                            WHERE isbn = '0-131-4966-9'))
```

Note that each subquery is completely surrounded by parentheses. The end of the query therefore contains two closing parentheses next to each other. The rightmost) closes the outer subquery; the) to its left closes the inner subquery.

The DBMS processes the innermost subquery first, returning a set of order numbers that contains the orders on which the ISBN in question appears. The middle SELECT (the outer subquery) returns a set of customer numbers for rows where the order number is any of those in the set returned by the innermost subquery. Finally, the outer query displays information about customers whose customer numbers are in the set produced by the outer subquery.

In general, the larger the tables in question (in other words, the more rows they have), the more performance benefit you will see if you assemble queries using subqueries rather than joins. How many levels deep can you nest subqueries? There is no theoretical limit. However, once a query becomes more than a few levels deep, it may become hard to keep track of what is occurring.

Replacing a Same-Table Join with Subqueries

The same-table join that you read about earlier in this chapter can also be replaced with subqueries. As you will remember, that query required a join between ORDERS and CUSTOMERS to obtain the customer name, a join between ORDERS and ORDER_LINES, and a join of the ORDER_LINES table to itself to find all orders that contained two desired ISBNs. Because there were three joins in the original query, the rewrite will require one nested subquery for each join.

```
SELECT customer_last_name, customer_first_name
FROM customers
WHERE customer_numb IN
        (SELECT customer_numb
        FROM orders
        WHERE order_numb IN
                (SELECT order_numb
                FROM order_lines
                WHERE isbn = '0-131-4966-9'
                AND order_numb IN
                        (SELECT order_numb
                        FROM order_lines
                        WHERE isbn = '0-191-4934-8')))
```

The innermost subquery retrieves a set of order numbers for the rows on which an ISBN of 0-191-4934-8 appears. The next level subquery above it retrieves rows from ORDER_LINES where the order number appears in the set retrieved by the innermost subquery and where the ISBN is 0-131-4966-9. These two subqueries therefore replace the same-table join.

The set of order numbers is then used by the outermost subquery to obtain a set of customer numbers for the orders whose numbers appear in the result set of the two innermost subqueries. Finally, the outer query displays customer information for the customers whose numbers are part of the outermost subquery's result set.

Notice that the two innermost subqueries are based on the same table. To process this query, the DBMS makes two passes through the ORDER_LINES table—one for each subquery—rather than joining a copy of the table to itself. When a table is very large, this syntax can significantly speed up performance because the DBMS does not need to create and manipulate a duplicate copy of the large table in main memory.

6

Advanced Retrieval Operations

To this point, the queries you have read about combine and extract data from relations in relatively straightforward ways. However, there are additional operations you can perform on relations that, for example, answer questions such as "show me the data that are not …" or "show me the combination of data that are … ." In this chapter you will read about several new relational algebra operations and the types of queries they support. You will, of course, also see the SQL syntax used to prepare these queries.

Union

The union operation creates a new table from two source tables by placing all rows from each table into a single result table. Rather than making new rows by combining rows from the source tables side by side, as does a join, union places the rows on top of one another.

The Relational Algebra Union Operation and Union Compatibility

As an example of how union works, assume that you have the two tables in Figure 6-1. The operation

```
in_print_books UNION out_of_print_books
```

then produces the result table in Figure 6-2.

```
In_print_books

isbn              author_name           title

0-153-2345-0      Jones,Harold          My Life
0-154-2020-X      Smith, Kathryn        Autobiographical Tales
0-456-2946-0      Johnson, Mark         About Me

Out_of_print_books

isbn              author_name           title
0-391-3847-2      Jones, Harold         Growing Up
0-381-4819-X      Jones, Harold         My Childhood
0-149-3857-5      Clark, Maggie         The Horrible Teen Years
```

Figure 6-1: Two tables that will be combined by a union

```
In_print_books

isbn              author_name           title

0-153-2345-0      Jones,Harold          My Life
0-154-2020-X      Smith, Kathryn        Autobiographical Tales
0-456-2946-0      Johnson, Mark         About Me
0-391-3847-2      Jones, Harold         Growing Up
0-381-4819-X      Jones, Harold         My Childhood
0-149-3857-5      Clark, Maggie         The Horrible Teen Years
```

Figure 6-2: The result of the union of the tables in Figure 6-1

For a union operation to be possible, the two source tables must be *union compatible*. In the relational algebra sense, this means that their columns must be defined over the same domains. The tables must have the same columns, but the columns do not necessarily need to be in the same order or be the same size.

In practice, however, the rules for union compatibility are stricter. The two source tables on which the union is performed must have columns with the same data types and sizes, in the same order. In SQL, the two source tables are actually virtual tables created by two independent SELECT statements, which are then joined by the keyword UNION.

Performing a Query That Includes a Union

When you want to include a union operation in a SQL query, you write two individual SELECT statements, joined by the keyword UNION:

```
SELECT column(s)
FROM table(s)
WHERE predicate
UNION
SELECT column(s)
FROM table(s)
WHERE predicate
```

The columns retrieved by the two SELECTs must have the same data types and sizes and be in the same order. For example, the following is legal as long as the customer numbers are the same data type (for example, integer) and the customer names are the same data type and length (for example, 30-character strings):

```
SELECT customer_numb, customer_name
FROM some_table
UNION
SELECT cust_number, cust_name
FROM some_other_table
```

Notice that the source tables of the two SELECTs don't need to be the same, nor do the columns need to have the same names. However, the following is not legal:

```
SELECT customer_numb, customer_first_name, customer_last_name
FROM customers
UNION
SELECT customer_numb, customer_phone
FROM customers
```

Although both SELECTS are taken from the same table, and the two base tables are therefore union compatible, the result tables returned by the SELECTs are *not* union compatible and the union therefore cannot be performed.

Performing Union Using the Same Source Tables

A typical use of UNION in interactive SQL is as a replacement for a predicate with an OR. As an example, consider the following query, the result of which can be found in Figure 6-3:

```
SELECT customer_first_name, customer_last_name
FROM order_lines JOIN orders JOIN customers
WHERE isbn = '0-131-4966-9'
UNION
SELECT customer_first_name, customer_last_name
FROM order_lines JOIN orders JOIN customers
WHERE isbn = '0-191-4934-8'
```

customer_first_name	customer_last_name
Anne	Smith
Mary	Johnson
Peter	Collins
Tom	Smith

Figure 6-3: The result of a query containing a union

The DBMS processes the query by performing the two SELECTs. It then combines the two individual result tables into one, eliminating duplicate rows. To remove the duplicates, the DBMS sorts the result table by every column in the table and then scans it for matching rows placed next to one another. (That is why the rows in Figure 6-3 are in alphabetical order by the author's first name.) The information returned by the preceding query is the same as the following:

```
SELECT customer_first_name, customer_last_name
FROM order_lines JOIN orders JOIN customers
WHERE isbn = '0-131-4966-9' OR isbn = '0-191-4934-8'
```

However, there are two major differences. The first can be seen in the result table in Figure 6-4. When you use a single SELECT with a predicate that contains an OR, duplicate rows are retained. In contrast, the query with the UNION operator removes them automatically.

customer_first_name	customer_last_name
Tom	Smith
Mary	Johnson
Mary	Johnson
Anne	Smith
Peter	Collins
Anne	Smith
Tom	Smith

Figure 6-4: Performing the query in Figure 6-3 with an OR

The second difference is in how the queries are processed. The query that performs a union makes two passes through the ORDER_LINES table, one for each of the individual SELECTs, making only a single comparison with the ISBN value in each row. The query that uses the OR in its predicate makes only one pass through the table but must make two comparisons when testing most rows.

Which query will execute faster? If you include a DISTINCT in the query with an OR predicate, then it will return the same result as the query that performs a union. In that case, both queries will perform about the same. However, if you can live with the duplicate rows and do not need to sort the result table, then the query with the OR predicate will be faster.

Performing Union Using Different Source Tables

Another common use of UNION is to pull together data from different source tables into a single result table. Suppose, for example, we wanted to obtain a list of all books that came from Ingram (a major book distributor) or that have been ordered by customer number 3. A query to obtain this data can be written as

```
SELECT author_name, title
FROM books JOIN sources
WHERE source_name = 'Ingram'
UNION
SELECT author_name, title
FROM orders JOIN order_lines JOIN books
WHERE customer_numb = 3
```

To process this query, the results of which appear in Figure 6-5, the DBMS performs each separate SELECT and then combines the individual result tables.

author_name	title
Bronte, Charlotte	Vilette
Bronte, Emily	Complete Poems of Emily Jane Bronte, The
Butler, Octavia	Clay's Ark
Butler, Octavia	Mind of My Mind
Cherryh, C. J.	Faded Sun, Shon'jir, The
Cherryh, C. J.	Heavy Time
Clavell, James	Gai-Jin
Clavell, James	Noble House
Clavell, James	Shogun
Clavell, James	Tai-Pan
Dumas, Alexandre	Black Tulip, The
Dumas, Alexandre	Corsican Brothers, The
Dumas, Alexandre	Count of Monte Cristo, The

Figure 6-5: The result of a union between result tables coming from different source tables

You *could* write this query in a single SELECT

```
SELECT author_name, title
FROM orders JOIN order_lines JOIN books JOIN sources
WHERE source_name = 'Ingram' OR customer_numb = 3
```

The result contains one more row than that produced by the query with a union because it doesn't remove duplicates. Nonetheless, in this case, the query with the OR predicate will be slower than the query with the union because it requires the join of four tables rather than three.

> *Conformance note: The preceding* UNION *syntax is part of the SQL-86 standard and is available with most SQL DBMSs. The Core SQL:1999 requires the* UNION *operator (with the qualifiers* ALL *and* DISTINCT*) as part of queries on tables as well as allowing views constructed with union-based queries.*

> *Note:* UNION *is available with MySQL 4.0.0 and later.*

Alternative SQL-92 Union Syntax

The SQL-92 syntax provides an alternative means of making two tables union compatible: the CORRESPONDING BY clause. This syntax can be used when the two source tables have some columns by the same names. However, the two source tables need not have completely the same structure.

> *Note: MySQL does not support* CORRESPONDING BY.

To use CORRESPONDING BY, you SELECT * from each of the source tables but then indicate the columns to be used for the union in the COR-RESPONDING BY clause

```
SELECT *
FROM table1
WHERE predicate
UNION CORRESPONDING BY (columns_for_union)
SELECT *
FROM table2
WHERE predicate
```

For example, the query to retrieve the names of all customers who
had ordered two specific books could be rewritten

```
SELECT *
FROM order_lines JOIN orders JOIN customers
WHERE isbn = '0-131-4966-9'
UNION CORRESPONDING BY (customer_first_name, customer_last_name)
SELECT *
FROM order_lines JOIN orders JOIN customers
WHERE isbn = '0-191-4934-8'
```

To process this query, the DBMS performs the two SELECTs, returning all columns in the tables. However, when the time comes to perform the union, it throws away all columns except those in the
parentheses following BY.

> Conformance note: The **CORRESPONDING BY** clause is required
> for intermediate level SQL-92 conformance, but not for entry
> level. However, this clause is not part of the Core SQL:1999
> standard.

Negative Queries

Among the most powerful database queries are those phrased in
the negative, such as "show me all the customers who have not
placed an order in the past year." This type of query is particularly
tricky because it is asking for data that are not in the database. (The
bookstore has data about customers who *have* ordered, but not
those who have not.) The only way to perform such a query is to request the DBMS to use the difference operation.

The Relational Algebra Difference Operation

The relational algebra difference operation retrieves all rows that
are in one table but not in another. For example, if you have a table
that contains all books (BOOKS) and another that contains the books
that *have* been ordered (ORDER_LINES), then the difference—

```
all_books MINUS books_that_have_been_ordered
```

—is the books that have *not* been ordered. When you remove the books that have been ordered from all books, what are left are the books that have not been ordered.

The difference operation looks at entire rows when it makes the decision whether to include a row in the result table. This means that the two source tables must be union compatible.

Performing Queries That Require a Difference

The traditional way to perform a query that requires a difference is to use subquery syntax with the NOT IN operator. SQL-92 adds a new operator—EXCEPT. Unfortunately, EXCEPT has not been implemented by today's DBMSs. You will therefore find coverage of it in Chapter 14.

When you want to use a subquery to perform a difference, the query takes the following general format:

```
SELECT columns
FROM table(s)
WHERE column NOT IN (SELECT column
                     FROM table(s)
                     WHERE predicate)
```

The outer query retrieves a list of all things of interest; the subquery retrieves those that meet the necessary criteria. The NOT IN operator then acts to include all those from the list of all things that *are not* in the set of values returned by the subquery.

As a first example, consider the query that retrieves the authors and titles of all books that have not been ordered:

```
SELECT author_name, title
FROM books
WHERE isbn NOT IN (SELECT isbn
                   FROM order_lines)
```

The outer query selects those rows from BOOKS (the list of all things) whose ISBNs are not in ORDER_LINES (the list of things that *are*). The result in Figure 6-6 contains the 31 books that do not appear at least once in the ORDER_LINES table.

author_name	title
Dumas, Alexandre	Titans, The
Dumas, Alexandre	Black Tulip, The
Clavell, James	Shogun
Clavell, James	Noble House
McCaffrey, Anne	Dragonsong
McCaffrey, Anne	Dragonquest
Rice, Anne	Interview with the Vampire
Rice, Anne	Cry to Heaven
Rice, Anne	Vampire Lestat, The
Twain, Mark	Dog's Tale, A
Twain, Mark	Innocents Abroad, The
Scott, Sir Walter	Ivanhoe
Bronte, Emily	Wuthering Heights
Burroughs, Edgar Rice	Tarzan the Magnificent
Burroughs, Edgar Rice	Tarzan of the Apes
Burroughs, Edgar Rice	War Chief, The
Ludlum, Robert	Parsifal Mosaic, The
Ludlum, Robert	Chancellor Manuscript, The
Barth, John	Chimera
Barth, John	Sabbatical: A Romance
Barth, John	Giles Goat-Boy
Butler, Octavia	Wild Seed
Butler, Octavia	Patternmaster
Lee, Tanith	Castle of Dark, The
Lee, Tanith	Electric Forest
Lee, Tanith	Winter Players, The
Cherryh, C. J.	Serpent's Reach
Cherryh, C. J.	Hunter of Worlds
Cherryh, C. J.	Brothers of Earth
Lee, Tanith	Book of the Damned, The

Figure 6-6: The result of the first SELECT that uses a NOT IN subquery

As a second example, we will retrieve a list of all publishers whose books have never been ordered, the result of which can be found in Figure 6-7:

```
SELECT publisher_name
FROM publishers
WHERE publisher_name NOT IN (SELECT publisher_name
                             FROM books
                             WHERE isbn IN (SELECT isbn
                             FROM order_lines))
```

```
publisher_name

World Pub. Co.
P. F. Collier & Son
Hart Publishing Co.
New English Library
Deutsch
Macmillan
```

Figure 6-7: The result of the second SELECT that uses a NOT IN subquery

In this case, the subquery requires a join between BOOKS and ORDER_LINES to obtain the publisher's name. The preceding query uses a subquery with the IN operator, but a direct join could have been used as well.

> *Note: The ability to process the preceding query is another reason why the Authors and Publishers tables have been included in the database. Not only can they be used for referential integrity validation, they are also necessary for queries that require complete unique lists of authors and publishers.*

Notice that in both of the sample queries there is no explicit syntax to make the two tables union compatible. However, the outer query's WHERE clause contains a predicate that compares a column taken from the result of the outer query with the same column taken from the result of the subquery. These two columns represent the union compatible tables.

As a final example, consider a query that retrieves the names of all customers who have not placed an order after 1/1/2005. When you are putting together a query of this type, your first thought might be to write the query as follows:

```
SELECT customer_numb, customer_first_name, customer_last_name
FROM customers JOIN orders
WHERE order_date < '2005-1-1'
```

This query, however, won't work as you intend. First of all, the join eliminates all customers who have never ordered, even though they should be included in the result. Second, the retrieval predicate identifies those customers who placed orders prior to 1/1/2005 but says nothing about who may or may not have placed an order after that date. Customers may have ordered prior to 1/1/2005, after 1/1/2005, or both.

The typical way to perform this query correctly is to use a difference: the difference between all customers and those who *have* ordered on or after 1/1/2005. The query—the result of which can be found in Figure 6-8—appears as follows:

```
SELECT customer_numb, customer_first_name, customer_last_name
FROM customers
WHERE customer_numb NOT IN
                    (SELECT customer_numb
                    FROM orders
                    WHERE order_date >= '2005-1-1');
```

customer_numb	customer_first_name	customer_last_name
3	Mary	Johnson
9	Mary	Collins
12	Peter	Smith
13	Jerry	Brown
14	Helen	Brown

Figure 6-8: The result of the third query using a NOT IN subquery

Conformance note: The NOT IN operator is part of the SQL-86 standard and should therefore be available with most SQL DBMSs. It is also part of the Core SQL:1999 specification.

Performing Negative Queries Using MySQL

Because versions of MySQL prior to 4.1 have no support for subqueries, you must use an alternative syntax to generate the same result with this product. The general technique to find all rows in T1 that are not in T2 involves a left outer join:

```
SELECT column(s)
FROM T1 LEFT JOIN T2 ON T1.key = T2.key
WHERE T2.key IS NULL
```

Note that you must use IS NULL rather than = NULL in the WHERE predicate.

As a first example, consider the query from the preceding section that lists the books that have not been ordered. The first part of the query produces an intermediate outer join table containing 118 rows, a portion of which can be seen in Figure 6-9:

```
SELECT author_name, title, t2.isbn
FROM books t1 LEFT JOIN order_lines t2 ON t1.isbn=t2.isbn;
```

Adding the where predicate removes the rows with null in the ISBN column. The result is the same as that in Figure 6-6. The complete query appears as

```
SELECT author_name, title, t2.isbn
FROM books t1 LEFT JOIN order_lines t2 ON t1.isbn=t2.isbn
WHERE t2.isbn IS NULL;
```

The second query in the preceding section could be rewritten

```
SELECT DISTINCT t3.publisher_name
FROM  publishers t3 LEFT JOIN books t2 ON t2.publisher_name =
    t3.publisher_name JOIN order_lines
WHERE t2.publisher_name IS NULL
```

This version of the query is much trickier than the version with the subqueries. The FROM line must contain the JOINs in the exact order you just saw. Since we are trying to get the equivalent of T3 MINUS (T2 JOIN T1), T3 must appear on the left-hand side of the LEFT JOIN operator. The left join tables must be followed immediately by the ON condition.

You can obtain the same result with a different order of joins on the FROM line if you use a right join rather than a left join:

```
SELECT DISTINCT t3.publisher_name
FROM  order_lines t1 JOIN books t2 RIGHT JOIN publishers t3 ON
    t2.publisher_name = t3. publisher_name
WHERE t2.publisher_name IS NULL
```

The final example in the preceding section translates to

```
SELECT customer_numb, customer_first_name, customer_last_name
FROM customers t1 LEFT JOIN orders t2 ON t2.customer_numb =
    t2.customer_numb and order_date >= '2005-1-1'
WHERE t2.customer_numb IS NULL
```

Dumas, Alexandre	Three Musketeers, The	0-123-1233-0
Dumas, Alexandre	Three Musketeers, The	0-123-1233-0
Dumas, Alexandre	Titans, The	NULL
Dumas, Alexandre	Count of Monte Cristo, The	0-126-3367-2
Dumas, Alexandre	Black Tulip, The	NULL
Dumas, Alexandre	Corsican Brothers, The	0-127-3948-2
Dumas, Alexandre	Corsican Brothers, The	0-127-3948-2
Clavell, James	Tai-Pan	0-128-4321-1
Clavell, James	Tai-Pan	0-128-4321-1
Clavell, James	Shogun	NULL
Clavell, James	Noble House	NULL
Clavell, James	Gai-Jin	0-128-3939-2
McCaffrey, Anne	Dragonsong	NULL
McCaffrey, Anne	Dragonsinger	0-129-4912-0
McCaffrey, Anne	White Dragon, The	0-130-2939-4
McCaffrey, Anne	White Dragon, The	0-130-2939-4
McCaffrey, Anne	Dragonflight	0-130-2943-2
McCaffrey, Anne	Dragonquest	NULL
Rice, Anne	Interview with the Vampire	NULL
Rice, Anne	Cry to Heaven	NULL
Rice, Anne	Vampire Lestat, The	NULL
Rice, Anne	Feast of All Saints, The	0-130-3941-7
Rice, Anne	Tale of the Body Thief, The	0-131-3021-2
Rice, Anne	Tale of the Body Thief, The	0-131-3021-2
Rice, Anne	Tale of the Body Thief, The	0-131-3021-2
Rice, Anne	Lasher	0-131-4966-9
Rice, Anne	Lasher	0-131-4966-9
Rice, Anne	Lasher	0-131-4966-9
Rice, Anne	Lasher	0-131-4966-9
Rice, Anne	Taltos	0-131-4912-X
Rice, Anne	Taltos	0-131-4912-X
Rice, Anne	Taltos	0-131-4912-X
Twain, Mark	Prince and the Pauper, The	0-132-3949-2
Twain, Mark	Prince and the Pauper, The	0-132-3949-2
Twain, Mark	Life on the Mississippi	0-132-9876-4
Twain, Mark	Celebrated Jumping Frog of Cal. County	0-124-2999-9
Twain, Mark	Dog's Tale, A	NULL
Twain, Mark	Innocents Abroad, The	NULL
Twain, Mark	Pudd'nhead Wilson	0-133-5935-2
Stevenson, Robert Louis	Child's Garden of Verses, A	0-134-3945-7
Stevenson, Robert Louis	Child's Garden of Verses, A	0-134-3945-7
Stevenson, Robert Louis	Child's Garden of Verses, A	0-134-3945-7
Stevenson, Robert Louis	Child's Garden of Verses, A	0-134-3945-7
Stevenson, Robert Louis	Treasure Island	0-135-2222-2
Stevenson, Robert Louis	Treasure Island	0-135-2222-2
Scott, Sir Walter	Rob Roy	0-137-1293-9
Stevenson, Robert Louis	Kidnapped	0-136-3956-1
Stevenson, Robert Louis	Strange Case of Dr. Jekyll and Mr. Hyde	0-136-3966-7

Figure 6-9: A portion of the outer join table

Notice that the condition regarding the date is included in the ON clause. Keep in mind when constructing these queries that the ON clause is applied as the join is being performed. The WHERE clause is used to remove rows *after* the join is complete.

> *Note: For the most part, it is conceptually simpler to use a sub-query to perform NOT queries. However, until MySQL 4.1 is available, the syntax you have seen in this section is the only way to write them.*

The EXISTS Operator

The EXISTS operator checks the number of rows returned by a sub-query. If the subquery contains one or more rows, then the result is true and a row is placed in the result table; otherwise, the result is false and no row is added to the result table.

For example, suppose the online bookstore wants to see a list of books that have been ordered. (You have already seen two syntaxes for this query, one using a join, the other using a subquery and the IN operator.)

To write the query using EXISTS, you would use

```
SELECT author_name, title
FROM books T1
WHERE EXISTS (SELECT *
FROM order_lines
WHERE T1.isbn = order_lines.isbn)
```

The preceding is a *correlated subquery*. Rather than completing the entire subquery and then turning to the outer query, the DBMS processes the query in the following manner:

1. Look at a row in the BOOKS table.
2. Use the ISBN from that row in the subquery's WHERE clause.

3. If the subquery finds at least one row in ORDER_LINES with the same ISBN, place a row in the result table. Otherwise, do nothing.

4. Repeat steps 1 through 3 for all rows in the BOOKS table.

The important thing to recognize here is that the DBMS repeats the subquery for every row in BOOKS. It is this repeated execution of the subquery that makes this a correlated subquery.

When you are using the EXISTS operator, it doesn't matter what follows SELECT in the subquery. EXISTS is merely checking to determine whether any rows are present in the subquery's result table. Therefore, it is easiest simply to use * rather than to specify individual columns.

How will this query perform? It will probably perform better than a query that joins BOOKS and ORDER_LINES, especially if the two tables are large. The query using IN, in contrast, contains an uncorrelated subquery that returns a set of ISBNs that the outer query searches. The more rows returned by the uncorrelated subquery, the closer the performance of the EXISTS and IN queries will be. However, if the uncorrelated subquery returns only a few rows, it will probably perform better than the query containing the correlated subquery.

> *Conformance note: The EXISTS operator is part of the SQL-86 standard and should be available with all SQL DBMSs. It is included in the Core SQL:1999 specifications.*
>
> *Note: Because MySQL does not support subqueries, it also does not support the EXISTS operator. The alternative is to use a simple SELECT with a WHERE predicate that includes multiple OR clauses.*

CASE Expressions

The SQL CASE expression, much like a CASE in a general-purpose programming language, allows a SQL statement to pick from among a variety of actions based on the truth of logical expression. The CASE expression has the following general syntax:

```
CASE
    WHEN logical condition THEN action
    WHEN logical condition THEN action
    :
    :
    ELSE default action
END
```

As an example, assume that the online bookstore wants to offer discounts to users based on the price of a book. The more the retail price of the item, the greater the discount. To include the discounted price in the output of a query, the bookstore might use

```
SELECT isbn,cost_each,
CASE
    WHEN cost_each < 20 THEN cost_each * .9
    WHEN cost_each >= 20 AND cost_each < 25 THEN cost_each * .8
    WHEN cost_each >= 35 AND cost_each < 30 THEN cost_each * .7
    ELSE cost_each * .6
END
FROM orders
WHERE order_numb = 8
```

The preceding query displays the ISBN and the normal cost of the book. It then evaluates the CASE expression by evaluating the first logical condition following WHEN. If that condition is true, the query performs the computation and exits the CASE. If the first condition is false, the query proceeds to the second WHEN, and so on. If none of the conditions are true, the query executes the action following ELSE. (The ELSE is optional.)

> *Note: You will read about SQL and computations in depth in Chapter 7.*

*Conformance note: Support for CASE is required for intermedi-
ate level SQL-92 conformance. It is also part of the Core
SQL:1999 specification.*

7

Calculations and Grouping Queries

Although SQL is not a complete programming language, it can perform some calculations and some data summarization. In this chapter you will read about adding computed columns to result tables, using SQL functions that perform computations on multiple rows of a table or that manipulate strings, and preparing queries that group data and compute summary measures about those groups.

> *Note: One of the goals of continued SQL development is to move it toward being a complete programming language. Many features that lead in that direction appear in SQL:1999. For details, see Chapter 15.*

Performing Arithmetic

SQL recognizes simple arithmetic expressions involving column names and literal values. (When you are working with embedded SQL, you can also use host language variables.) For example, if we wanted to compute the line cost of an item on an order placed with the online bookstore, the computation could be written

```
cost_each * quantity
```

You could then incorporate this into a query as

```
SELECT order_numb, isbn, quantity, cost_each, (cost_each * quantity)
FROM order_lines
WHERE order_numb = 3
```

The result of the preceding query can be found in Figure 7-1. Notice that the computation has been applied to each row and a new column for the computed value added to the result table. (The exact title of the column depends on your DBMS.) These computed values exist only in the result table; they are not stored in the database.

order_numb	isbn	quantity	cost_each	cost_each*quantity
3	0-131-4966-9	1	23.95	23.95
3	0-191-4934-8	1	23.95	23.95
3	0-180-4712-X	2	19.95	39.90
3	0-150-5948-9	1	19.95	19.95

Figure 7-1: Output of a query that includes a computed column

> Note: If you want to store the line cost in the database, the easiest way is to have an application program use embedded SQL to perform the computation and then update the associated row in the base table.

Arithmetic Operators

SQL recognizes the arithmetic operators in Table 7-1. Compared with a general-purpose programming language, this list is fairly limited. For example, there are no operators for exponentiation or modulo division. This means that if you need more sophisticated arithmetic manipulations, you will probably need to use embedded SQL, retrieve the data into host language variables, and perform the arithmetic using the host programming language.

Operator	Meaning	Example
+	Unary +: Preserve the sign of the value	`+balance`
–	Unary –: Change the sign of the value	`-balance`
*	Multiplication: Multiply two values	`balance * tax_rate`
/	Division: Divide one value by another	`balance / numb_items`
+	Addition: Add two values	`balance + new_charge`
–	Subtraction: Subtract two values	`balance - payment`

Table 7-1: SQL arithmetic operators

> *Note: MySQL provides some extensions to the SQL-92 standard for arithmetic manipulation. For example, you can use the % operator for modulo division. There are also functions for exponentiation, logarithms, absolute value, and so on. See http:// www.mysql.com/doc/M/a/Mathematical_functions.html for a full list of available arithmetic operators and functions.*

Operator Precedence

The rows in Table 7-1 appear in the general order of the operators' precedence. (Both unary operators have the same precedence, followed by multiplication and division. Addition and subtraction have the lowest precedence.) This means that when multiple operators appear in the same expression, the DBMS evaluates them according to their predetermined order. For example, because the unary operators have the same precedence, for the expression

```
-balance * tax_rate
```

the DBMS will first change the sign in the BALANCE column and then multiply it by the value in the TAX_RATE column.

When more than one operator of the same precedence appears in the same expression, they are evaluated from left to right. Therefore, in the expression

```
balance + new_charges — payments
```

the DBMS will first add the new charges to the balance and then subtract the payments from the sum.

Sometimes the default precedence can produce unexpected results. Assume that you want to evaluate the expression

```
12 / 3 * 2
```

When the operators are evaluated from left to right, the DBMS divides 12 by 3 and then multiplies the 4 by 2, producing an 8. However, what if you really wanted to perform the multiplication first, followed by the division? (The result would be 2.)

To change the order of evaluation, you use parentheses to surround the operations that should be performed first:

```
12 / (3 * 2)
```

Whenever the DBMS sees a set of parentheses, it knows to evaluate what is inside the parentheses first, regardless of the precedence of the operators.

You can nest one set of parentheses within another:

```
12 / (3 * (1 + 2))
```

In this example, the DBMS evaluates the innermost parentheses first (the addition), moves to the outer set of parentheses (the multiplication), and finally evaluates the division.

There is no limit to how deep you can nest parentheses. However, be sure that each opening parenthesis is paired with a closing parenthesis.

String Manipulations

The SQL-92 standard contains one operator and several functions for manipulating character strings.

Concatenation

As you saw in Chapter 5 when we were discussing joins using concatenated foreign keys, the concatenation operator—||—pastes one string on the end of another. It can be used to format output as well as concatenate keys for searching. For example, the online bookstore could get an alphabetical list of customer names formatted as *last, first* (see Figure 7-2) with

```
SELECT customer_last_name || ', ' || customer_first_name
FROM customers
ORDER BY customer_last_name, customer_first_name
```

customer_last_name||', '||customer_first_name

Brown, Helen
Brown, Jerry
Collins, Mary
Collins, Peter
Hayes, Edna
Hayes, Franklin
Johnson, Mary
Johnson, Peter
Jones, Emily
Jones, Jane
Smith, Anne
Smith, John
Smith, Peter
Smith, Tom

Figure 7-2: The result of a concatenation

Note: Don't forget that MySQL uses | | as the OR operator and therefore requires that you use the CONCAT( ) function to perform concatenation.

Notice that the concatenation includes a literal string to place the comma and space between the last and first names. The concatenation operation knows nothing about normal English spacing; it simply places one string on the end of another. Therefore, it is up to the user to include any necessary spacing and punctuation.

> *Conformance note: Support for concatenation is required only at the SQL-92 intermediate level. However, most DBMSs, even those that are only SQL-86 compliant, do support it. Character concatenation is also part of the Core SQL:1999 standard.*

UPPER and LOWER

When a DBMS evaluates a literal string against stored data, it performs a *case-sensitive* search. This means that upper- and lowercase letters are different and that JONES is not the same as Jones. You can get around these problems using the UPPER and LOWER functions to convert stored data to a single case.

For example, assume that someone at the online bookstore is not certain of the case in which customer names are stored. To perform a case-insensitive search for a single customer, the person could use

```
SELECT customer_numb, customer_first_name, customer_last_name,
    customer_street, customer_city
FROM customers
WHERE UPPER(customer_last_name) = 'JONES'
```

The result (see Figure 7-3) includes rows for customers whose last names contain the characters J-O-N-E-S, regardless of case. The UPPER function converts the data stored in the database to uppercase before making the comparison in the WHERE predicate. You obtain the same effect by using LOWER instead of UPPER.

customer _numb	customer_first _name	customer_last _name	customer_street	customer_city
1	Jane	Jones	125 W. 8th Blvd.	Anytown
5	Emily	Jones	7921 First Road	Anytown

Figure 7-3: The result of a case-insensitive search

Conformance note: Support for UPPER and LOWER is required only for full SQL-92 conformance, although you may find similar functions with DBMSs with lower levels of conformance. In addition, these functions are required for Core SQL:1999 conformance.

Note: MySQL performs case-insensitive text searches. To perform a case-sensitive search, you typecast character strings to binary strings by placing the word BINARY in front of the string (a column name or string expression).

TRIM

The TRIM function removes leading and/or trailing characters from a string. The various syntaxes for this function and their effects are summarized in Table 7-2.

Function	Result	Comments
TRIM (' word ')	'word'	Default: removes both leading and trailing blanks
TRIM (BOTH ' ' FROM ' word ')	'word'	Removes leading and trailing blanks
TRIM (LEADING ' ' FROM ' word ')	'word '	Removes leading blanks
TRIM (TRAILING ' ' FROM ' word ')	' word'	Removes trailing blanks
TRIM (BOTH '*' FROM '*word*')	'word'	Removes leading and trailing *

Table 7-2: The various forms of the SQL TRIM function

You can place TRIM in any expression that contains a string. For example, if you are using characters to store a serial number with leading 0s (for example, 0012), you can strip those 0s when performing a search:

```
SELECT item_description
FROM items
WHERE TRIM (LEADING '0' FROM item_numb) = '25'
```

Conformance note: The TRIM *function is required only for full SQL-92 conformance, although you may find it supported at lower levels. This function is part of the Core SQL:1999 standard.*

SUBSTRING

The SUBSTRING function extracts portions of a string. It has the following general syntax:

```
SUBSTRING (source_string,FROM starting_position FOR
    number_of_characters)
```

For example, if the online bookstore wanted to extract the first character of a customer's name, the function call would be written

```
SUBSTRING (customer_first_name FROM 1 FOR 1)
```

The substring being created begins at the first character in the column and is one character long.

You could then incorporate this into a query with

```
SELECT SUBSTRING (customer_first_name FROM 1 FOR 1) || '. ' ||
    customer_last_name
FROM customers
```

The results can be found in Figure 7-4.

Conformance note: The **SUBSTRING** *function is required for intermediate level SQL-92 conformance. However, you may find this function, or something very similar, implemented by DBMSs with lower levels of conformance. This function is also required for Core SQL:1999 conformance.*

Note: MySQL supports a wide range of string functions. For documentation, see http://www.mysql.com/doc/S/t/String_functions.html.

```
substring (customer_first_name from 1 for 1) || '. ' || customer_last_name
```

J. Jones
T. Smith
M. Johnson
J. Smith
E. Jones
P. Johnson
E. Hayes
F. Hayes
M. Collins
P. Collins
A. Smith
P. Smith
J. Brown
H. Brown

Figure 7-4: Output of a query including the SUBSTRING function

Date and Time Manipulation

SQL DBMSs provide column data types for dates and times. When you store data using these data types, you make it possible for SQL to perform chronological operations on those values. You can, for example, subtract two dates to find out the number of days between them or add an interval to a date to advance the date a specified number of days. In this section you will read about the types of date manipulations that SQL provides along with a simple way to get current date and time information from the computer.

SQL-92 specifies four column data types that relate to dates and times (jointly referred to as "datetime" data types):

♦ DATE: A date only
♦ TIME: A time only
♦ TIMESTAMP: A combination of date and time
♦ INTERVAL: The interval between two of the preceding data types

As you will see in the next two sections, these can be combined in a variety of ways.

Date and Time System Values

To help make date and time manipulations easier, SQL lets you retrieve the current date and/or time with the following three keywords:

- ◆ CURRENT_DATE: Returns the current system date
- ◆ CURRENT_TIME: Returns the current system time
- ◆ CURRENT_TIMESTAMP: Returns a combination of the current system date and time

For example, to see all orders placed on the current day, the online bookstore uses the following query:

```
SELECT customer_first_name, customer_last_name, order_numb
FROM orders JOIN customers
WHERE order_date = CURRENT_DATE
```

You can also use these system date and time values when performing data entry, as you will read about beginning in Chapter 8.

> *Conformance note: Support for* CURRENT_DATE, CURRENT_TIME, *and* CURRENT_TIMESTAMP *is required at the SQL-92 intermediate level. However, intermediate level conformance does not require support for fractions of seconds, which is required only for full comformance. The Core SQL:1999 specifications require* CURRENT_DATE, LOCALTIME, *and* LOCALTIMESTAMP.

Date and Time Arithmetic

The types of date and time arithmetic available with SQL are summarized in Table 7-3. Unfortunately, expressions involving these operations aren't as straightforward as they might initially appear. When you use date and time arithmetic, you must also specify the portions of the date and/or time that you want.

Expression	Result
DATETIME — DATETIME	INTERVAL
DATETIME ± INTERVAL	DATETIME
INTERVAL ± INTERVAL	INTERVAL
INTERVAL * numeric_data_type	INTERVAL
INTERVAL / numeric_data_type	INTERVAL

Table 7-3: Datetime arithmetic

Each datetime column is made up of the following fields:

- YEAR
- MONTH
- DAY
- HOUR
- MINUTE
- SECOND

When you write an expression that includes an interval, you can either indicate that you want the interval expressed in one of those fields (for example, DAY for the number of days between two dates) or specify a range of fields (for example, YEAR TO MONTH to give you an interval in years and months). The *start field* (the first field in the range) can be only YEAR, DAY, HOUR, or MINUTE. The second field in the range (the *end field*) must be a chronologically smaller unit than the start field.

> Note: There is one exception to the preceding rule. If the start field is YEAR, then the end field must be MONTH.

To see the number of years between a customer's orders and the current date, the online bookstore might use

```
SELECT CURRENT_DATE — order_date YEAR
FROM orders
WHERE customer_numb = 6
```

To see the same interval expressed in years and months, the query would be rewritten as

```
SELECT CURRENT_DATE – order_date YEAR TO MONTH
FROM orders
WHERE customer_numb = 6
```

To add 7 days to an order date to give a customer an approximate delivery date, the online bookstore would write a query like

```
SELECT order_date + INTERVAL '7' DAY
FROM orders
WHERE order_numb = 3
```

Notice that when you include an interval as a literal, you precede it with the keyword INTERVAL, put the interval's value in single quotes, and follow it with the datetime unit in which the interval is expressed.

> *Note: The syntax for date and time arithmetic varies considerably from one DBMS to another. You should therefore check your DBMS's documentation carefully to determine whether it adheres to the syntax specified in the SQL-92 standard or uses a syntax of its own.*

> *Note: MySQL provides a larger collection of date and time functions than required by the SQL standard. For documentation, see http://www.mysql.com/doc/D/a/Date_and_time_functions.html.*

Set Functions

SQL includes a set of set functions (summarized in Table 7-4) that compute a variety of measures based on values in a column in multiple rows. The result of using one of these set functions is a computed column that appears only in a result table.

The basic syntax for the set functions is

```
function_name (input_argument)
```

Function	Action
COUNT	Returns the number of rows
SUM	Returns the total of the values in a column from a group of rows
AVG	Returns the average of the values in a column from a group of rows
MIN	Returns the minimum value in a column from among a group of rows
MAX	Returns the maximum value in a column from among a group of rows

Table 7-4: SQL set functions

You place the function call following SELECT, just as you would for an arithmetic calculation. What you use for an input argument depends on which function you are using.

COUNT

The COUNT function is somewhat different from the other SQL set functions in that instead of making computations based on data values, it counts the number of rows in a table. To use it, you place COUNT (*) in your query. COUNT's input argument is always an asterisk.

For example, the following query counts the number of rows in the ORDER_LINES table:

```
SELECT COUNT (*)
FROM order_lines
```

The response appears as

```
count (*)
87
```

To count a subset of the rows in a table, you can apply a WHERE clause:

```
SELECT COUNT (*)
FROM order_lines
WHERE isbn = '0-180-4712-X'
```

The result—

```
count (*)
2
```

—tells you that the book with an ISBN of 0-180-4712-X appears on two orders. It does *not* tell you how many copies of the book have been ordered because the query is simply counting the number of rows in which the ISBN appears. It does not take into account the value in the QUANTITY column.

Alternatively, the online bookstore could determine the number of distinct items contained in a specific order with a query like

```
SELECT COUNT (*)
FROM order_lines
WHERE order_numb = 8
```

Keep in mind that once again this does not tell you the total number of items ordered because it does not look at the value in the QUAN-TITY column.

When you use * as an input parameter to the COUNT function, the DBMS includes all rows. However, if you want to exclude rows that have nulls in a particular column, you can use the name of the column as an input parameter:

```
SELECT COUNT (publisher_name)
FROM books
```

If every row in the table has a value in the PUBLISHER_NAME column, then COUNT (PUBLISHER_NAME) is the same as COUNT (*). However, if any rows contain null, then the count will exclude those rows.

You can also use COUNT to determine how many unique values appear in any given column by placing the keyword DISTINCT in front of the column name used as an input parameter. For example, to find out how many different books appear in the ORDER_LINES table, the online bookstore would use

```
SELECT COUNT (DISTINCT isbn)
FROM order_lines
```

The result—51—is the number of unique ISBNs in the table. (As you saw earlier in this section, the table has 87 rows.) Note that any rows that contain null in the specified column are excluded from the count.

SUM

If someone at the online bookstore wants to know the total number of items in an order, then the easiest way to obtain this value is to add up the values in the QUANTITY column:

```
SELECT SUM (quantity)
FROM order_lines
WHERE order_numb = 3
```

The result appears as

```
sum (quantity)
5
```

If you COUNT the number of lines in order number 3, you will discover that there are only four rows for the order. The SUM of the QUANTITY column is larger because one of the four rows contains an order for two copies.

In the preceding example, the input argument to the SUM function was a single column. However, it can also be an arithmetic operation. For example, to find the total value of an order, the online bookstore could use the following query:

```
SELECT SUM (cost_each * quantity)
FROM order_lines
```

```
WHERE order_numb = 3
```

The result—

```
sum (cost_each*quantity)
107.75
```

—is the total of the multiplication of the COST_EACH and QUANTITY columns for each row belonging to ORDER_NUMBER 3.

If we need to add tax to the order, a query could then multiply the result of the SUM by the tax rate:

```
SELECT SUM (cost_each * quantity) * 1.0725
FROM order_lines
WHERE order_numb = 3
```

producing a final result of 115.561875.

> *Note: Rows that contain null in any columns involved in a SUM are excluded from the computation.*

AVG

The AVG function computes the average value in a column. For example, to find out the average price of a book, the online bookstore could use a query like

```
SELECT AVG (retail_price)
FROM books
```

The result is 21.8512345679012 (approximately $21.85).

MIN and MAX

The MIN and MAX functions return the minimum and maximum values in a column or expression. For example, to see the maximum price of a book, the online bookstore could use a query like

```
SELECT MAX (retail_price)
```

```
FROM books
```

The result is a single value: $27.95.

The MIN and MAX functions are not restricted to columns or expressions that return numeric values. If the online bookstore wanted to see the latest date on which an order had been placed, then

```
SELECT MAX (order_date)
FROM orders
```

returns the chronologically latest date (in our particular sample data, using a year 2000–compliant DBMS, 07/21/05).

By the same token, if you use

```
SELECT MIN (customer_last_name)
FROM customers
```

you will receive the alphabetically first customer last name (Brown).

> Conformance note: SQL-86 supports the preceding set functions. However, the use of the keyword DISTINCT in the COUNT function is required only at the SQL-92 intermediate level. At that level the argument following DISTINCT may be limited to a single column. Support for expressions is required only for full compliance. The Core SQL:1999 specifications include AVG, COUNT, MAX, MIN, and SUM, along with the ALL and DISTINCT qualifiers.

Set Functions in Predicates

Set functions can also be used in WHERE predicates to generate values against which stored data can be compared. Assume, for example, that the online bookstore wants to see the titles and cost of all books that were ordered that cost more than the average cost of a book.

The strategy for preparing this query is to use a subquery that returns the average cost of an ordered book and to compare the cost of each book in the ORDER_LINES table to that average:

```
SELECT order_numb, title, cost_each
FROM order_lines JOIN books
WHERE cost_each > (SELECT AVG (cost_each)
                    FROM order_lines)
                   ORDER BY order_numb
```

The DBMS processes this query by first computing the average cost of ordered books. (This is therefore an uncorrelated subquery.) It can then compare that value to rows in the ORDER_LINES table. In all likelihood, the join to BOOKS will be the final step. You can find the result in Figure 7-5.

Changing Data Types: Using CAST

One of the problems with the output of the SUM and AVG functions that you saw earlier in this chapter is that they give you no control over the *precision* (number of places to the right of the decimal point) of the output. One way to solve that problem is to change the data type of the result to something that has only two places to the right of the decimal point using the CAST function.

CAST has the general syntax

```
CAST (source_data AS new_data_type)
```

To restrict the output of the average price of books to a precision of 2, you could then use

```
CAST (AVG (retail_price) AS DECIMAL (10,2))
```

and incorporate it into a query using

```
SELECT CAST (AVG (retail_price) AS DECIMAL(10,2))
FROM books
```

order_numb	title	cost_each
1	Strange Case of Dr. Jekyll and Mr. Hyde	23.95
2	Taltos	24.95
3	Lasher	23.95
3	Heavy Time	23.95
4	Waverly Novels	27.95
5	Waverly Novels	27.95
6	Heavy Time	23.95
7	Treasure Island	24.95
7	Heavy Time	23.95
8	Taltos	24.95
8	Floating Opera and The End of the Road, The	24.95
8	Book of the Dead, The	22.95
9	Waverly Novels	27.95
10	Kidnapped	22.95
11	Sot-Weed Factor, The	27.95
12	Holcroft Covenant, The	24.95
13	Gemini Contenders, The	24.95
14	Feast of All Saints, The	24.95
14	Taltos	24.95
16	Tai-Pan	22.95
16	Tale of the Body Thief, The	24.95
17	Tale of the Body Thief, The	24.95
17	Bourne Identity, The	23.95
17	Book of the Beast, The	22.95
18	Tai-Pan	22.95
18	Book of the Dead, The	22.95
19	Tale of the Body Thief, The	24.95
19	Aquitaine Progression, The	25.95
19	Holcroft Covenant, The	24.95
20	Hellburner	23.95
21	Lasher	23.95
23	Gai-Jin	25.95
23	Lasher	23.95
23	Treasure Island	24.95
23	Letters: A Novel	27.95
23	Sot-Weed Factor, The	27.95
24	Lasher	23.95
24	Letters: A Novel	27.95
24	Hellburner	23.95

Figure 7-5: Output of a query that uses a set function in a subquery

The preceding specifies that the result should be displayed as a decimal number with a maximum of 10 characters with two digits to the right of the decimal point. The result is 21.85, a more meaningful currency value than the original 21.8512345679012.

CAST can also, for example, be used to convert a string of characters into a date. The expression

```
CAST ('10-20-99' AS DATE)
```

returns a datetime value.

Valid conversions for commonly used data types are represented by the light gray boxes in Table 7-5. Those conversions that may be possible if certain conditions are met are represented by the dark gray boxes. In particular, if you are attempting to convert a character string into a shorter string, the result will be truncated.

Original data type	New data type						
	Integer or fixed point	Floating point	Variable-length character	Fixed-length character	Date	Time	Time-stamp
Integer or fixed point	valid	valid	valid	valid			
Floating point	valid	valid	valid	valid			
Character (fixed or variable length)	valid	valid	may be valid	may be valid	valid	valid	valid
Date			valid	valid	valid		valid
Date			valid	valid		valid	valid
Timestamp			valid	valid	valid	valid	valid

Table 7-5: Valid data type conversions for commonly used data types (light gray boxes are valid; dark gray boxes may be valid)

> *Conformance note: Support for* CAST *is required for intermediate level SQL-92 conformance and for Core SQL:1999 conformance.*

Grouping Queries

SQL can group rows based on matching values in specified columns and compute summary measures for each group. When these *grouping queries* are combined with the set functions that you saw earlier in this chapter, SQL can provide simple reports without requiring any special programming.

Forming Groups

To form a group, you add a GROUP BY clause to a SELECT statement, followed by the columns whose values are to be used to form the groups. All rows whose values match on those columns will be placed in the same group.

For example, if the online bookstore wants to see how many copies of each book have been ordered, it can use a query like

```
SELECT title, COUNT (*)
FROM order_lines JOIN books
GROUP BY title
ORDER BY title
```

The preceding query joins ORDER_LINES to BOOKS and then forms groups by matching book titles. The query displays the title and the number of rows for each group (see Figure 7-6).

There is a major restriction that you must observe with a grouping query: You can display values only from columns that are used to form the groups. For example, if the online bookstore used the ISBN column to form the groups—a more reliable way to identify individual books than titles, which may duplicate—there would be no way to display the titles for each group. This is because the DBMS cannot require that all books with the same ISBN have the same title. (We as humans know that they do, but the DBMS does not.)

title	count (*)
Apache Devil	3
Aquitaine Progression, The	1
Bandit of Hell's Bend, The	1
Black Unicorn	2
Book of the Beast, The	1
Book of the Dead, The	2
Bourne Identity, The	2
Celebrated Jumping Frog of Calaveras County	1
Child's Garden of Verses, A	4
Clay's Ark	4
Complete Poems of Emily Jane Bronte, The	1
Corsican Brothers, The	2
Count of Monte Cristo, The	1
Cyteen	1
Dragonflight	1
Dragonsinger	1
East of Midnight	1
Faded Sun, Kesrith, The	1
Faded Sun, Shon'jir, The	1
Feast of All Saints, The	1
Floating Opera and the End of the Road, The	1
Gai-Jin	1
Gemini Contenders, The	1
Heavy Time	3
Hellburner	2
Holcroft Covenant, The	2
Jane Eyre	2
Kidnapped	1
Kindred	1
Lasher	4
Letters: A Novel	2
Life on the Mississippi	1
Mind of My Mind	2
Out of Time's Abyss	1
People That Time Forgot, The	3
Prince and the Pauper, The	2
Pudd'nhead Wilson	1
Rimrunners	1
Rob Roy	1
Sot-Weed Factor, The	2
Strange Case of Dr. Jekyll and Mr. Hyde	1
Survivor	1
Tai-Pan	2
Tale of the Body Thief, The	3

Figure 7-6:   Counting the members of a group

Taltos	3
Tarzan and the Forbidden City	1
Three Musketeers, The	2
Treasure Island	2
Vilette	1
Waverly Novels	3
White Dragon, The	2

Figure 7-6: (Continued) Counting the members of a group

You can use any of the set functions in a grouping query. For example, the online bookstore could see the total cost for each order in the ORDER_LINES table with

```
SELECT order_numb, SUM (cost_line)
FROM order_lines
GROUP BY order_numb
```

The result can be found in Figure 7-7.

order_numb	sum(cost_line)
1	59.85
2	64.90
3	107.75
4	27.95
5	68.85
6	121.70
7	258.45
8	170.60
9	47.90
10	83.80
11	65.85
12	88.80
13	84.80

Figure 7-7: Summing the members of a group

You can form nested groups by including more than one column in the GROUP BY clause. For example, if the online bookstore wanted to see the total cost of orders placed by each customer per day, the query could be written

```
SELECT customer_numb, order_date, SUM (cost_line)
FROM order_lines JOIN orders
GROUP BY customer_numb, order_date
```

Because the CUSTOMER_NUMBER column is listed first in the ORDER BY clause, its values are used to create the outer groupings. The DBMS then groups orders by date *within* customer numbers. The default output (see Figure 7-8) is somewhat hard to interpret because the outer groupings are not in order. However, if you add an ORDER BY clause to sort the output by customer number, you can see the ordering by date for each customer (see Figure 7-9).

customer_numb	order_date	sum(cost_line)
1	12/5/04	59.85
2	3/18/05	27.95
2	11/12/04	107.75
1	7/6/05	64.90
4	11/22/04	170.60
3	12/2/04	258.45
3	8/15/04	121.70
2	7/6/05	68.85
6	3/12/05	88.80
6	9/19/04	65.85
5	3/12/05	83.80
4	1/6/05	47.90
8	10/12/04	131.70
7	1/9/05	15.95
7	12/13/04	111.75
6	7/21/05	84.80
11	2/21/05	172.65
11	9/19/04	31.90
10	3/4/05	67.85
10	11/15/04	43.90
9	7/15/04	115.75
8	5/13/05	83.80
8	2/22/05	71.85
12	10/10/04	41.90
11	5/14/05	75.85

Figure 7-8: Grouping by two columns (default row order)

Restricting Groups

The grouping queries you have seen to this point include all the rows in the table. However, you can restrict the rows that are included in grouped output using one of two strategies:

customer_numb	order_date	sum(cost_lines)
1	12/5/04	59.85
1	7/6/05	64.90
2	11/12/04	107.75
2	3/18/05	27.95
2	7/6/05	68.85
3	8/15/04	121.70
3	12/2/04	258.45
4	11/22/04	170.60
4	1/6/05	47.90
5	3/12/05	83.80
6	9/19/04	65.85
6	3/12/05	88.80
6	7/21/05	84.80
7	12/13/04	111.75
7	1/9/05	15.95
8	10/12/04	131.70
8	2/22/05	71.85
8	5/13/05	83.80
9	7/15/04	115.75
10	11/15/04	43.90
10	3/4/05	67.85
11	9/19/04	31.90
11	2/21/05	172.65
11	5/14/05	75.85
12	10/10/04	41.90

Figure 7-9:   **Grouping by two columns (rows sorted by outer grouping column)**

◆ Restrict the rows before groups are formed.
◆ Allow all groups to be formed and then restrict the groups.

The first strategy is performed with the WHERE clause in the same way we have been restricting rows to this point. The second requires a HAVING clause, which contains a predicate that applies to groups after they are formed.

Assume, for example, that the online bookstore wants to see the number of books ordered at each price over $22. One way to write the query is to use a WHERE clause to throw out rows with a cost less than or equal to $22:

```
SELECT cost_each, count (*)
FROM order_lines
WHERE cost_each > 22
GROUP BY cost_each
```

Alternatively, you could let the DBMS form the groups and then throw out the groups that have a cost less than or equal to $22 with a HAVING clause:

```
SELECT cost_each, count (*)
FROM order_lines
GROUP BY cost_each
HAVING cost_each > 22
```

The result in both cases is the same (see Figure 7-10). However, the way in which the query is processed is different. When you use WHERE, the restriction on rows is performed *before* rows are grouped. When you use HAVING, the groups are formed and then the predicate following HAVING is applied to the groups.

cost_each	count(*)
23.95	11
27.95	7
24.95	13
22.95	6
25.95	2

Figure 7-10: Restricting rows to books that cost more than $22

There are two important implications of this distinction. First, the predicate following HAVING must pertain to the criteria used to form the groups because the restriction is placed on the group as a whole. In the preceding example, a predicate in a HAVING clause could involve only the COST_EACH column because that is the only piece of data that pertains to the groups.

Second, depending on the distribution of your data, the performance of the two methods may be very different. If most of the rows in the table will be included in groups and you want to display data from most of the groups, then a query will perform better if you form the groups first and then discard the few that are not wanted. However, if the groups will be formed from just a few of the rows, then you will get better performance if you restrict the rows first and then form the groups.

In some cases, you may need to use both WHERE and HAVING clauses in the same query. For example, if the bookstore wants to see how many books costing more than $22 and published after 1980 have been ordered, the query could be written

```
SELECT cost_each, count(*)
FROM order_lines JOIN books
WHERE publication_year > '1980'
GROUP BY cost_each
HAVING cost_each > 22
```

There is no choice but to place the predicate involving the publication year in a WHERE clause: The column is not used for forming groups. As you can see in Figure 7-11, adding the extra restriction indeed limits the rows used to form the groups. (Compare Figure 7-11 with Figure 7-10.)

cost_each	count(*)
23.95	9
24.95	8
22.95	3
25.95	2

Figure 7-11:   Output of a query using both WHERE and HAVING clauses

Conformance note: Grouping queries are required for Core SQL:1999 conformance, including the HAVING clause. The GROUP BY clause must be able to support columns not in the SELECT list.

8

Data Modification

SQL includes three statements for modifying the data in tables: IN-SERT, UPDATE, and DELETE. Most of the time, application programs provide forms-driven data modification, removing the need for SQL data modification statements. (As you will see, that is a good thing because using SQL data modification statements is rather clumsy.) Nonetheless, when manipulating database data from within an application program, you will often need to construct the appropriate SQL statements. This chapter therefore shows you how to use SQL commands to modify stored data.

Inserting Rows

The SQL INSERT statement has two variations: one that inserts a single row into a table and a second that copies one or more rows from another table.

Inserting One Row

To add one row to a table, you use the general syntax

```
INSERT into table_name VALUES (value_list)
```

In the preceding form, the value list contains one value for every column in the table, in the order in which the columns were created. For example, to insert a new row into the BOOKS table you might use

```
INSERT INTO books VALUES ('0-200-3939-2','Bronte, Emily','My Very
    Best Work','Harper','1810','hb',2,18.95,6)
```

There are two things to keep in mind when inserting data in this way:

- ◆ The format of the values in the value list must match the data types of the columns into which the data will be placed. In the current example, the first six columns require character data. Therefore, the values have been surrounded by single quotes. The last three values are numeric and therefore are not in quotes.
- ◆ When you insert a row of data, the DBMS checks any integrity constraints that you have placed on the table. In this case, it will verify that the author exists in the AUTHORS table and that the publisher exists in the PUBLISHERS table. If the constraints are not met, you will receive an error message and the row will not be added to the table. It will also verify that the primary key (the ISBN) is unique and nonnull.

If you do not want to insert data into every column of a table, you can specify the columns into which data should be placed:

```
INSERT INTO table_name (column_list) VALUES (value_list)
```

There must be a one-to-one correspondence between the columns in the column list and values in the value list because the DBMS matches them by their relative positions in the lists.

As an example, assume that you want to insert a row into the BOOKS table but do not have a supplier or retail price for the book as yet. The SQL would then be written

```
INSERT INTO books (isbn, author_name, title, publisher,
    publication_year, binding) VALUES ('0-200-3939-2','Bronte,
    Emily','My Very Best Work', 'Harper', '1810','hb')
```

There are six columns in the column list and therefore six values in the value list. The first value in the value list will be inserted in the ISBN column, the second value in the AUTHOR_NAME column, and so on. The columns omitted from the lists will remain null. You must therefore at least be sure to place values in primary key columns. Otherwise, the DBMS will not permit the insertion to occur.

Although it is not necessary to list column names when inserting values for every column in a table, there is one good reason to do so, especially when embedding the INSERT statement in an application program. If the structure of the table changes—if columns are added or rearranged—then an INSERT without column names will no longer work properly. By always specifying column names, you can avoid unnecessary program modifications as your database changes to meet your changing needs.

Copying Multiple Rows

The SQL INSERT statement can also be used to copy one or more rows from one table to another. The rows that will be copied are specified with a SELECT, giving the statement the following general syntax:

```
INSERT INTO table_name SELECT complete_SELECT_statement
```

The columns in the SELECT must match the columns of the table. For the purposes of this example, we will add a simple table to the online bookstore database:

```
Summary (isbn, how_many)
```

This table will contain summary information gathered from the ORDER_LINES table. To add rows to the new table, the INSERT statement can be written

```
INSERT INTO summary
SELECT isbn, COUNT(*)
FROM order_lines
GROUP BY isbn
```

The result is 51 rows copied into the SUMMARY table, one for each unique book in the ORDER_LINES table.

> *Note: Should you store summary data like that placed in the Summary table? The answer is,"it depends." If it takes a long time to generate the summary data and you use the data frequently, then storing it probably makes sense. But if you can generate the summary data easily and quickly, then it is just as easy not to store it and to create the data whenever it is needed for output.*

Placement of New Rows

Where do new rows go when you add them? That depends on your DBMS. A typical scheme is to assign each new row an internal identifier (something akin to the combination of a row number and a table identifier) that gives the DBMS information about where the row is physically stored in the database's file. These identifiers continue to increase in value. As rows are deleted from the table, there will be gaps in the sequence of row identifiers. However, the DBMS does not reuse them (to "fill in the holes") until it has used up all available identifiers. As a result, new rows generally appear to go on the end of a table. But if a database is very old, very large, and/

or very active, the DBMS will run out of new identifiers and will then start to reuse those made available by deleted rows. In that case, new rows may appear anywhere in the table. This means that you can never count on the physical position of rows in a table. Given that you can view rows in any order by using the ORDER BY clause, it should make absolutely no difference to an end user or an application program where a new row is added.

> *Conformance note: Support for the INSERT statement is required for Core SQL:1999 conformance.*

Updating Data

Although most of today's end users modify existing data using an on-screen form, it is not unusual for an application program to perform embedded SQL updates out of sight of the user. For example, as a user adds rows to a line items table, the application may compute the order total and then insert that total into the row in the orders table that describes the order.

The SQL UPDATE statement affects one or more rows in a table, based on row selection criteria in a WHERE predicate. UPDATE has the following general syntax:

```
UPDATE table_name
SET column1 = new_value, column2 = new_value, …
WHERE row_selection_predicate
```

If the WHERE predicate contains a primary key expression, then the UPDATE will affect only one row. For example, to change a customer's address, the online bookstore could use

```
UPDATE customers
SET street = '195 Main Street',
    city = 'New Town',
    zip = '11111'
WHERE customer_numb = 5
```

However, if the WHERE predicate identifies multiple rows, each row that meets the criteria in the predicate will be modified. To change all 23.95 prices to 24.25, the online bookstore might write a query as

```
UPDATE books
SET retail_price = 24.25
WHERE retail_price = 23.95
```

Notice that it is possible to modify the value in a column being used to identify rows. The DBMS will select the rows to be modified before making any changes to data.

If you leave the WHERE clause off an UPDATE, the same modification will be applied to every row in the table. For example, the following statement increases the price of every book by 10 percent:

```
UDPATE books
SET retail_price = retail_price * 1.1
```

The expression in the SET clause takes the current value in the RETAIL_PRICE column for each row, multiplies it by 1.1, and replaces the existing value with the new computed value.

> *Conformance note: Support for the UPDATE statement, including the ability to use a WHERE clause to search for the rows to be affected by the command, is required for Core SQL:1999 conformance.*

Deleting Rows

Like the UPDATE statement, the DELETE statement affects one or more rows in a table based on row selection criteria in a WHERE predicate. The general syntax for DELETE is

```
DELETE FROM table_name
WHERE row_selection_predicate
```

For example, if a customer decided to remove a book from an order, the online bookstore could use a statement like

```
DELETE FROM order_lines
WHERE isbn = '0-151-1111-2' AND order_numb = 12
```

In this case, the WHERE predicate contains a primary key expression. Therefore, only one row is deleted.

When the criteria in a WHERE predicate identify multiple rows, all those matching rows are removed. If the customer wanted to cancel all contents of order 12, then the SQL would be written

```
DELETE FROM order_lines
WHERE order_numb = 12
```

DELETE is a potentially dangerous operation. If you leave off the WHERE clause—DELETE FROM ORDER_LINES—you will delete every row in the table! (The table remains in the database without any rows.)

Deletes and Referential Integrity

The preceding examples of DELETE involve a table that has no foreign keys referencing it from another table. It does contain two foreign keys of its own (ISBN referencing the primary key of BOOKS and ORDER_NUMB referencing the primary key of ORDERS). You can delete foreign keys without any effect on the rest of the database, but what happens when you attempt to delete rows that *do* have foreign keys referencing them?

Assume, for example, that a customer cancels an order. Your first thought might be to delete the row for that order from the ORDERS table. However, this will "orphan" the rows in the ORDER_LINES table that are related to that order. There will be no primary key for them to reference and referential integrity will be violated.

What actually happens in such a situation depends on what was specified when the table containing the primary key being referenced was created. The SQL-92 standard provides four options for handling the deletion of primary key rows that have foreign key rows that reference them:

- ♦ SET NULL: The values of all foreign keys that reference the deleted primary key row are set to null. In our particular example, this is not a viable option because the foreign key in the ORDER_LINES table is part of its own primary key and therefore cannot be null.
- ♦ SET DEFAULT: The values of all foreign keys that reference the deleted primary key row are set to a default value. This is also not a reasonable solution for our example because we need to relate order lines to a specific order, rather than some generic order.
- ♦ CASCADE: When the primary key row is deleted, all foreign key rows that reference it are deleted as well. This alternative makes sense for our example. When a customer cancels an order, we want to get rid of the order lines, too. There is no reason to keep them.
- ♦ NO ACTION: Disallow the deletion of a primary key row if there are foreign key rows that reference it. This alternative makes sense for the CUSTOMER table, for example, because we do not want to delete any customers who have orders in the ORDERS table. By the same token, we would probably use this option for the BOOKS table so that we do not delete data about any books that are on order.

Conformance note: Support for the DELETE statement, and a WHERE clause to search for rows, is required for Core SQL:1999 conformance.

Part Three

Managing Database Structure

9

Schemas and Tables

As a complete data manipulation language, SQL contains statements that let you create, modify, and delete structural elements in a database. In this chapter we will begin the discussion of a database's structural elements by looking at schemas and the permanent base tables that you create within them. This discussion will be concluded in Chapter 10, which covers additional structural elements such as views, temporary tables, and indexes.

The actual file structure of a database is implementation dependent, as is the procedure needed to create database files. Therefore, the discussion in this chapter assumes that the necessary database files are already in place.

Database Object Hierarchy

The objects in a database maintained by SQL-92 are arranged in a hierarchy, diagrammed in Figure 9-1. The smallest units with which a database works—the columns and rows—appear in the center. These in turn are grouped into tables and views.

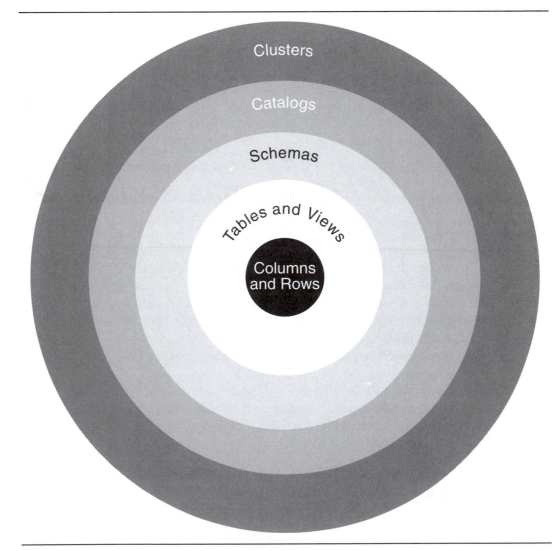

Figure 9-1: The SQL-92 database object hierarchy

The tables and views that constitute a single logical database are collected into a *schema*. Multiple schemas are grouped into *catalogs*, which can then be grouped into *clusters*. A catalog usually contains information describing all the schemas handled by one DBMS. Catalog creation is implementation dependent and therefore not part of the SQL-92 standard.

Prior to SQL-92, clusters often represented database files, and the clustering of objects into files was a way to increase database performance by placing objects accessed together in the same physical file. The SQL-92 concept of a cluster, however, is a group of catalogs that are accessible using the same connection to a database server. Under SQL-92, none of the groupings of database objects are related to physical storage structures. If you are working with a centralized mainframe DBMS, you may find multiple catalogs stored in the database file. However, on smaller or distributed systems, you are just as likely to find one catalog or schema per database file or to find a catalog or schema split between multiple files.

Clusters, catalogs, and schemas are not required elements of a database environment. In a small installation where there is one collection of tables serving a single purpose, for example, it may not even be necessary to create a schema to hold them.

Naming and Identifying Objects

The way in which you name and identify database objects is in some measure dictated by the object hierarchy:

- ◆ Column names must be unique within the table.
- ◆ Table names must be unique within the schema.
- ◆ Schema names must be unique within their catalog.
- ◆ Catalog names must be unique within their cluster.

As you saw when you were reading about data retrieval, when a column name appears in more than one table in a query, you must specify the table from which a column should be taken (even if it makes no difference which table is used). The general form for qualifying duplicate names is

```
table_name.column_name
```

If an installation has more than one schema, then you must also indicate the schema in which a table resides:

```
schema_name.table_name.column_name
```

This naming convention means that two different schemas can include tables with the same name.

By the same token, if an installation has multiple catalogs, you will need to indicate the catalog from which an object comes:

```
catalog_name.schema_name.table_name.column_name
```

The names that you assign to database elements can include the following:

- ◆ Letters
- ◆ Numbers
- ◆ Underscores (_)

Names can be up to 128 characters long. They are not case sensitive. (In fact, many SQL command processors convert names to all upper- or lowercase characters before submitting a SQL statement to a DBMS for processing.)

> *Note: Some DBMSs also allow pound signs (#) and dollar signs ($) in element names, but neither is recognized by SQL queries so their use should be avoided.*

Schemas

To a database designer, a schema represents the overall, logical design of a complete database. As far as SQL is concerned, however, a schema is nothing more than a container for tables, views, and other structural elements. It is up to the database designer to place a meaningful group of elements within each schema.

A schema is not required to create tables and views. In fact, if you are installing a database for an environment in which there is likely to be only one logical database, then you can just as easily do without one. However, if more than one database will be sharing the same DBMS and the same server, then organizing database elements into schemas can greatly simplify the maintenance of the individual databases.

Creating a Schema

To create a schema, you use the CREATE SCHEMA statement. In its simplest form, it has the syntax

```
CREATE SCHEMA schema_name
```

as in

```
CREATE SCHEMA bookstore
```

By default, a schema belongs to the user who created it (the user ID under which the schema was created). The owner of the schema is the only user ID that can modify the schema unless the owner grants that ability to other users.

To assign a different owner to a schema, you add an AUTHORIZATION clause:

```
CREATE SCHEMA schema_name AUTHORIZATION owner_user_ID
```

For example, to assign the bookstore schema to the user ID DBA, someone could use

```
CREATE SCHEMA bookstore AUTHORIZATION dba
```

When creating a schema, you can also create additional database elements at the same time. To do so, you use braces to group the CRE-ATE statements for the other elements, as in

```
CREATE SCHEMA schema_name AUTHORIZATION owner_user_ID
{
    other create statements go here
}
```

This automatically assigns the elements within the braces to the schema.

> *Conformance note: Entry level SQL-92 conformance requires support for schemas, but not for naming them. In that case, the name of the schema defaults to the user ID of the user creating the schema. At intermediate level conformance, named schemas are required. The CREATE SCHEMA statement is also required for Core SQL:1999 conformance.*

Identifying the Schema You Want to Use

One of the nicest things about a relational database is that you can add or delete database structure elements at any time. There must therefore be a way to specify a current schema for new database elements after the schema has been created initially with the CREATE SCHEMA statement.

One way to do this is with the SET SCHEMA statement:

```
SET SCHEMA schema_name
```

To use SET SCHEMA, the user ID under which you are working must have authorization to work with that schema.

Alternatively, you can qualify the name of a database element with the name of the schema. For example, if you are creating a table, then you would use something like

```
CREATE TABLE schema_name.table_name
```

For DBMSs that do not support SET SCHEMA, this is the only way to attach new database elements to a schema after the schema has been created.

> *Conformance note: Support for* SET SCHEMA *is required only for*
> *full conformance to the SQL-92 standard. The SQL:1999 stan-*
> *dard does not include* SET SCHEMA. *Users must therefore qual-*
> *ify element names with the name of the schema to which they*
> *will belong, as described in the preceding section.*

Domains

A *domain* is an expression of the permitted values for a column in a
relation. When you define a table, you assign each column a data
type (for example, character or integer) that provides a broad domain.

A DBMS will not store data that violate that constraint. The SQL-92
standard introduced the concept of user-defined domains, which
can be viewed as user-defined data types that can be applied to columns in tables. (This means you have to create a domain before you
can assign it to a column!)

Domains can be created as part of a CREATE SCHEMA statement or, if
your DBMS supports SET SCHEMA, at any time after a schema has
been defined.

To create a domain, you use the CREATE DOMAIN statement, which has
the following general syntax:

```
CREATE DOMAIN domain_name data_type
CHECK (expression_to_validate_values)
```

The CHECK clause is actually a generic way to express a condition
that data must meet. It can include a SELECT to validate data against
other data stored in the database or it can include a simple logical
expression. In that expression, the keyword VALUE represents the
data being checked.

For example, if the online bookstore wanted to validate the price of
a book, someone might create the following domain:

```
CREATE DOMAIN price numeric (6,2)
CHECK (VALUE >= 5.95)
```

After creating this domain, a column in a table can be given the data type of PRICE. The DBMS will then check to be certain that the value in that column is always greater than or equal to 5.95. (We will leave a discussion of the data type used in the preceding SQL statement until we cover creating tables in the next section of this chapter.)

The domain mechanism is very flexible. Assume, for example, that you want to ensure that telephone numbers are always stored in the format xxx-xxx-xxxx. A domain to validate that format might be created as

```
CREATE DOMAIN telephone char (12)
CHECK (SUBSTRING (VALUE FROM 4 FOR 1 = '-') AND
    SUBSTRING (VALUE FROM 8 FOR 1 = '-'))
```

You can use the CREATE DOMAIN statement to give a column a default value. For example, the following statement sets up a domain that holds either Y or N and defaults to Y:

```
CREATE DOMAIN boolean char (1)
DEFAULT 'Y'
CHECK (UPPER(VALUE) = 'Y' OR UPPER(VALUE) = 'N')
```

> *Conformance note: Domains are required for intermediate level SQL-92 conformance. However, the move toward user-defined data types and, in particular, classes, in SQL:1999 has meant that domains are not included in the most recent standard. Domains have not been deprecated explicitly, but there seems to be tacit agreement that no further development of domain support will occur.*

Tables

The most important structure within a relational database is the table. Tables contain just about everything, including business data and the data dictionary.

The SQL-92 standard divides tables into three categories:

- ◆ Permanent base tables: Permanent base tables are tables whose contents are stored in the database and remain permanently in the database unless they are explicitly deleted.
- ◆ Global temporary tables: Global temporary tables are tables used for working storage that are destroyed at the end of a SQL session. The definitions of the tables are stored in the data dictionary, but their data are not. The tables must be loaded with data each time they are going to be used. Global temporary tables can be used only by the current user, but they are visible to an entire SQL session (either an application program or a user working with an interactive query facility).
- ◆ Local temporary tables: Local temporary tables are similar to global temporary tables. However, they are visible only to the specific program module in which they are created. Temporary base tables are subtly different from views, which assemble their data by executing a SQL query. You will read more about this difference and how temporary tables are created and used in Chapter 10.

Conformance note: Support for temporary tables is required only for full SQL-92 conformance, although you may find them available with DBMSs that are otherwise only at intermediate level conformance. Only permanent base tables are required for Core SQL:1999 conformance. Temporary tables are, however, part of the full standard specification.

Most of the tables you use will be permanent base tables. You create them with the CREATE TABLE statement:

```
CREATE TABLE table_name (column1_name column1_data_type
    column_constraints, column2_name column2_data_type
    column_constraints, …
    table_constraints)
```

The constraints on a table include declarations of primary and foreign keys. The constraints on a column include whether values in the column are mandatory as well as other constraints you may decide to include in a CHECK clause.

Column Data Types

Each column in a table must be given a data type. Although data types are somewhat implementation dependent, you can expect to find most of the following:

- ♦ INTEGER (abbreviated INT): A positive or negative whole number. The number of bits occupied by the value is implementation dependent. On today's desktop computers, an integer is either 16 or 32 bits. Large computers use only 32-bit integers.
- ♦ SMALLINT: A positive or negative whole number. A small integer is usually half the size of a standard integer. Using small integers when you know you will need to store only small values can save space in the database.
- ♦ NUMERIC: A fixed-point positive or negative number. A numeric value has a whole number portion and a fractional portion. When you create it, you must specify the total length of the number (including the decimal point) and how many of those digits will be to the right of the decimal point (its *precision*). For example,

```
numeric (6,2)
```

creates a number in the format XXX.XX. The DBMS will store exactly two digits to the right of the decimal point.
- ♦ DECIMAL: A fixed-point positive or negative number. A decimal number is similar to a numeric value. However, the DBMS may store more digits to the right of the decimal than you specify. Although there is no guarantee that you will get the extra precision, its presence can provide more accurate results in computations.
- ♦ REAL: A "single precision" floating point value. A floating-point number is expressed in the format

$$\pm X.XXXXX * 10^{YY}$$

where YY is the power to which 10 is raised. Because of the way in which computers store floating-point numbers, a real number will never be an exact representation of a value, but only a close approximation. The range of values that can be stored is implementation dependent, as is the precision. You therefore cannot specify a size for a real number column.

♦ DOUBLE PRECISION (abbreviated DOUBLE): A "double precision" floating-point number. The range and precision of double-precision values are implementation dependent, but generally both will be greater than with single-precision real numbers.

♦ FLOAT: A floating-point number for which you can specify the precision. The DBMS will maintain at least the precision that you specify. (It may be more.)

♦ BIT: Storage for a fixed number of individual bits. You must indicate the number of bits, as in

```
BIT (n)
```

where n is the number of bits. (If you do not, you will have room for only one bit.)

♦ BIT VARYING: Storage for a varying number of bits, up to a specified maximum, as in

```
BIT VARYING (n)
```

where n is the maximum number of bits. In some DBMSs, columns of this type can be used to store graphic images.

♦ DATE: A date.

♦ TIME: A time.

♦ TIMESTAMP: The combination of a date and a time.

♦ CHARACTER (abbreviated CHAR): A fixed-length space to hold a string of characters. When declaring a CHAR column, you need to indicate the width of the column:

```
CHAR (n)
```

where n is the amount of space that will be allocated for the column in every row. Even if you store less than n characters, the column will always take up n bytes and the column will be padded with blanks to fill up empty space. The maximum number of characters allowed is implementation dependent.

♦ CHARACTER VARYING (abbreviated VARCHAR): A variable length space to hold a string of characters. You must indicate the maximum width of the column—

```
VARCHAR (n)
```

—but the DBMS stores only as many characters as you insert, up to the maximum n. The overall maximum number of characters allowed is implementation dependent.

♦ INTERVAL: A date or time interval. An interval data type is followed by a qualifier that specifies the size of the interval and optionally the number of digits. For example,

```
INTERVAL YEAR
INTERVAL YEAR (n)
INTERVAL MONTH
INTERVAL MONTH (n)
INTERVAL YEAR TO MONTH
INTERVAL YEAR (n) TO MONTH
INTERVAL DAY
INTERVAL DAY (n)
INTERVAL DAY TO HOUR
INTERVAL DAY (n) TO HOUR
INTERVAL DAY TO MINUTE
INTERVAL DAY (n) TO MINUTE
INTERVAL MINUTE
INTERVAL MINUTE (n)
```

In the preceding examples, n specifies the number of digits. When the interval covers more than one date/time unit, such as YEAR TO MONTH, you can specify a size for only the first unit. Year/month intervals can include years, months, or both. Time intervals can include days, hours, minutes, and/or seconds.

Most current DBMSs do not support the BOOLEAN data type. This means that if you need to use a column as a flag, the best solution is to create a BOOLEAN domain like the one you saw earlier in this chapter in the section on domains.

In Figure 9-2 you will find bare-bones CREATE TABLE statements for the online bookstore database. These statements include only column names and data types. SQL will create tables from statements in this format, but because the tables have no primary keys, many DBMSs will not let you enter data.

> *Note: Support for all the preceding data types—with the exception of BIT, BIT VARYING, and INTERVAL—is required for Core SQL:1999 conformance. INTERVAL, BIT, BOOLEAN, and large object (BLOB and CLOB) are included in the full standard.*

Default Values

As you are defining columns, you can designate a default value for individual columns. To indicate a default value, you add a DEFAULT keyword to the column definition, followed by the default value. For example, in the ORDERS relation the ORDER_DATE column defaults to the current system date. The column declaration is therefore written

```
order_date date DEFAULT CURRENT_DATE
```

Notice that this particular declaration is using the SQL value CURRENT_DATE. However, you can place any value after DEFAULT that is a valid instance of the column's data type.

> *Conformance note: The Core SQL:1999 specifications require support for column default values.*

NOT NULL Constraints

The values in primary key columns must be unique and not null. In addition, there may be columns for which you want to require a value. You can specify such columns by adding NOT NULL after the column declaration. Since the online bookstore wants to ensure that an order date is always entered, the complete declaration for that column in the ORDERS table is

```
CREATE TABLE books
    (isbn char (12),
    author_name varchar (40),
    title varchar (60),
    publisher_name varchar (40),
    publication_year char (4),
    binding char (2),
    source_numb integer,
    retail price numeric (6,2),
    number_on_hand integer)

CREATE TABLE authors
    (author_name varchar (40))

CREATE TABLE publishers
    (publisher_name varchar (40))

CREATE TABLE customers
    (customer_numb integer,
    customer_first_name varchar (15),
    customer_last_name varchar (15),
    customer_street varchar (30),
    customer_city varchar (15),
    customer_state char (2),
    customer_zip char (5)
    customer_phone char (12),
    customer_email varchar (40))

CREATE TABLE sources
    (source_numb integer,
    source_name varchar (30),
    source_street varchar (30),
    source_city varchar (20),
    source_state char (2),
    source_zip char (5),
    source_phone varchar (12))

CREATE TABLE orders
    (order_numb integer,
    customer_numb integer,
    order_date date,
    credit_card_numb varchar (15),
    credit_card_expiration_date char (5),
    order_filled char (1))
```

Figure 9-2:   Initial CREATE TABLE statements for the online bookstore

```
CREATE TABLE order_lines
    (order_numb integer,
    isbn char (12),
    quantity integer,
    cost_each numeric (6,2),
    cost_line numeric (6,2),
    shipped char (1))
```

Figure 9-2: (Continued) Initial CREATE TABLE statements for the online

order_date date NOT NULL DEFAULT CURRENT_DATE

> *Conformance note: Support for the* NOT NULL *constraint is required for Core SQL:1999 conformance.*

Primary Keys

To specify a table's primary key, you add a PRIMARY KEY clause to a CREATE TABLE statement. The keywords PRIMARY KEY are followed by the names of the primary key column or columns, surrounded by parentheses.

In Figure 9-3 you will find the CREATE TABLE statements for the online bookstore database including primary key declarations. Notice that in the ORDER_LINES table, which has a concatenated primary key, both primary key columns have been included in the PRIMARY KEY clause.

> *Conformance note: DBMSs that are at entry level conformance require that all primary key columns be designated as NOT NULL as well as being part of the primary key constraint. At the intermediate level, NOT NULL is not required for primary key columns. Core SQL:1999 requires implicit support for NOT NULL in primary keys.*

Foreign Keys

As you know, a foreign key is a column (or concatenation of columns) that is exactly the same as the primary key of another table.

```
CREATE TABLE books
    (isbn char (12),
    author_name varchar (40),
    title varchar (60),
    publisher_name varchar (40),
    publication_year char (4),
    binding char(2),
    source_numb integer,
    retail price numeric (6,2),
    number_on_hand integer,
    PRIMARY KEY (isbn))

CREATE TABLE authors
    (author_name varchar (40),
    PRIMARY KEY (author_name))

CREATE TABLE publishers
    (publisher_name varchar (40),
    PRIMARY KEY (publisher_name))

CREATE TABLE customers
    (customer_numb integer,
    customer_first_name varchar (15) NOT NULL,
    customer_last_name varchar (15) NOT NULL,
    customer_street varchar (30),
    customer_city varchar (15),
    customer_state char (2),
    customer_zip char (5),
    customer_phone char (12) NOT NULL,
    customer_email varchar (40),
    PRIMARY KEY (customer_numb))

CREATE TABLE sources
    (source_numb integer,
    source_name varchar (30) NOT NULL,
    source_street varchar (30),
    source_city varchar (20),
    source_state char (2),
    source_zip char (5),
    source_phone varchar (12) NOT NULL,
    PRIMARY KEY (source_numb))
```

Figure 9-3:   CREATE TABLE statements for the online bookstore database including primary key declarations

```
CREATE TABLE orders
    (order_numb integer,
    customer_numb integer NOT NULL,
    order_date date NOT NULL DEFAULT CURRENT_DATE,
    credit_card_numb varchar (15),
    credit_card_expiration_date char (5),
    order_filled char (1) NOT NULL DEFAULT 'N',
    PRIMARY KEY (order_numb))

CREATE TABLE order_lines
    (order_numb integer,
    isbn char (12),
    quantity integer NOT NULL,
    cost_each numeric (6,2) NOT NULL,
    cost_line numeric (6,2),
    shipped char (1) NOT NULL DEFAULT 'N',
    PRIMARY KEY (order_numb, isbn))
```

Figure 9-3: (Continued) CREATE TABLE statements for the online bookstore database including primary key declarations

When a foreign key value matches a primary key value, we know that there is a logical relationship between the database objects represented by the matching rows.

One of the major constraints on a relation is referential integrity, which states that every nonnull foreign key value must reference an existing primary key value. Early implementations of SQL and the SQL-86 standard did not include support for foreign keys. Validation of referential integrity was left up to application programmers. However, it is far better to have foreign keys identified in the data dictionary and referential integrity enforced directly by a DBMS. Referential integrity was therefore added to the SQL-89 standard.

To specify a foreign key for a table, you add a FOREIGN KEY clause:

```
FOREIGN KEY foreign_key_name (foreign_key_columns)
REFERENCES primary_key_table (primary_key_columns)
ON UPDATE update_action
ON DELETE delete_action
```

The names of the foreign key columns follow the keywords FOREIGN KEY. The REFERENCES clause contains the name of the primary key table being referenced. If the primary key columns are named in the

PRIMARY KEY clause of their table, then you don't need to list the column names. However, if the columns aren't part of a PRIMARY KEY clause, you must list the primary key columns in the REFERENCES clause.

The final part of the FOREIGN KEY specification indicates what should happen when a primary key value being referenced by the foreign key is deleted or updated. There are three options that apply to both updates and deletions and one additional option for each:

- ♦ SET NULL: Replace the foreign key value with null. This isn't possible when the foreign key is part of the primary key of its table.
- ♦ SET DEFAULT: Replace the foreign key value with the column's default value.
- ♦ CASCADE: Delete or update all foreign key rows.
- ♦ NO ACTION: On update, make no modification of foreign key values.
- ♦ RESTRICT: Do not allow deletion of the primary key row.

The complete declarations for the online bookstore database tables, which include foreign key constraints, can be found in Figure 9-4. Notice that although there are no restrictions on how to name foreign keys, the foreign keys in this database have been named to indicate the tables involved. This makes them easier to identify if you need to delete or modify a foreign key at a later date.

> *Conformance note: Support for foreign keys is required by the SQL-89 standard and beyond. However, support for named foreign keys is required only for intermediate level SQL-92 conformance. The Core SQL:1999 requires support only for* NO ACTION *on delete or update of a primary key value referenced by a foreign key.*

```
CREATE TABLE books
    (isbn char (12),
    author_name varchar (40),
    title varchar (60),
    publisher_name varchar (40),
    publication_year char (4),
    binding char (2),
    source_numb integer,
    retail_price numeric (6,2),
    number_on_hand integer,
    PRIMARY KEY (isbn)
    FOREIGN KEY books2authors (author_name)
        REFERENCES authors
        ON UPDATE CASCADE
        ON DELETE RESTRICT,
    FOREIGN KEY book2publishers (publisher_name)
        REFERENCES publishers
        ON UPDATE CASCADE
        ON DELETE RESTRICT,
    FOREIGN KEY books2sources (source_numb)
        REFERENCES sources
        ON DELETE RESTRICT)

CREATE TABLE authors
    (author_name varchar (40),
    PRIMARY KEY (author_name))

CREATE TABLE publishers
    (publisher_name varchar (40),
    PRIMARY KEY (publisher_name))

CREATE TABLE customers
    (customer_numb integer,
    customer_first_name varchar (15) NOT NULL,
    customer_last_name varchar (15) NOT NULL,
    customer_street varchar (30),
    customer_city varchar (15),
    customer_state char (2),
    customer_zip char (5)
    customer_phone char (12) NOT NULL,
    customer_email varchar (40),
    PRIMARY KEY (customer_numb))
```

Figure 9-4: Complete CREATE TABLE statements for the online bookstore database including primary and foreign key declarations

```
CREATE TABLE sources
    (source_numb integer,
    source_name varchar (30) NOT NULL,
    source_street varchar (30),
    source_city varchar (20),
    source_state char (2),
    source_zip char (5),
    source_phone varchar (12) NOT NULL,
    PRIMARY KEY (source_numb))

CREATE TABLE orders
    (order_numb integer,
    customer_numb integer NOT NULL,
    order_date date NOT NULL DEFAULT CURRENT_DATE,
    credit_card_numb varchar (15),
    credit_card_expiration_date char (5),
    order_filled char (1) NOT NULL DEFAULT 'N',
    PRIMARY KEY (order_numb)
    FOREIGN KEY orders2customers (customer_numb)
        REFERENCES customers
        ON UPDATE CASCADE
        ON DELETE RESTRICT)

CREATE TABLE order_lines
    (order_numb integer,
    isbn char (12),
    quantity integer NOT NULL,
    cost_each numeric (6,2) NOT NULL,
    cost_line numeric (6,2),
    shipped char (1) NOT NULL DEFAULT 'N',
    PRIMARY KEY (order_numb, isbn),
    FOREIGN KEY orderlines2books (isbn)
        REFERENCES books
        ON DELETE RESTRICT,
    FOREIGN KEY orderlines2orders (order_numb)
        REFERENCES orders
        ON UPDATE CASCADE
        ON DELETE RESTRICT)
```

Figure 9-4: (Continued) Complete CREATE TABLE statements for the online bookstore database including primary and foreign key declarations

Additional Column Constraints

There are additional constraints that you can place on columns in a table beyond primary and foreign key constraints. These include requiring unique values and predicates in CHECK clauses.

Requiring Unique Values

If you want to ensure that the values in a non–primary key column are unique, then you can use the UNIQUE keyword. UNIQUE verifies that all nonnull values are unique. For example, if you were storing social security numbers in an employees table that used an employee ID as the primary key, you could also enforce unique social security numbers with

```
ssn CHAR (11) UNIQUE
```

The UNIQUE clause can also be placed at the end of the CREATE TABLE statement, along with the primary key and foreign key specifications.

In that case, it takes the form

```
UNIQUE (column_names)
```

Conformance note: Support for the UNIQUE *constraint is required for Core SQL:1999 conformance.*

Check Clauses

The CHECK clause to which you were introduced earlier in this chapter in the Domains section can also be used with individual columns to declare column-specific constraints. To add a constraint, you place a CHECK clause after the column declaration, using the keyword VALUE in a predicate to indicate the value being checked. For example, to verify that a column used to hold true/false values is limited to T and F, you could write a CHECK clause as

```
CHECK (UPPER(VALUE) = 'T' OR UPPER(VALUE) = 'F')
```

Conformance note: Support for the CHECK *clause is required for Core SQL:1999 conformance.*

10

Views, Temporary Tables, and Indexes

A database is made up of more than just a schema and permanent base tables. It can contain views, temporary tables, and indexes. This chapter begins by looking at those structural elements and then turns to modifying all parts of a schema. The chapter concludes by discussing the granting and revoking of access rights to database objects.

Views

A view is a virtual table that is produced by executing a SQL query. It is stored in the data dictionary as a named SELECT. Whenever a SQL query contains the name of a view, the DBMS executes the

179

query associated with the view's definition to create its virtual result table. That table can then be used as a source table by the remainder of the query in which its name appears.

Why We Use Views

There are several important reasons for using views in a database environment:

♦ Views provide a way to store commonly used complex queries in the database. Users can use a simple query such as

```
SELECT * FROM
view_name
```

instead of typing a complex SQL statement.

♦ Views can help you tailor the database environment to individual users, groups of users, or uses. You create views that package the data needed by specific people or for specific purposes, making it easier for those users to access their data.

♦ Views can help maintain database security. Rather than giving users access to entire base tables, you can create views that provide users with exactly the data they need to see. You then grant users access to the views but not to the base tables. (A complete discussion of granting and revoking access rights can be found later in this chapter.)

Another major benefit of using a view is that because view tables are created at the instant they are named in a SQL statement, they are always up to date. View tables always use the most current data stored in the base tables on which they are based.

Creating Views

To create a view whose columns have the same name as the columns in the base tables from which it is derived, you give the view a name and include the SQL query that defines its contents:

```
CREATE VIEW  AS
    SELECT …
```

For example, if the online bookstore wanted to create a view that included hardcover books, the SQL is written

```
CREATE VIEW hardcovers AS
    SELECT author_name, title, isbn, retail_price
    FROM books
    WHERE binding = 'hc'
```

If you want to rename the columns in the view, you include the new column names in the CREATE VIEW statement:

```
CREATE VIEW hardcovers (author, title, isbn, price) AS
    SELECT author_name, title, isbn, retail_price
    FROM books
    WHERE binding = 'hc'
```

The preceding statement will produce a view with four columns named AUTHOR, TITLE, ISBN, and PRICE. Notice that if you want to change even one column name, you must include *all* the column names in the parentheses following the view name. The DBMS will match the columns following SELECT with the view column names by their position in the list.

Views can be created from any SQL query, including those that perform joins, unions, and grouping. For example, to simplify looking at sales figures, the online bookstore might create a view like the following:

```
CREATE VIEW sales_summary AS
    SELECT customer_numb, orders.order_numb, orders.order_date, SUM
    (cost_each)
    FROM order_lines JOIN orders
    GROUP BY customer_numb, orders.order_date, orders.order_numb
```

The view table will then contain grouped data along with a computed column.

Conformance note: Support for views, including views with grouping queries, is included in the Core SQL:1999 specifications.

Querying Views

You use a view in a SQL SELECT just as you would use a base table. For example, to see the entire contents of the SALES_SUMMARY view created in the preceding section, the online bookstore could use the simple query

```
SELECT * FROM sales_summary
```

which produces the result table in Figure 10-1.

customer_numb	order_numb	order_date	expression
1	1	12/5/04	59.85
1	2	7/6/05	44.90
2	3	11/12/04	87.80/05/05
2	4	3/18/00	27.95
2	5	7/6/00	68.85
3	6	8/15/04	105.75
3	7	12/2/04	70.85
4	8	11/22/04	170.60
4	9	1/6/00	47.90
5	10	3/12/00	83.80
6	11	9/19/04	65.85
6	12	3/12/00	88.80
6	13	7/21/00	84.80
7	14	12/13/04	111.75
7	15	1/9/00	15.95
8	16	10/12/04	111.75
8	17	2/22/00	71.85
8	18	5/13/00	83.80
9	19	7/15/04	115.75
10	20	11/15/04	43.90
10	21	3/4/00	67.85
11	22	9/19/04	15.95
11	23	2/21/00	172.65
11	24	5/14/00	75.85
12	25	10/10/04	41.90

Figure 10-1: The output of querying a view that includes grouping and a calculated column

You can apply additional predicates to a view, as in the following example that restricts rows by date:

```
SELECT *
FROM sales_summary
WHERE order_date BETWEEN '04/7/1' AND '04/12/31'
```

The result is the 12 rows in Figure 10-2.

customer_numb	order_numb	order_date	expression
1	1	12/5/04	59.85
2	3	11/12/04	87.80
3	6	8/15/04	105.75
3	7	12/2/04	70.85
4	8	11/22/04	170.60
6	11	9/19/04	65.85
7	14	12/13/04	111.75
8	16	10/12/04	111.75
9	19	7/15/04	115.75
10	20	11/15/04	43.90
11	22	9/19/04	15.95
12	25	10/10/04	41.90

Figure 10-2: The output of adding additional row selection criteria to a view

View Updatability Issues

Theoretically, you should be able to perform INSERT, UPDATE, and DE-LETE on views as well as SELECT. However, not all views are *updatable* (capable of being used for updating). Keep in mind that a view table exists only in main memory. If it is to be used for updates, then the DBMS must be able to propagate the update back to the view's base tables.

The SQL-92 standard places the following conditions on updatable views:

- ◆ The view must be created from only one base table. Views that include joins, for example, are not updatable.
- ◆ The view must include only one query. Views that include UNION, for example, are not updatable.
- ◆ If you have created a view based on another view, then the underlying view must also be updatable.

♦ The SELECT clause must contain only column names. It cannot contain calculated columns or set functions.
♦ The view cannot be based on a grouping query.
♦ The view's query cannot require DISTINCT rows.
♦ The view's query can include a subquery, but only if that subquery uses the same table as the outer query.

In addition, you will be unable to insert rows into views that do not contain the primary key columns of their base tables. (Doing so will violate the base table's primary key constraint.) Although updates and deletes are possible when the primary key columns aren't present in a view, performing such modifications may have unexpected results because you can't be certain which rows will be affected.

The Core SQL:1999 standard does not remove the preceding restrictions. However, the full standard includes a provision for the updatability of views that are derived from grouping queries as well as those derived from more than one table (in particular, JOIN and UNION operations).

Temporary Tables

A temporary table is a base table that is not stored in the database, but instead exists only while the database session in which it was created is active. At first glance, this may sound like a view, but views and temporary tables are rather different:

♦ A view exists only for a single query. Each time you use the name of a view, its table is recreated from existing data.
♦ A temporary table exists for the entire database session in which it was created.
♦ A view is automatically populated with the data retrieved by the query that defines it.
♦ You must add data to a temporary table with SQL INSERT commands.

♦ Only views that meet the criteria for view updatability can be used for data modification.

♦ Because temporary tables are base tables, all of them can be updated.

♦ Because the contents of a view are generated each time the view's name is used, a view's data are always current.

♦ The data in a temporary table reflect the state of the database at the time the table was loaded with data. If the data from which the temporary table was loaded are modified after the temporary table has received its data, then the contents of the temporary table may be out of sync with other parts of the database.

If the contents of a temporary table become outdated when source data change, why use a temporary table at all? Wouldn't it be better simply to use a view whose contents are continually regenerated? The answer lies in performance. It takes processing time to create a view table. If you are going to use data only once during a database session, then a view will actually perform better than a temporary table because you don't need to create a structure for it. However, if you are going to be using the data repeatedly during a session, then a temporary table provides better performance because it needs to be created only once. The decision therefore results in a trade-off. Using a view repeatedly takes more time but provides continually updated data; using a temporary table repeatedly saves time, but you run the risk that the table's contents may be out of date.

Creating Temporary Tables

Creating a temporary table is very similar to creating a permanent base table. You do, however, need to decide on the *scope* of the table. A temporary table can be *global*, in which case it is accessible to the entire application program that created it. Alternatively, it can be *local*, in which case it is accessible only to the program module in which it was created.

VIEWS, TEMPORARY TABLES, AND INDEXES

186   VIEWS, TEMPORARY TABLES, AND INDEXES

To create a global temporary table, you add the keywords GLOBAL TEMPORARY to the CREATE TABLE statement:

```
CREATE GLOBAL TEMPORARY TABLE
    (remainder of CREATE statement)
```

By the same token, you create a local temporary table with

```
CREATE LOCAL TEMPORARY TABLE
    (remainder of CREATE statement)
```

For example, if the online bookstore was going to use the sales summary information repeatedly, they might create the following temporary table instead of using a view:

```
CREATE GLOBAL TEMPORARY TABLE sales_summary
    (customer_numb INTEGER,
    order_numb INTEGER,
    order_date DATE,
    order_total NUMERIC (6,2),
    PRIMARY KEY (customer_numb, order_numb))
```

Loading Temporary Tables with Data

To place data in a temporary table, you use one or more SQL INSERT statements. For example, to load the SALES_SUMMARY table created in the preceding section, you could write

```
INSERT INTO sales_summary
    SELECT customer_numb, orders.order_numb, orders.order_date,
    SUM (cost_each)
    FROM order_lines JOIN orders
    GROUP BY customer_numb, orders.order_date, orders.order_numb
```

You can now query and manipulate the SALES_SUMMARY table just as you would a permanent base table.

Disposition of Temporary Table Rows

When you write embedded SQL, you have control over the amount of work that the DBMS considers to be a unit (a *transaction*). We will discuss transactions in depth in Chapter 11. However, to understand what happens to the rows in a temporary table, you do need to know that a transaction can end in one of two ways: It can be *committed* (its changes made permanent) or it can be *rolled back* (its changes undone).

By default, the rows in a temporary table are purged whenever a transaction is committed. You can, however, instruct the DBMS to retain the rows by including ON COMMIT PRESERVE ROWS to the end of the table creation statement:

```
CREATE GLOBAL TEMPORARY TABLE sales_summary
    (customer_numb INTEGER,
    order_numb INTEGER,
    order_date DATE,
    order_total NUMERIC (6,2),
    PRIMARY KEY (customer_numb, order_numb),
ON COMMIT PRESERVE ROWS)
```

Because a rollback returns the database to the state it was in before the transaction began, a temporary table will also be restored to its previous state (with or without rows).

> *Conformance note: Temporary tables are not part of the Core SQL:1999 standard. They are, however, included in the full SQL:1999 specification.*

Indexes

An *index* is a data structure that provides a fast access path to rows in a table based on the values in one or more columns (the index key). Because an index stores key values in order, the DBMS can use a fast search technique to find the values rather than being forced to search each row in an unordered table sequentially.

The conceptual operation of an index is diagrammed in Figure 10-3. (The different weights of the lines have no significance other than to make it easier for you to follow the crossed lines.) In this illustration, you are looking at the BOOKS relation and an index that provides fast access to rows in the table based on the author's name.

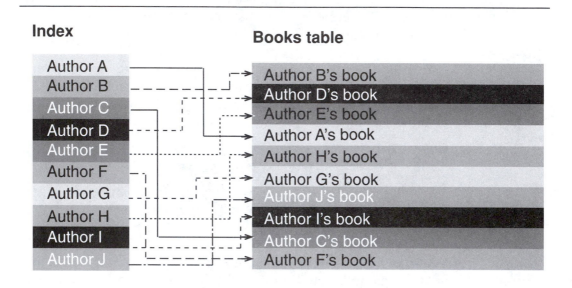

Index

Books table

Figure 10-3: The operation of an index to a relation

The index itself contains an ordered list of keys (the authors' names) along with the locations of the associated rows in the BOOKS table. The rows in the books table are in relatively random order. However, because the index is in alphabetical order by author name, it can be searched quickly to locate a specific author. Then the DBMS can use the information in the index to go directly to the correct row or rows in the BOOKS table, thus avoiding a slow sequential scan of the base table's rows.

Once you have created an index, the DBMS's query optimizer will use the index whenever it determines that using the index will speed up data retrieval. You never need to access the index again yourself unless you want to delete it.

When you create a primary key for a table, the DBMS automatically creates an index for that table using the primary key column or columns as the index key. The first step in inserting a new row into a table is therefore verification that the index key (the primary key of the table) is unique to the index. In fact, uniqueness is enforced by requiring the index entries to be unique, rather than by actually searching the base table. This is much faster than attempting to verify uniqueness directly on the base table, because the ordered index can be searched much more rapidly than the unordered base table.

Deciding Which Indexes to Create

You have no choice about whether the DBMS creates indexes for your primary keys; you get them whether you want them or not. In addition, you can create indexes to provide fast access to any column or combination of columns you want. However, before you jump head- first into creating indexes on every column in every table, there are some trade-offs to consider:

- ♦ Indexes take up space in the database. Given that disk space is inexpensive today, this is usually not a major drawback.
- ♦ When you insert, modify, or delete data in indexed columns, the DBMS must update the index as well as the base table. This may slow down data modification operations, especially if the tables have a lot of rows.
- ♦ Indexes definitely speed up access to data.

The trade-off therefore is generally between update speed and retrieval speed. A good rule of thumb is to create indexes for foreign keys and for other columns that are used frequently in WHERE clause predicates. If you find that update speed is severely affected, you may choose at a later time to delete some of the indexes you created.

Creating Indexes

You create indexes with the CREATE INDEX statement:

```
CREATE INDEX index_name ON table_name (index_key_columns)
```

For example, to create an index on the AUTHOR_NAME column in the BOOKS table, the online bookstore would use

```
CREATE INDEX author_name ON books (author_name)
```

By default, the index will allow duplicate entries and sort the entries in ascending order. To require unique index entries, add the keyword UNIQUE after CREATE:

```
CREATE UNIQUE INDEX author_name ON books (author_name)
```

To sort in descending order, insert DESC after the column whose sort order you want to change. For example, the online bookstore might want to create an index on ORDER_DATE in the ORDERS relation in descending order so that the most recent orders are first:

```
CREATE INDEX order_date ON orders (order_date DESC)
```

If you want to create an index on a concatenated key, you include all the columns that should be part of the index key in the column list. For example, the following creates an index organized by author and book title:

```
CREATE INDEX author_title ON books (author_name, title)
```

Although you do not need to access an index directly unless you want to delete it from the database, it helps to give indexes names that tell you something about their keys. This makes it easier to remember them should you need to get rid of the indexes.

> *Conformance note: Indexes are actually not part of the SQL standard. However, they have been available with virtually every SQL-based DBMS since SQL first appeared.*

Modifying Database Elements

With the exception of tables, structural database elements are largely unchangeable. When you want to modify them, you must delete them from the database and create them from scratch. In contrast, just about every characteristic of a table can be modified without deleting the table using the ALTER TABLE statement.

Adding New Columns

To add a new column to a table, you use the ALTER TABLE statement with the following syntax:

```
ALTER TABLE table_name
ADD column_name column_data_type column_constraints
```

For example, if the online bookstore wanted to add a telephone number column to the PUBLISHERS table, they would use

```
ALTER TABLE publishers
ADD phone CHAR (12)
```

To add more than one column at the same time, simply separate the clauses with commas:

```
ALTER TABLE publishers
ADD phone CHAR (12),
ADD publisher_street VARCHAR (30),
ADD publisher_city VARCHAR (30),
ADD publisher_state CHAR (2),
```

There is one caveat that goes along with adding columns: If you have any application programs that use the SELECT * syntax, then any new columns that you add to a table will be included in the output of that query. The result may be either the disclosure of data you wanted to keep secret or application programs that no longer work properly. Because SQL allows you to add columns to tables without restriction, you should avoid using the SELECT * syntax.

Adding Table Constraints

You can add table constraints such as foreign keys at any time. To do so, include the new constraint in the ADD clause of an ALTER TABLE statement:

```
ALTER TABLE table_name
ADD table_constraint
```

Assume, for example, that the online bookstore created a new table named STATES and included in it all the two-character U.S. state abbreviations. The bookstore would then need to add references to that table from both the CUSTOMERS and PUBLISHERS tables:

```
ALTER TABLE customers
    ADD FOREIGN KEY customers2states (customer_state)
    REFERENCES states (state_name)
ALTER TABLE publishers
    ADD FOREIGN KEY publishers2states (publisher_state)
    REFERENCES states (state_name)
```

When you add a foreign key constraint to a table, the DBMS verifies that all existing data in the table meet that constraint. If they do not, the ALTER TABLE will fail.

Modifying Columns

You can modify columns by changing any characteristic of the column, including its data type, size, and constraints:

♦ To replace a complete column definition, use the MODIFY command with the current column name and the new column characteristics. For example, to change the customer number in the CUSTOMERS table from an integer to a character column, the online bookstore could use

```
ALTER TABLE customers
MODIFY customer_numb CHAR (4)
```

♦ To add or change a default value only (without changing the data type or size of the column), include the DEFAULT keyword:

```
ALTER TABLE customers
MODIFY customer_numb DEFAULT 0
```

◆ To switch between allowing nulls and not allowing nulls without changing any other column characteristics, add NULL or NOT NULL as appropriate:

```
ALTER TABLE customers
MODIFY customer_zip NOT NULL
```

or

```
ALTER TABLE customers
MODIFY customer_phone NULL
```

◆ To modify a column constraint without changing any other column characteristics, include a CHECK clause:

```
ALTER TABLE books
MODIFY retail_price
CHECK (VALUE >= 10.95)
```

When you change the data type of a column, the DBMS will attempt to convert any existing values to the new data type. If the current values cannot be converted, then the table modification will not be performed. In general, most columns can be converted to characters. However, conversions from a character data type to numbers or datetimes require that existing data represent legal values in the new data type.

Deleting Elements

You can also delete structural elements from a table as needed:

◆ To delete a column:

```
ALTER TABLE order_lines
DELETE line_cost
```

◆ To delete a CHECK table constraint (a CHECK that has been applied to an entire table rather than to a specific column):

```
ALTER TABLE customers
DELETE CHECK
```

To remove the UNIQUE constraint from one or more columns:

```
ALTER TABLE books
DELETE UNIQUE (title)
```

◆ To remove a table's PRIMARY KEY:

```
ALTER TABLE customers
DELETE PRIMARY KEY
```

Although you can delete a table's primary key, keep in mind that if you do not add a new one, you will not be able to modify any data in that table.

◆ To delete a foreign key:

```
ALTER TABLE books
DELETE FOREIGN KEY books2publishers
```

Renaming Elements

You can rename both tables and columns:

◆ To rename a table, place the new table name after the RE-NAME keyword:

```
ALTER TABLE order_lines
RENAME line_items
```

◆ To rename a column, include both the old and new column names separated by the keyword TO:

```
ALTER TABLE books
RENAME title TO book_title
```

Note: The SQL-92 standard does include an ALTER DOMAIN statement that has not been implemented by most DBMSs, even those that support the creation and deletion of domains.

Conformance note: Support for ALTER TABLE is required for intermediate level SQL-92 conformance. Although it was not part of previous standards, many DBMSs have supported it in a minimal way, usually allowing users to add columns and increase column widths.

The Core SQL:1999 standard requires support only for adding columns. However, the full standard includes all of the ALTER TABLE *features described in the preceding section, as well as the ability to remove columns from a table.*

Deleting Database Elements

To delete a structural element from a database, you *drop* the element. For example, to delete a table, you would type

```
DROP TABLE table_name
```

Dropping a table is irreversible. In most cases, the DBMS will not bother to ask "Are you sure?" but will immediately delete the structure of the table and all of its data.

You can remove the following structural elements from a database with the DROP statement:

- ◆ Tables
- ◆ Views

  ```
  DROP VIEW view_name
  ```

- ◆ Indexes

  ```
  DROP INDEX index_name
  ```

- ◆ Domains

  ```
  DROP DOMAIN domain_name
  ```

A DROP of a table or view will fail if the element being dropped is currently in use by another user.

The action of a DBMS when you attempt to DROP a table or view depends to some extent whether the table or view contains primary keys with foreign key references and what action was specified when the table or view was created. If the action is RESTRICT, then the DROP will fail. In contrast, for example, if the action was CASCADE, related foreign key rows will be deleted from their table(s) when the primary key table is dropped.

> *Conformance note: Dropping tables and views with* `RESTRICT` *is required for Core SQL:1999 conformance. Other options (*`CASCADE`*,* `SET NULL`*, and so on) are required for full conformance.*

Granting and Revoking Access Rights

When you create an element of database structure, the user name under which you are working becomes that element's owner. The owner has the right to do anything to that element; all other users have no rights at all. This means that if tables and views are going to be accessible to other users, you must *grant* them access rights.

Types of Access Rights

There are six types of access rights that you can grant:

- ◆ SELECT: Allows a user to retrieve data from a table or view.
- ◆ INSERT: Allows a user to insert new rows into a table or updatable view. Permission may be granted to specific columns rather than the entire database element.
- ◆ UPDATE: Allows a user to modify rows in a table or updatable view. Permission may be granted to specific columns rather than the entire database element.
- ◆ DELETE: Allows a user to delete rows from a table or updatable view.
- ◆ REFERENCES: Allows a user to reference a table as a foreign key in a table he or she creates. Permission may be granted to specific columns rather than the entire table.
- ◆ ALL PRIVILEGES: Gives a user all of the preceding rights to a table or view.

By default, granting access rights to another user does not give that user the right to pass on those rights to others. If, however, you add a WITH GRANT OPTION clause, you give the user the ability to grant the rights that he or she has to another user.

Storing Access Rights

Access rights to tables and views are stored in the data dictionary. Although the details of the data dictionary tables vary from one DBMS to another, you will usually find access rights split between two system tables named something like SYSTABLEPERM and SYSCOLPERM.

The first table is used when access rights are granted to entire tables or views; the second is used when rights are granted to specific columns within a table or view.

A SYSTABLEPERM table has a structure similar to the following:

```
systableperm (table_id, grantee, grantor, selectauth, insertauth,
    deleteauth, updateauth, updatecols, referenceauth)
```

The columns represent

- ◆ TABLE_ID: An identifier for the table or view.
- ◆ GRANTEE: The user ID to which rights have been granted.
- ◆ GRANTOR: The user ID granting the rights.
- ◆ SELECTAUTH: The grantee's SELECT rights.
- ◆ INSERTAUTH: The grantee's INSERT rights.
- ◆ DELETEAUTH: The grantee's DELETE rights.
- ◆ UPDATEAUTH: The grantee's UPDATE rights.
- ◆ UPDATECOLS: Indicates whether rights have been granted to specific columns within the table or view. When this value is Y (yes), the DBMS must also look in SYSCOLPERM to determine whether a user has the rights to perform a specific action against the database.
- ◆ REFERENCEAUTH: The grantee's REFERENCE rights.

The columns that hold the access rights take one of three values: Y (yes), N (no), or G (yes with grant option).

Whenever a user makes a request to the DBMS to manipulate data, the DBMS first consults the data dictionary to determine whether the user has the rights to perform the requested action. (SQL-based DBMSs are therefore said to be *data dictionary driven*.) If the DBMS cannot find a row with a matching user ID and table identifier, then the user has no rights at all to the table or view. If a row with a matching user ID and table identifier exists, then the DBMS checks for the specific rights that the user has to the table or view and—based on the presence of Y, N, or G in the appropriate column—either permits or disallows the requested database access.

Granting Rights

To grant rights to another user, a user that either created the database element (and therefore has all rights to it) or that has GRANT rights issues a GRANT statement:

```
GRANT type_of_rights
ON table_or_view_name TO user_ID
```

For example, if the DBA of the online bookstore wanted to allow the accounting manager (who has a user ID of ACCTG_MGR) to access the sales summary view, the DBA would type

```
GRANT SELECT
ON sales_summary TO acctg_mgr
```

To allow the accounting manager to pass those rights on to other users, the DBA would need to add one line to the SQL:

```
GRANT SELECT
ON sales_summary TO acctg_mgr
WITH GRANT OPTION
```

If the online bookstore wanted to give some student interns limited rights to some of the base tables, the GRANT might be written

```
GRANT SELECT, UPDATE (retail_price, source)
```

```
ON books TO intern1, intern2, intern3
```

The preceding example grants SELECT rights to the entire table but gives UPDATE rights only on two specific columns. Notice also that you can grant multiple rights in the same command as well as give the same group of rights to more than one user. However, a single GRANT applies to only one table or view.

In most cases, rights are granted to specific user IDs. You can, however, make database elements accessible to anyone by granting rights to the special user ID PUBLIC. For example, the following statement gives every authorized user the rights to see the SALES_SUMMARY view:

```
GRANT SELECT
ON sales_summary TO PUBLIC
```

Revoking Rights

To remove previously granted rights, you use the REVOKE statement, whose syntax is almost opposite to that of GRANT:

```
REVOKE access_rights
FROM table_or_view_name FROM user_ID
```

For example, if the online bookstore's summer interns have finished their work, the DBA might want to remove their access from the database:

```
REVOKE SELECT, UPDATE (retail_price, source)
ON books FROM intern1, intern2, intern3
```

If the user from which you are revoking rights has the GRANT option for those rights, then you also need to make a decision about what to do if the user has passed on those rights. In the following case, the REVOKE will be disallowed if the ACCTG_MGR user has passed on his or her rights:

```
REVOKE SELECT
ON sales_summary FROM acctg_mgr
RESTRICT
```

In contrast, the syntax

```
REVOKE SELECT
ON sales_summary FROM acctg_mgr
CASCADE
```

will remove the rights from the ACCTG_MGR ID along with any user IDs to which ACCTG_MGR granted rights.

> *Conformance note: Granting and revoking access rights, including WITH GRANT OPTION, is required for Core SQL:1999 conformance.*

Part Four

Program-Based Data Manipulation

11

Users, Sessions, and Transaction Control

An end user can interact with a database either by issuing SQL statements directly by typing them or by running an application program in which SQL has been embedded. In either case, the database must recognize the user as an authorized database user, the user must connect to the database to establish a database session, and there must be control over the user's transactions. As an introduction, this chapter begins with a discussion of the environment in which multiple users operate and what a DBMS has to do to preserve data integrity when multiple users attempt to modify the same data. The chapter then turns to SQL specifics as a prelude to the discussion of embedded SQL in Chapter 12.

The Concurrent Use Data Environment

A *transaction* is a unit of work submitted as a whole to a database for processing. (A database session consists of one or more transactions.) When more than one user or application program is interacting with the database at one time, we say that their transactions are running *concurrently*. Concurrent transactions can run in one of two ways:

- ◆ They may run *serially*, in which case one transaction completes its work before the second begins.
- ◆ They may run *interleaved*, in which case the actions of both transactions alternate.

Ideally, the result of interleaved transaction execution should be the same as that of serial execution (regardless of which transaction went first). If interleaved transaction execution produces such a result, the transactions are said to be *serializable*.

Unfortunately, some very nasty things can happen if no controls are placed on interleaved execution. As an example, consider what might happen to the online bookstore when there is only one copy of a book in stock and two customers place an order for that one copy (see Figure 11-1).

The first customer retrieves data about the book over the World Wide Web and sees in his or her browser that the book is available for immediate shipment. A short time later, a second customer does exactly the same thing. After the second customer's retrieval, the first customer places an order for the book. The database application program subtracts the quantity ordered from the quantity in stock, producing a result of 0.

Moments later, the second customer places an order for the same book, also thinking that it is in stock for immediate shipment. This time, when the database application subtracts the ordered copy, the inventory level drops to −1. The second customer has actually ordered a book that is no longer available for sale because it was sold

Customer #1

Retrieve book
info; see that
book is in stock: Order book

1 copy on hand   0 copies on hand

TIME ⟶

                        Retrieve book   Order book
                        info; see that
                        book is in stock: -1 copies on hand

                        1 copy on hand

Customer #2

Figure 11-1: A lost update

to the first customer. As a result, the second customer will need to wait for the book to be ordered from the distributor, causing a shipment delay and an unhappy customer.

This problem, known as a *lost update*, occurred because the second customer's update was based on old data; the second customer did not see the first customer's purchase and therefore could not know that the book had already been sold.

The most common solution is to use *locking*, where transactions receive control over database elements they are using to prevent other transactions from updating and/or viewing the same data. Transactions that modify data usually obtain *exclusive*, or *write*, locks that prevent both viewing and modification of data by other transactions while the locks are in place.

To see how locking solves the book ordering problem, take a look at Figure 11-2. This time, when the first customer retrieves data about the book, the transaction receives a lock on the book's data that prevents the second customer from viewing the data. The second customer's transaction is placed in a *wait state* by the DBMS until the transaction holding lock finishes and releases the lock. At that point, the second customer's transaction can proceed, but when it retrieves the data about the book, the second customer sees that the shipping time is now 2 to 3 weeks because the book must be reordered from the distributor.

Customer #1

Retrieve book info;
get lock:

1 copy on hand

Order book;
end transaction and
release lock:

0 copies on hand

TIME

Retrieve book info;
get lock;

Try to retrieve   WAIT   See that book is not
book info; info is   ───────────────► in stock; decide not
locked; wait: to order

1 copy on hand   0 copies on hand

Customer #2

Figure 11-2:   Solving a lost update problem with locking

The second customer decides not to order the book. Although the second customer may be unhappy about not being able to get the book, he or she is probably less upset than if the book were promised quickly and not delivered.

For locking to be effective, a transaction must hold all its locks for the entire length of the transaction. Part of the process that ends a transaction is therefore to release all of the locks, making the data held by the transaction available for other transactions.

In the preceding example, you saw an exclusive lock used to prevent both viewing and updating a part of the database. DBMSs also place *shared*, or *read*, locks that allow many transactions to view a part of the database but allow none to modify it while a shared lock is in place. A DBMS will use a shared lock instead of an exclusive lock wherever it can because a shared lock allows more concurrent use of database elements.

In many cases, the DBMS will place a shared lock on data when a transaction retrieves the data and then upgrade that lock to an exclusive lock only when the transaction issues a data modification command. This scheme, known as *two-phase locking*, helps ensure that exclusive locks are held for as short a time as possible and thus promotes the highest level of concurrent use.

The size of the database element on which a lock is placed (the *granularity* of the lock) varies from one DBMS to another and with the types of actions you are performing. It may be as large as an entire disk page (as in early versions of DB2) or it may be as small as a single row in a single table. The smaller the granularity, the more "pieces" there are to lock and the more concurrent use a database can support. However, the DBMS must spend time maintaining locks and keeping track of which transactions are waiting for locks. Therefore, the smaller the granularity and the more locks in place, the more processing time the DBMS must devote to locks rather than data manipulation.

Muddying the Waters: Isolation Levels

At first glance, it may seem that concurrency control is straightforward: Either you have serializable transactions or you don't. However, the SQL-92 standard muddies the water a bit by allowing you to specify that a transaction can read data modified by another, uncommitted transaction. The degree to which a transaction has access to such data is known as its *isolation level*.

There are four isolation levels:

- ◆ SERIALIZABLE: A serializable transaction is fully isolated from other transactions. It acts exactly as described in the preceding section of this chapter.
- ◆ REPEATABLE READ: A repeatable read transaction can read the same data more than once, retrieving rows that satisfy a WHERE predicate. If another transaction has inserted or updated rows and been committed between the first transaction's reads, then the repeated read of the data may return different rows than the first. Depending on

the nature of the transactions, such behavior may be desirable. This effect is known as a *phantom read*.

◆ READ COMMITTED: A read committed transaction can also read the same data more than once, but in this case the read returns the same rows. However, the second read may produce different values if the data have been updated by another transaction that committed between the first and second reads by the transaction in question. Again, depending on the nature of the transaction, this may be something that you want. This effect is known as a *nonrepeatable read*. Such transactions also permit phantom reads.

◆ READ UNCOMMITTED: A read uncommitted transaction can read the same data more than once and read updates made to data by other uncommitted transactions. The danger here is that the uncommitted transactions may be rolled back, voiding their updates. This effect is known as a *dirty read*. Such transactions also permit nonrepeatable reads and phantom reads.

The default isolation level is SERIALIZABLE. To set a lower level, you use the SET TRANSACTION command:

```
SET TRANSACTION ISOLATION LEVEL isolation_level
```

Choose the isolation level from one of the four just discussed, as in

```
SET TRANSACTION ISOLATION LEVEL REPEATABLE READ
```

> *Conformance note: The Core SQL:1999 standard requires only the SERIALIZABLE isolation level. Other isolation level support appears in the full standard.*

Database User IDs

Most DBMS are shipped with only one or two authorized users (often DBA and/or SYSTEM) that have access to an entire database. However, the SQL standard does not specify exactly how additional users should be added. Today, there are two general strategies for supporting users:

- ◆ A user's database ID is the same as the user's operating system user name. This type of scheme is found in large systems, such as IBM's DB2.
- ◆ The DBMS has its own set of user IDs, separate from those required to gain access to the operating system. This type of scheme is found in DBMSs such as Oracle and Sybase.

When a DBMS requires its own user IDs, you will typically find that the DBMS has extended the GRANT command to support adding user-level access. For example,

```
GRANT CONNECT TO john_doe
IDENTIFIED BY every_man
```

creates the database user ID JOHN_DOE with a password of EVERY_MAN. (Keep in mind that this user ID–password pair is completely distinct from the user name and password that a user may use to log on to the operating system.) The user now has the right to connect to the database but cannot use any database elements unless he or she is granted access to them by another user.

Having the right to connect to a database usually does not automatically confer the right to create database elements. Someone with DBA rights must grant that ability:

```
GRANT RESOURCE TO john_doe
```

DBA rights permit a user to grant connect and resource rights to others:

```
GRANT DBA TO john_doe
```

> Note: Please remember that the preceding extensions of the GRANT statement are not part of the SQL standard but are commonly implemented.

Database Sessions and Connections

To interact with a database, a user *connects* to it. When the user is finished, he or she *disconnects*. The time between the connection and disconnection is a database *session*.

SQL for Connecting and Disconnecting

To establish a connection to a database, you use the keyword CON-NECT. For example, to connect under a specific user ID, a user or application program would enter

```
CONNECT TO USER user_ID
```

The SQL-92 standard includes considerable flexibility in the CON-NECT command syntax. If the DBMS has its own way of naming connections, then CONNECT may be enough. If the DBMS requires you to name connections, then you might use

```
CONNECT AS connection_identifier
```

You should consult your DBMS's documentation for the specific syntax required for a database connection.

> Note: The CONNECT command assumes that there is some imple-mentation-specific way to identify the database with which a user will interact once connected and that the database specifi-cation occurs before the user attempts to make a database con-nection.

To terminate a connection, you use the DISCONNECT command. If you specified a connection name, then the command is written

```
DISCONNECT connection_identifier
```

If you took the default connection or connected with a user name, then DISCONNECT by itself is usually enough.

Conformance note: Support for a standard connection and disconnection syntax is required only for full SQL-92 conformance. However, most DBMSs currently have support for some variation of the CONNECT and DISCONNECT statements.

Session Length Considerations

There are two possible strategies governing the length of a database connection that come with their own sets of trade-offs:

♦ An end user working with a SQL command processor or an application program can connect to the database at the beginning of work and stay connected until work is completed. This eliminates the overhead of repeated connections and disconnections but prevents another user from taking advantage of the connection when the connected user is idle. This strategy is therefore a problem if the number of concurrent users authorized for your DBMS is considerably smaller than the number of people who need to access the database.

♦ An end user working with a SQL command processor or an application program can connect to the database just before a database interaction occurs and disconnect immediately after completing the interaction. (Don't forget that temporary tables exist only during a single database session.) This creates additional overhead for processing the connection and disconnection. However, it ties up the connection for the smallest amount of time necessary and allows more people to access the database.

The bottom line is this: If your DBMS is authorized for the same number of users as people who need to use the database, then you can connect and stay connected. There's no reason not to. However, if you have more people than your software will allow at any one time, you will get less variance in your response times by connecting and disconnecting for each group of database actions.

Transaction Control

Most interactive SQL command processors consider each individual SQL command as a distinct transaction or give the end user a way to "Save changes" after entering a series of commands. However, when you are writing an embedded SQL program, the length of a transaction is totally under your direct control. You also have control over whether the transaction can read and write data, or read only.

Transaction Read/Write Permissions

By default, transactions can both read and write data. However, read-only transactions never require exclusive (write) locks and therefore in most cases permit higher concurrent use of a database. It therefore can be beneficial to indicate that a retrieval transaction is read only.

If you want a transaction that is read only, you can set that property with the SET TRANSACTION command:

```
SET TRANSACTION READ ONLY
```

If you are also setting the transaction's isolation level, you can do so with the same command by separating the options with commas, as in:

```
SET TRANSACTION ISOLATION LEVEL READ COMMITTED, READ ONLY
```

> *Conformance note: READ ONLY and READ WRITE transactions are required for Core SQL:1999 conformance.*

Transaction Termination

Transactions end in one of two ways:

♦ If a transaction is *committed*, then any changes the transaction made to the database become permanent.

♦ If a transaction is *rolled back*, then any changes the transaction made are undone, restoring the database to the state it was in before the transaction began.

By definition, a committed transaction is never rolled back. To be able to roll back a transaction, a DBMS needs a log of every action taken by a transaction. This log, known more formally as a *before-image file*, contains information about all database transactions currently in progress. When a transaction is committed, its records are purged from the log and the vacated space is used for data about subsequent transactions. When a transaction is rolled back, the DBMS starts at the transaction's last record in the log file and replaces each current value with its old value from the log file. The process repeats, moving forward in the log file, until the DBMS reaches the log record that indicates the start of the transaction. At this point, the log records can be purged.

Starting Transactions

The SQL-92 standard and the Core SQL:1999 specification do not specify any command for starting a transaction. Transactions therefore start automatically whenever there is no current transaction and a user or application program issues a command that requires database interaction.

The full SQL:1999 standard, however, does include a START TRANS-ACTION statement:

```
START TRANSACTION mode
```

The mode of a transaction can include its isolation level and whether it is read only or read/write.

Ending Transactions

If you are working with an interactive SQL command processor, you probably request the end of a transaction by issuing a "Save changes" command. If the DBMS can process your updates—if they do not violate any integrity constraints—then the DBMS automatically commits your transaction. If there are integrity violations, the the DBMS rolls back your transaction.

In an application program, you typically make the decision whether to commit or roll back based on an error code returned by the DBMS. (You will read more about these error codes in Chapter 12.) Once the decision has been made, a program issues COMMIT or COMMIT WORK to commit the transaction.

> *Conformance note: The keyword* WORK *following* COMMIT *is required at the SQL-92 entry level. However, it is optional at the full and intermediate levels. The* COMMIT *statement (with the optional* WORK *keyword) is required for Core SQL:1999 conformance.*

To undo everything done by a transaction, you issue either ROLLBACK or ROLLBACK WORK.

> *Conformance note: DBMSs that are SQL-92 entry level compliant may require the* WORK *keyword following* ROLLBACK. *It must be optional for full and intermediate level compliance. The* ROLLBACK *statement (with the optional* WORK *keyword) is required for Core SQL:1999 conformance.*

Transaction Length Considerations

One of the questions that always arises in a discussion of transactions is how long they should be. In general, they should be short, and there are two important reasons why:

♦ A transaction is *the unit of recovery*. When you perform a rollback, you must undo the entire transaction, not just part of it. You stand to lose a lot of processing if you must roll back a long transaction.
♦ As you read earlier in this chapter, for locking to be effective a transaction must hold all its locks until the transaction ends. Long transactions therefore tie up large portions of the database, cutting down on the amount of concurrent use the database can provide. Because all locks are released when a transaction terminates, shorter transactions maximize the number of users that can share the same database elements.

Note: Locking is essential for data consistency and integrity when multiple transactions are running concurrently. It is therefore not an option to remove the locking mechanism.

Programmers often wonder if it is necessary to end a transaction quickly if all the transaction is doing is retrieving data. The answer is "yes," because retrieval transactions lock database elements. Although they typically allow other transactions to view the locked data, they prevent update of the data. Therefore, you should always commit a retrieval transaction immediately after bringing the data from the database in a query result table, freeing up the tables or views used for other users to modify.

Note: There is rarely any reason to roll back a retrieval transaction. The undo process just takes up processing time without affecting the contents of the database.

12

Embedded SQL

Although a knowledgeable SQL user can accomplish a great deal with an interactive command processor, much interaction with a database is through application programs that provide a predictable interface for non–technologically sophisticated users. In this chapter you will read about the preparation of programs that contain SQL statements and the special things you must do to fit SQL within a host programming language.

The Embedded SQL Environment

SQL statements can be embedded in a wide variety of languages (*host languages*). Some are general-purpose programming languages, such as COBOL or C++. Others are special-purpose database programming languages such as the PowerScript language used by PowerBuilder or Oracle's SQL/Plus.

The way in which you handle source code depends on the type of host language you are using. Special-purpose database languages like PowerScript or SQL/Plus need no special processing. Their language translators recognize embedded SQL statements and know what to do with them. However, general-purpose language compilers are not written to recognize syntax that isn't part of the original language. When a COBOL or C++ compiler encounters a SQL statement, it generates an error.

The solution to the problem has several aspects:

- ♦ Support for SQL statements is provided by a set of program library modules. The input parameters to the modules represent the portions of a SQL statement that are set by the programmer.
- ♦ SQL statements embedded in a host language program are translated by a *precompiler* into calls to routines in the SQL library.
- ♦ The host language compiler can accept the calls to library routines and therefore can compile the output produced by the precompiler.
- ♦ During the linking phase of program preparation, the library routines used to support SQL are linked to the executable file along with any other libraries used by the program.

To make it easier for the precompiler to recognize SQL statements, each one is preceded by EXEC SQL. The way in which you terminate the statement varies from one language to another. The typical terminators are summarized in Table 12-1.

> *Note: For the examples in this book, we will use a semicolon as an embedded SQL statement terminator.*

Language	Terminator
Ada	Semicolon
C, C++	Semicolon
COBOL	`END-EXEC`
Fortran	None
MUMPS	Close parenthesis
Pascal	Semicolon
PL/1	Semicolon

Table 12-1: Embedded SQL statement terminators

> *Conformance note: The Core SQL:1999 standard requires embedded SQL support for Ada, C, COBOL, Fortran, MUMPS, Pascal, and PL/1.*

Using Host Language Variables

General-purpose programming languages require that you redeclare any host language variables used in embedded SQL statements. The declarations are bracketed between two SQL statements, using the following format:

```
EXEC SQL BEGIN DECLARE SECTION;
    declarations go here
EXEC SQL END DECLARE SECTION;
```

The specifics of the variable declarations depend on the host language being used. (The syntax typically conforms to the host language's syntax for variable declarations.)

When you use a host language variable in a SQL statement, you must precede it by a colon so that it is distinct from table, view, and column names. For example, the following statement updates one row in the CUSTOMERS table with a value stored in the variable

NEW_PHONE, using a value stored in the variable WHICH_CUSTOMER to identify the row to be modified:

```
EXEC SQL UPDATE customers
    SET customer_phone = :new_phone
    WHERE customer_numb = :which_customer;
```

This use of a colon applies both to general-purpose programming languages and to database application languages (even those that don't require a precompiler).

The host language variables that contain data for use in SQL statements are known as *dynamic parameters*. The values that are sent to the DBMS, for example, as part of a WHERE predicate, are known as *input parameters*. The values that accept data being returned by the DBMS, such as the data returned by a SELECT, are known as *output parameters*.

DBMS Return Codes

When you are working with interactive SQL, error messages appear immediately on your screen. You then read the message and make any necessary changes to your SQL syntax to correct the problem. However, when SQL is embedded in a program, the end user has no access to the SQL and therefore can't make any corrections. Technologically unsophisticated users also may become upset when they see the usually cryptic DBMS errors appearing on the screen. Programs in which SQL is embedded therefore need to be able to intercept the error codes returned by the DBMS and to handle them before the errors reach the end user.

The SQL-86 standard included a DBMS status variable named SQL-CODE. Any embedded SQL program could read the contents of the variable, which were set by the DBMS immediately after executing every SQL statement. SQLCODE contained 0 if a SQL command executed successfully. If a retrieval returned no rows, SQLCODE was set to 100. However, other SQLCODE values were implementation dependent.

The SQL-92 standard attempts to standardize return codes by introducing a new status variable: SQLSTATE. SQLSTATE is a five-character string. The first two characters represent the class of the error. The rightmost three characters are the subclass, which provides further detail about the state of the database. For example, 00000 means that the SQL statement executed successfully. A class of 22 indicates a data exception. The subclasses of class 22 include 003 (numeric value of out range) and 007 (invalid datetime format). A complete listing of the SQLSTATE return codes can be found in Appendix B.

In most cases, an application program should check the contents of SQLSTATE each time it executes a SQL statement. For example, after performing the update example you saw in the preceding section, a C++ program might do the following:

```
if (strcmp(SQLSTATE,'00000') == 0)
    EXEC SQL COMMIT;
else
{
    // some error handling code goes here
}
```

> *Conformance note: Support for* SQLSTATE *is part of the Core SQL:1999 specification.*

Retrieving a Single Row

When the WHERE predicate in a SELECT statement contains a primary key expression, the result table will contain at most one row. For such a query, all you need to do is specify host language variables into which the SQL command processor can place the data it retrieves. You do this by adding an INTO clause to the SELECT.

For example, if the online bookstore wanted to retrieve the e-mail address of a specific customer, a program might include

```
EXEC SQL SELECT customer_email
INTO :email
FROM customers
WHERE customer_numb = 12;
```

The INTO clause is followed by the names of the host language variables in which data will be placed. In the preceding example, data are being retrieved from only one column and the INTO clause therefore contains just a single variable name.

If you want to retrieve data from multiple columns, you must provide one host language variable for each column, as in the following:

```
EXEC SQL SELECT customer_first_name, customer_last_name,
    customer_email
INTO :first, :last, :email
FROM customers
WHERE customer_numb = 12;
```

The names of the host language variables are irrelevant. The SQL command processor places data into them by position. In other words, data from the first column following SELECT is placed in the first variable following INTO, data from the second column following SELECT is placed in the second variable following INTO, and so on. Keep in mind that all host language variables are preceded by colons to distinguish them from the names of database elements.

After executing a SELECT that contains a primary key expression in its WHERE predicate, an embedded SQL program should check to determine whether a row was retrieved. Assuming we are using C or C++, the code might be written

```
if (strcmp (SQLSTATE,'00000') == 0)
EXEC SQL COMMIT;
else
{
EXEC SQL ROLLBACK;
return; // retrieval failed; stop processing
}
// continue processing here
```

At this point, the program can continue its work using the data stored in the host language variables.

Indicator Variables

The SQLSTATE variable is not the only way in which a DBMS can communicate the results of a retrieval to an application program. Each host variable into which you place data can be associated with an *indicator variable*. When indicator variables are present, the DBMS stores a 0 to indicate that a data variable has valid data or a −1 to indicate that the row contained a null in the specified column and that the contents of the data variable are unchanged.

To use indicator variables, first declare host language variables of an integer data type to hold the indicators. Then, follow each data variable in the INTO clause with the keyword INDICATOR and the name of the indicator variable. For example, to use indicator variables with the customer data retrieval query:

```
EXEC SQL SELECT customer_first_name, customer_last_name,
    customer_email
INTO :first INDICATOR :firstInd, :last INDICATOR :lastInd, :email
    INDICATOR :lastInd
FROM customers
WHERE customer_numb = 12;
```

You can then use host language syntax to check the contents of each indicator variable to determine whether you have valid data to process in each data variable.

> Note: The INDICATOR *keyword is optional. Therefore, the syntax* INTO :first :firstInd, :last :lastInd, *and so on is acceptable. The use of* INDICATOR *is nonetheless clearer.*

Indicator variables can also be useful for telling you when character values have been truncated. For example, assume that the host language variable FIRST has been declared to accept a 10-character string but that the database column CUSTOMER_FIRST_NAME is 15 characters long. If the database column contains a full 15 characters, only the first 10 will be placed in the host language variable. The indicator variable will contain 15, indicating the size of the column (and the size to which the host language variable should have been set).

Conformance note: Support for the embedded single-row SE-LECT statement is part of the Core SQL:1999 standard.

Retrieving Multiple Rows: Cursors

SELECT statements that may return more than one row present a bit of a problem when you embed them in a program: Host language variables can hold only one value at a time and the SQL command processor cannot work with host language arrays. The solution provides you with a pointer (a *cursor*) to a SQL result table that allows you to extract one row at a time for processing.

The procedure for creating and working with a cursor is as follows:

1. *Declare* the cursor by specifying the SQL SELECT to be executed. This does not execute the retrieval.
2. *Open* the cursor. This step actually executes the SELECT and creates the result table in main memory. It positions the cursor just above the first row in the result table.
3. *Fetch* the next row in the result table and process the data in some way.
4. Repeat step 3 until all rows in the result table have been accessed and processed.
5. *Close* the cursor. This deletes the result table from main memory but does not destroy the declaration. You can therefore reopen an existing cursor, recreate the result table, and work with the data without redeclaring the SELECT.

    Note: There is no way to "undeclare" a cursor. A cursor's declaration disappears when the program module in which it was created terminates.

By default, a cursor fetches the "next" row in the result table. The SQL-92 standard, however, has added *scrollable* cursors. You can therefore fetch the "next," "prior," "first," or "last" row. In addition, you can fetch by specifying a row number in the result table or by giving an offset from the current row. This in large measure eliminates the need to close and reopen the cursor to reposition the cursor above its current location.

Declaring a Cursor

Declaring a cursor is similar to creating a view in that you include a SQL statement that defines a virtual table. The DECLARE statement has the following general format in its simplest form:

```
DECLARE cursor_name CURSOR FOR
SQL SELECT statement
```

For example, assume that the online bookstore wanted to prepare labels for a mass mailing to its customers. The program that prints the mailing labels needs each customer's name and address from the database, which it can then format for labels. A cursor to hold the data might be declared as:

```
EXEC SQL DECLARE address_data CURSOR FOR
SELECT customer_first_name, customer_last_name, customer_street,
    customer_city, customer_state, customer_zip
FROM customers;
```

The name of a cursor must be unique within the program module in which it is created. A program can therefore manipulate an unlimited number of cursors at the same time.

> *Conformance note: Declaring a cursor with implicit "next" movement is required for Core SQL:1999 conformance.*

Scrolling Cursors

One of the options available with a cursor is the ability to retrieve rows in other than the default "next" order. To enable a scrolling cursor, you must indicate that you want scrolling when you declare the cursor by adding the keyword SCROLL after the cursor name:

```
EXEC SQL DECLARE address_data SCROLL CURSOR FOR
SELECT customer_first_name, customer_last_name, customer_street,
    customer_city, customer_state, customer_zip
```

```
FROM customers;
```

You will find more about using scrolling cursors a bit later in this chapter when we talk about fetching rows.

> *Conformance note: Scrolling cursor support is not required for Core SQL:1999 conformance, but is part of the full standard.*

Enabling Updates

The data in a cursor are by default read only. However, if the SELECT meets all updatability criteria, you can use the cursor for data modification. (You will find more about the updatability criteria in the *Modification Using Cursors* section later in this chapter.)

To enable modification for a cursor, add the keywords FOR UPDATE at the end of the cursor's declaration:

```
EXEC SQL DECLARE address_data SCROLL CURSOR FOR
SELECT customer_first_name, customer_last_name, customer_street,
    customer_city, customer_state, customer_zip
FROM customers
FOR UPDATE;
```

To restrict updates to specific columns, add the names of the columns following UPDATE:

```
EXEC SQL DECLARE address_data SCROLL CURSOR FOR
SELECT customer_first_name, customer_last_name, customer_street,
    customer_city, customer_state, customer_zip
FROM customers
FOR UPDATE customer_street, customer_city, customer_state,
    customer_zip;
```

Sensitivity

Assume, for example, that a program for the online bookstore contains a module that computes the average price of the books and changes prices based on that average: If a book's price is more than 20 percent higher than the average, the price is discounted 10 percent; if the price is only 10 percent higher, it is discounted 5 percent.

A programmer codes the logic of the program in the following way:

1. Declare and open a cursor that contains the ISBNs and prices for all books whose price is greater than the average. The SELECT that generates the result table is

```
SELECT isbn, retail_price
FROM books
WHERE retail_price >
    (SELECT avg (retail_price)
    FROM books;)
```

2. Fetch each row and modify its price.

The question at this point is: What happens to the result table as data are modified? As prices are lowered, some rows will no longer meet the criteria for inclusion in the table. More important, the average retail price will drop. If this program is to execute correctly, however, the contents of the result table must remain fixed once the cursor has been opened.

The SQL-92 standard introduced two types of cursors in this regard: *insensitive,* in which the contents of the result table are fixed, and *indeterminate* (ASENSITIVE), in which the effects of updates made by the same transaction on the result table are left up to each individual DBMS. The default is indeterminate, which means that you cannot be certain that the DBMS will not alter your result table before you are through with it.

The solution is to request specifically that the cursor be insensitive:

```
EXEC SQL DECLARE address_data SCROLL INSENSITIVE CURSOR FOR
SELECT customer_first_name, customer_last_name, customer_street,
    customer_city, customer_state, customer_zip
FROM customers
FOR UPDATE;
```

> *Note: There is currently no such thing as a "sensitive" cursor that is always updated whenever underlying data change.*

Opening a Cursor

To open a cursor, place the cursor's name following the keyword OPEN:

```
EXEC SQL OPEN address_data;
```

Fetching Rows

To retrieve the data from the next row in a result table, placing the data into host language variables, you use the FETCH statement:

```
FETCH FROM cursor_name
INTO host_language_variables;
```

For example, to obtain a row of data from the list of customer names and addresses, the online bookstore program could use

```
EXEC SQL FETCH FROM address_data
INTO :first, :last, :street, :city, :state, :zip;
```

Notice that as always the host language variables are preceded by colons to distinguish them from table, view, or column names. In addition, the host language variables must match the database columns as to data type. The FETCH will fail if, for example, you attempt to place a string value into a numeric variable.

If you want to fetch something other than the next row, you can specify the row by adding the direction in which you want the cursor to move after the keyword FETCH:

♦ To fetch the first row

```
EXEC SQL FETCH FIRST FROM address_data
INTO :first, :last, :street, :city, :state, :zip;
```

♦ To fetch the last row

```
EXEC SQL FETCH LAST FROM address_data
INTO :first, :last, :street, :city, :state, :zip;
```

♦ To fetch the prior row

```
EXEC SQL FETCH PRIOR FROM address_data
INTO :first, :last, :street, :city, :state, :zip;
```

♦ To fetch a row specified by its position (row number) in the result table

```
EXEC SQL FETCH ABSOLUTE 12 FROM address_data
INTO :first, :last, :street, :city, :state, :zip;
```

The preceding fetches the twelfth row in the result table.

♦ To fetch a row relative to and below the current position of the cursor

```
EXEC SQL FETCH RELATIVE 5 FROM address_data
INTO :first, :last, :street, :city, :state, :zip;
```

The preceding fetches the row five rows below the current position of the cursor.

♦ To fetch a row relative to and above the current position of the cursor

```
EXEC SQL FETCH RELATIVE -5 FROM address_data
INTO :first, :last, :street, :city, :state, :zip;
```

The preceding fetches the row five rows above the current position of the cursor.

Note: If you use FETCH without an INTO clause, you will move the cursor without retrieving any data.

If there is no row containing data at the position of the cursor, the DBMS returns a "no data" error (SQLSTATE = '02000'). The general strategy for processing a table of data is therefore to create a loop that continues to fetch rows until a SQLSTATE of something other than '00000' occurs. Then you can test to see whether you've simply finished processing or whether some other problem has arisen. In C/C++, the code would look something like

```
EXEC SQL FETCH FROM address_data
INTO :first, :last, :street, :city, :state, :zip;
while (strcmp (SQLSTATE,'00000') == 0)
{
    // Process one row's data in appropriate way
    EXEC SQL FETCH FROM address_data
    INTO :first, :last, :street, :city, :state, :zip;
}
if (strcmp (SQLSTATE,'02000') == 0)
    EXEC SQL COMMIT;
else
{
    // Do some more error checking if necessary
    EXEC SQL ROLLBACK;
}
```

Note: One common error that beginning database programmers make is to write loops that use a specific error code as a terminating value. This can result in an infinite loop if some other error condition arises. We therefore typically write loops to stop on any error condition and then check to determine exactly which condition occurred.

Note: You can use indicator variables in the INTO clause of a FETCH statement, just as you do when executing a SELECT that retrieves a single row.

Conformance note: Scrolling cursors are required only for intermediate level SQL-92 conformance. Other levels need only support fetching in the "next" direction.

Closing a Cursor

To close a cursor, removing its result table from main memory, use

```
CLOSE cursor_name;
```

as in

```
EXEC SQL CLOSE address_data;
```

Embedded SQL Data Modification

Although many of today's database development environments make it easy to create forms for data entry and modification, situations still arise in which you need to include data modification in an underlying application program. For example, as a customer of the online bookstore chooses books to purchase, an application program must multiply the number of items purchased by the cost of the item to generate the contents of the COST_LINE column and then insert that value into the correct row in the ORDER_LINES table.

Data modification can be performed using the SQL UPDATE command to change one or more rows. In some cases, you can update the data in a cursor's result table and have those updates propagated back to the underlying base tables.

Direct Modification

To perform direct data modification using the SQL UPDATE command, you simply include the command in your program. For example, if the line cost of a purchased item is stored in the host language variable LINE, the order number in WHICH_ORDER, and the ISBN in BOOK_NUMB, you could update the database column with

```
EXEC SQL UPDATE order_lines
SET cost_line = :line
WHERE order_numb = :which_order AND isbn = :book_numb;
```

The preceding statement will update one row in the table because its WHERE predicate contains a primary key expression. To modify multiple rows, you use an UPDATE with a WHERE predicate that identifies multiple rows, such as the following, which increases all retail prices by two percent for books written after 1970:

```
EXEC SQL UPDATE books
SET retail_price = retail_price * 1.02
WHERE publication_year > 1970;
```

Indicator Variables and Data Modification

Indicator variables, which hold information about the result of embedded SQL retrievals, can also be used when performing embedded SQL modification. Their purpose is to indicate that you want to store a null in a column. For example, assume that the online bookstore writes a program that stores new rows in the BOOKS table. Sometimes the user of the program doesn't have complete information about a book and therefore wants to leave some of the columns null.

To do this, the program declares an indicator variable for each column in the table. If the data variable holds a value to be stored, the program sets the indicator variable to 0; if the column is to be left null, the program sets the indicator variable to –1.

> Note: In truth, any negative value will do, but the –1 is most likely to be compatible with upcoming changes to the SQL standard.

Sample pseudocode for performing this embedded INSERT can be found in Figure 12-1.

Modification Using Cursors

The similarity between a cursor and a view doesn't end with the fact that both are SQL statements whose execution creates a virtual table. Just as some views can be modified and the changes saved to the database, so can rows in a cursor's table be modified.

For the most part, updatable cursors must conform to the same rules as updatable views:

- ♦ The cursor must be created from only one base table or view.
- ♦ If the cursor is based on a view, then the view must be updatable.

```
// Data variables
// Initialize all strings to null, all numeric variables to 0
string isbn, author_name, title, publisher_name,
    publication_year, binding;
int source_numb;
float retail_price;
// Indicator variables
// Initialize all to 0
int isbnInd, author_nameInd, titleInd, publisher_nameInd,
    publication_yearInd, bindingInd, source_numbInd,
    retail_priceInd;
// Collect data from user, possibly using on-screen form,
// and store in data variables
if (strcmp (isbn,"") == 0) isbnInd = -1;
if (strcmp (author_name,"") == 0) author_nameInd = -1;
// ... continue by checking each data variable and setting
// indicator variable if necessary
EXEC SQL INSERT INTO books VALUES (:isbn INDICATOR :isbnInd,
    :author_name INDICATOR :author_nameInd, :title INDICATOR
    :titleInd, :publisher_name INDICATOR :publisher_nameInd,
    :publication_year INDICATOR :publication_yearInd, :binding
    INDICATOR :bindingInd, :source_numb INDICATOR
    :source_numbInd, :retail_price INDICATOR :retail_priceInd);
// Finish by checking SQLSTATE to see if insert worked to
// decide whether to commit or rollback
```

Figure 12-1: Using indicator variables to send nulls to a table

- The query cannot include summary functions or GROUP BY and HAVING clauses.
- The query cannot include DISTINCT.
- The query cannot include SCROLL, INSENSITIVE, or ORDER BY.
- The cursor must be created from only one SELECT (no UNION).
- No column name can be used in the SELECT clause more than once.

Assuming that you have an updatable cursor, you can then use FETCH without an INTO clause to move the cursor to the row you want to update. Then you can use an UPDATE command whose WHERE predicate specifies the row pointed to by the cursor. For example, to change the address of the fifteenth row in the ADDRESS_DATA cursor's result table, the online bookstore would use

```
EXEC SQL FETCH 15 FROM address_data;
EXEC SQL UPDATE customers
    SET customer_street = '123 Main Street',
    customer_city = 'New Home',
    customer_state = 'MA',
    customer_zip = '02111'
    WHERE CURRENT OF address_data;
```

The clause CURRENT OF CURSOR_NAME instructs SQL to work with the row in CUSTOMERS currently being pointed to by the named cursor. If there is no valid corresponding row in the CUSTOMERS table, the update will fail.

Deletion Using Cursors

You can apply the technique of modifying the row pointed to by a cursor to deletions as well as updates. To delete the current row, you use

```
DELETE FROM table_name WHERE CURRENT OF cursor_name;
```

The deletion will fail if the current row indicated by the cursor isn't a row in the table named in the DELETE. For example,

```
EXEC SQL DELETE FROM customers WHERE CURRENT OF address_data;
```

will probably succeed but

```
EXEC SQL DELETE FROM books WHERE CURRENT OF address_data;
```

will certainly fail.

> *Conformance note: Support for positioned updates and deletes using cursors is required for Core SQL:1999 conformance.*

13

Dynamic SQL

The embedded SQL that you have seen to this point is "static," in that the entire SQL commands have been specified within the source code. However, there are often times when you don't know exactly what a command should look like until a program is running.

Consider, for example, the screen in Figure 13-1. The user fills in the fields on which he or she wishes to base a search of the online bookstore's inventory. When the user clicks the Search button, the application program managing the window (be it a local program or a program working over the World Wide Web) checks the contents of the fields on the window and uses the data it finds to create a SQL query.

The query's WHERE predicate will differ depending on which of the fields have values in them. It is therefore impossible to completely

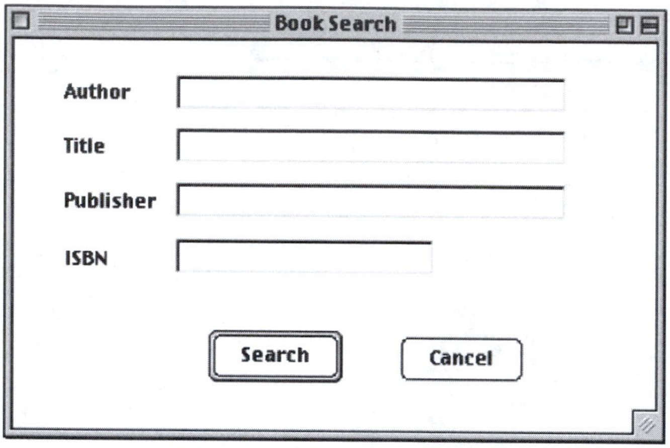

Figure 13-1: A typical window for gathering information for a dynamic SQL query

specify the query within a program. This is where dynamic SQL comes in.

> *Conformance note: Support for dynamic SQL is required for intermediate level SQL-92 conformance. Entry level conforming DBMSs need not support it. It is not included in the Core SQL:1999 specifications, but instead appears in the full standard.*

Immediate Execution

The easiest way to work with dynamic SQL is the EXECUTE IMMEDIATE statement. To use it, you store a SQL command in a host language string variable and then submit that command for processing:

```
EXEC SQL EXECUTE IMMEDIATE variable_containing_command;
```

For example, assume that a user fills in a data entry form with a customer number and the customer's new address. A program could process the update with code written something like the pseudocode in Figure 13-2. Notice the painstaking way in which the logic of the code examines the values the user entered and builds a syntactically correct SQL UPDATE statement. By using the dynamic SQL, the program can update just those columns for which the user has supplied new data. (Columns whose fields on the data entry form are left empty aren't added to the SQL statement.)

```
String theSQL;
theSQL = "UPDATE customers SET ";
boolean needsComma = false;

if (valid_contents_in_street_field)
{
    theSQL = theSQL + "customer_street = " +
        contents_of_street_field;
    needsComma = true;
}
if (valid_contents_in_city_field)
{
    if (needsComma)
        theSQL = theSQL + ", ";
    theSQL = theSQL + "customer_city = " + contents_of_city_field;
    needsComma = true;
}
if (valid_contents_in_state_field)
{
    if (needsComma)
        theSQL = theSQL + ", ";
    theSQL = theSQL + "customer_state = " +
        contents_of_state_field;
    needsComma = true;
}
if (valid_contents_in_zip_field)
{
    if (needsCommas)
                                        theSQL = theSQL + ", ";
    theSQL = "customer_zip = " + contents_of_zip_field;
}
EXEC SQL EXECUTE IMMEDIATE :theSQL;
```

Figure 13-2: Pseudocode to process a dynamic SQL update

There are two major limitations to EXECUTE IMMEDIATE:

♦ The SQL command cannot contain input parameters or output parameters. This means that you can't use SELECT or FETCH statements.

♦ To repeat the SQL statement, the DBMS has to perform the entire immediate execution process again. You can't save the SQL statement, except as a string in a host language variable. This means that such statements execute more slowly than static embedded SQL statements because the SQL command processor must examine them for syntax errors at runtime rather than during preprocessing by a precompiler.

Each time you EXECUTE IMMEDIATE the same statement, it must be scanned for syntax errors again. Therefore, if you need to execute a dynamic SQL statement repeatedly, you will get better performance if you can have the syntax checked once and save the statement in some way.

Dynamic SQL with Dynamic Parameters

If you want to repeat a dynamic SQL statement or if you need to use dynamic parameters (as you would to process the form in Figure 13-1), you need to use a more involved technique for preparing and executing your commands.

The process for creating and using a repeatable dynamic SQL statement is as follows:

1. Store the SQL statement in a host language string variable using question marks in places where dynamic parameters should appear.
2. (Optional) Allocate a *SQL descriptor area* that the DBMS can use to store information about any dynamic parameters that your statement may use. Make the area big enough to store the total number of parameters your statement needs.
3. *Prepare* the SQL statement. This process checks the statement for syntax and assigns it a name by which it can be referenced.
4. (Optional unless you are using a descriptor area) *Describe* input and output parameters for storage in the descriptor area.

5. *Execute* the statement.

6. If through with the statement, deallocate the descriptor area and deprepare the statement.

Creating the Statement String

If your dynamic SQL statement will have a WHERE predicate that returns only one row, you include the INTO clause as part of the statement string, again using question marks where the parameters will appear:

```
theQuery = "SELECT author, title, retail_price FROM books INTO ?, ?,
    ? WHERE isbn = ?";
```

The preceding query has one input parameter (the ISBN) and three output parameters (variables to hold the results of the SELECT).

The query form in Figure 13-1, however, may produce a result table with multiple rows. A program that handles that query must therefore use a cursor to perform the retrieval. You can find a pseudocode version of code that creates a SQL command from that form in Figure 13-3. Notice that what ends up in the THEQUERY parameters should appear occupied by question marks. In this case, there are no output parameters; the output parameters will be part of an associated FETCH.

There are a few limitations to the use of dynamic parameters in a statement of which you should be aware:

♦ You cannot use a dynamic parameter in a SELECT clause. For example, the following is *not* valid:

```
SELECT ?, ?, ? …
```

♦ You cannot place a dynamic parameter on both sides of a relationship operator, as in ? = ?, ? > ?, and so on.

♦ You cannot use a dynamic parameter as an argument in a summary function. For example, SUM(?) is not allowed.

```
string theQuery, dynamicCursor
boolean hasWhere = false;
String authorVal = null, titleVal = null, publisherVal = null,
isbnVal = null;
theQuery = SELECT author, title, publisher, isbn FROM books ";
if (author_field_has_value)
{
    if (!hasWhere)
        theQuery = theQuery + "WHERE ";
    theQuery = theQuery + "?";
    authorVal = contents_of_author_field;
}
if (title_field_has_value)
{
    if (!hasWhere)
        theQuery = theQuery + "WHERE ";
    else
        theQuery = theQuery + ", ";
    theQuery = theQuery + "?";
    titleVal = contents_of_title_field;
}
if (publisher_field_has_value)
{
    if (!hasWhere)
        theQuery = theQuery + "WHERE ";
    else
        theQuery = theQuery + ", ";
    theQuery = theQuery + "?";
    publisherVal = contents_of_publisher_field;
}
if (isbn_field_has_value)
{
    if (!hasWhere)
        theQuery = theQuery + "WHERE ";
    else
        theQuery = theQuery + ", ";
    theQuery = theQuery + "?";
    isbnVal = contents_of_isbn_field;
}
```

Figure 13-3: Pseudocode for processing a dynamic SQL query

♦ You cannot test a dynamic parameter against null. In other words,

```
? = NULL
```

is not allowed.

♦ In general, you cannot compare a dynamic parameter with itself. Expressions such as

```
BETWEEN ? AND ?
```

are not allowed.

Setting up Parameter Descriptor Areas

One way to keep track of the parameters used by a dynamic SQL statement is to store information about them in a descriptor area. Doing so is optional, but it does simplify coding when the time comes to actually execute a dynamic SQL statement.

To allocate a descriptor area for dynamic parameter storage, you use the ALLOCATE DESCRIPTOR statement:

```
ALLOCATE DESCRIPTOR descriptor_name;
```

For example, if you wanted to create a descriptor area named SELECT_AREA, you could use

```
EXEC SQL ALLOCATE DESCRIPTOR select_area;
```

The name of the descriptor area can also be stored in a host language variable, in which case you must precede the variable name with a colon when using it in the SQL statement.

The default number of parameters that can be accommodated by a given descriptor area is implementation dependent. To make sure that you have enough room for all your parameters, you can supply a maximum value. For example, if a statement requires 20 parameters, then you might use

```
EXEC SQL ALLOCATE DESCRIPTOR select_area WITH MAX 20;
```

> *Conformance note: SQL-92 intermediate level conformance requires only literals for the descriptor area name and the maximum number of parameters. Support for host language variables is required only for full conformance.*

Preparing the Statement

Preparing a dynamic SQL statement for execution allows the DBMS to examine the statement for syntax errors and to perform query optimization. Once a query is prepared and stored with a name, it can be reused while the program is still running.

To prepare a statement, you use the PREPARE statement:

```
PREPARE statement_name FROM :variable_containing_statement;
```

Therefore, to prepare the two statements we have been using as examples, a program would include:

```
EXEC SQL PREPARE single_row_query FROM :theQuery;
:
EXEC SQL PREPARE multi_row_query FROM :theQuery;
```

By default, the scope of a prepared statement is limited to the program module in which it is created. However, if you want to extend the scope of the entire database session, you can add the keyword GLOBAL:

```
EXEC SQL PREPARE GLOBAL multi_row_query FROM :theQuery;
```

Declaring a Dynamic Cursor

The multirow query that we just prepared requires a cursor because it can return multiple rows. Once the statement is prepared, you can declare the cursor:

```
EXEC SQL DECLARE CURSOR multi_row_cursor FROM multi_row_query;
```

The only difference between this version of the statement and that used with static SQL is that the query specification is a prepared SQL statement rather than a variable or a literal containing the SQL.

Describing, Setting, and Accessing Parameters

If you are using a descriptor area to store information about dynamic parameters, then you must get that information from a prepared statement into the descriptor area. This is known as "describing" the parameters.

You describe the parameters in a dynamic SQL statement with the DESCRIBE OUTPUT and DESCRIBE INPUT statements. When you execute the command, the DBMS scans a prepared SQL statement, looking for input or output dynamic parameters. Information about the parameters is then copied to the descriptor area.

Keep in mind, however, that simply describing the parameters doesn't give them values. You must do that separately with the SET DESCRIPTOR statement. By the same token, you can retrieve values from the descriptor area with the GET DESCRIPTOR statement.

Describing Parameters

The purpose of a DESCRIBE statement is to associate a prepared SQL statement with a descriptor area. When you do so, the DBMS counts the number of parameters (input or output) and numbers them in the order in which they appeared in the prepared statement. This numbering is essential. You will use a parameter's number to reference it when you store or retrieve a value.

During the describe, the DBMS also looks at various characteristics of the parameters. For example, it can look at the column names following SELECT and figure out the data types of the statement's output parameters.

To describe output parameters, you use

```
DESCRIBE OUTPUT prepared_SQL_statement
USING SQL DESCRIPTOR descriptor_name;
```

For example, to use the previously allocated SELECT_AREA for the query MULTI_ROW_QUERY, you would code:

```
EXEC SQL DESCRIBE OUTPUT multi_row_output
USING SQL DESCRIPTOR select_area;
```

Describing output parameters is similar

```
EXEC SQL DESCRIBE INPUT multi_row_input
USING SQL DESCRIPTOR select_area;
```

Changing Descriptor Values

Before you execute a prepared SQL statement that contains input parameters, you must load the descriptor area with the values you want the DBMS to place in your dynamic SQL statement. A descriptor area stores a great many pieces of descriptive information about a parameter. However, there are only a few that you will use commonly:

- ◆ DATA: The value of the parameter
- ◆ INDICATOR: The value of the associated indicator parameters, if any
- ◆ TYPE: The data type of the parameter
- ◆ LENGTH: The length of the parameter
- ◆ TITLE: The name of the database column associated with the parameter

In most cases, all you will need to do is initialize each parameter's actual value. Note as well that when you change any value other than DATA, the value in DATA becomes undefined.

To give a parameter in a descriptor area a value use SET DESCRIPTOR *DESCRIPTOR_NAME*:

```
VALUE parameter_number
DATA = data_value;
```

The parameter number is the number assigned to the parameter when the prepared SQL statement was described to the descriptor area. It is equivalent to the parameter's position in the SQL statement.

Note: To include other values in the SET DESCRIPTOR state-ment, separate them by commas.

With the book query we have been using as an example, setting pa-rameter values gets a bit tricky because we initially do not know how many there are or exactly which ones have been used. Howev-er, we do know the order in which they are placed in the statement. Therefore, the code to set the parameters needs to examine each search term to see if it has been included in the parameter list. Pseudocode for this process can be found in Figure 13-4.

```
GET DESCRIPTOR descriptor_name
VALUE parameter_number
:target_variable = DATA;
int paramNumb = 1;
if (authorVal != NULL)
{
    EXEC SQL SET DESCRIPTOR multi_row_input VALUE :paramNumb
    DATA = :authorVal;
    paramNumb = paramNumb + 1;
}
if (titleVal != NULL)
{
    EXEC SQL SET DESCRIPTOR multi_row_input VALUE :paramNumb
    DATA = :titleVal;
    paramNumb = paramNumb + 1;
}
if (publisherVal != NULL)
{
    EXEC SQL SET DESCRIPTOR multi_row_input VALUE :paramNumb
    DATA = :publisherVal;
    paramNumb = paramNumb + 1;
}
if (isbnVal != NULL)
{
    EXEC SQL SET DESCRIPTOR multi_row_input VALUE :paramNumb
    DATA = :isbnVal;
}
```

Figure 13-4: Setting parameters for the book query

Note: The entire parameter identification process in Figure 13-4 relies on there being nulls in the variables that correspond to fields that are not being used. Another, and perhaps more reli-able, method of doing the same would be to use a Boolean for each field, setting it to true if the field is used and false if it is not.

Retrieving Values

Assuming that you have executed a prepared SQL statement that is using descriptor areas (the details of which you will find in the next section), the data returned by the execution are placed in a descriptor area. Your program can then retrieve them with GET DESCRIPTOR.

For example, to retrieve data for a row in the book query's result table, we might use the pseudocode in Figure 13-5.

```
int paramNumb = 1;
if (authorVal != NULL)
{
    EXEC SQL GET DESCRIPTOR multi_query_output VALUE :paramNumb
    :authorVal = DATA;
    paramNumb = paramNumb + 1;
}
if (titleVal != NULL)
{
    EXEC SQL GET DESCRIPTOR multi_query_output VALUE :paramNumb
    :titleVal = DATA;
    paramNumb = paramNumb + 1;
}
if (publisherVal != NULL)
{
    EXEC SQL GET DESCRIPTOR multi_query_output VALUE :paramNumb
    :publisherVal = DATA;
    paramNumb = paramNumb + 1;
}
if (isbnVal != NULL)
{
    EXEC SQL GET DESCRIPTOR multi_query_output VALUE :paramNumb
    :isbnVal = DATA;
    paramNumb = paramNumb + 1;
}
```

Figure 13-5: Extracting data from a SQL descriptor area

Executing the Statement

The way in which you execute a dynamic SQL statement depends on whether it uses a cursor. The syntax also varies slightly depending on whether you are using a descriptor area.

Statements without Cursors or a Descriptor Area

To execute a prepared statement that does not use either a cursor or a descriptor area, use the EXECUTE statement:

```
EXECUTE statement_name
USING input_parameter_list
INTO output_parameter_list;
```

The USING and INTO clauses are optional. However, you must include a USING clause if your statement has input parameters and an INPUT clause if your statement has output parameters. The number and data type of the parameters in each parameter list must be the same as the number of parameters in the query.

For example, assume that you want to execute the statement named SINGLE_ROW_QUERY that was prepared earlier in this chapter. The query has one input parameter and three output parameters. It can therefore be executed with

```
EXEC SQL EXECUTE single_row_query
USING '12-34454-123'
INTO :authorVal, :titleVal, :priceVal;
```

The parameters can be contained in host language variables or specified as literals.

Statements without Cursors but Using a Descriptor Area

If your parameters have already been placed in a descriptor area, then all you need to do to execute a statement that does not use a cursor is to add the name of the appropriate descriptor area to the EXECUTE statement:

```
EXEC SQL EXECUTE single_row_query
USING input_descriptor_area
INTO output_descriptor_area;
```

Statements with Cursors

Using a cursor in dynamic SQL is very similar to using one with static embedded SQL. First, you open the cursor. Then you fetch the rows, one at a time, much like the pseudocode in Figure 13-6.

```
EXEC SQL OPEN CURSOR multi_row_cursor;
EXEC SQL FETCH NEXT FROM multi_row_cursor
USING :authorVal, :titleVal, :publisherVal, :isbnVal;
while (more_rows)
{
    EXEC SQL FETCH NEXT FROM multi_row_cursor
    USING :authorVal, :titleVal, :publisherVal, :isbnVal;
    // process data
}
```

Figure 13-6: Processing results using a dynamic cursor

If you happen to be using a descriptor area, you replace the list of output parameters with the name of the descriptor area:

```
FETCH NEXT FROM multi_row_cursor USING multi_row_output;
```

Removing Dynamic SQL Elements from Main Memory

Once a program has finished with a dynamic SQL statement, it can free up the memory used by the prepared statement and its descriptor areas (if any). To get rid of a descriptor area use

```
DEALLOCATE DESCRIPTOR descriptor_name;
```

To get rid of a prepared SQL statement use

```
DEALLOCATE PREPARE statement_name;
```

> *Conformance note: Support for* DEALLOCATE PREPARE *is required only for full SQL-92 compliance, and appears in only the complete SQL:1999 standard.*

Part Five

Additional Language Features

14

Unimplemented SQL-92 Features

Portions of the SQL-92 standard are currently not implemented by most DBMSs, even though the standard has been updated. In this chapter you will find coverage of those features that appear on the author's "I wish my DBMS did this" list.

Additional Relational Algebra Operations

Throughout the main portion of this book, you have read about a number of relational algebra operations. Five are of particular importance: restrict, project, join, union, and difference. A DBMS that supports these five is said to be relationally *complete*.

In fact, there is no need for a DMBS to support any of the other relational algebra operations, including the product operation that was discussed in Chapter 5. Their functionality can be provided through combinations of the others. Nonetheless, SQL does provide some support for direct use of additional relational algebra manipulations. (If you really want a product, for example, you can obtain one by using the keyword CROSS JOIN between two table names in the FROM clause.)

In this section of this chapter you will read about three additional relational algebra operations that are nice to have but not essential to being able to query a relational database.

The Union Join

The SQL-92 standard introduced a new operation—the union join—that is a combination of a union and a join. It combines the two source tables both horizontally and vertically. You get all rows from both tables, matched with all the columns from both tables.

As an example, consider the following query:

```
SELECT author_name, title, source_name
FROM books UNION JOIN sources
WHERE author_name = 'Clavell, James'
```

It produces the result in Figure 14-1. (The empty spaces are nulls, not blanks!) Notice that the DBMS made no attempt to match the rows in any way. It simply included all rows from every table, placing nulls in the columns from the "other" table.

author_name	title	source
Clavell, James	Tai-Pan	
Clavell, James	Shogun	
Clavell, James	Noble House	
Clavell, James	Gai-Jin	
		Ingram
		Baker and Taylor
		Jostens
		Brodart

Figure 14-1: The result of a union join

Note: Unless one or both of the source tables have no rows, the result of a union join can never be a legal relation because every column will have null in at least one row.

Conformance note: The union join is required of intermediate level SQL-92 conformance but not of entry level.

Except

The SQL-92 syntax has added an operator—EXCEPT—that performs a difference operation directly between two union compatible tables. Queries using EXCEPT look very much like a union:

```
SELECT author_name, title
FROM books
EXCEPT
SELECT author_name, title
FROM books JOIN order_lines
```

or

```
SELECT *
FROM books
EXCEPT CORRESPONDING BY (author_name, title)
SELECT *
FROM books JOIN order_lines
```

In the first syntax, you include two complete SELECT statements that are joined by the keyword EXCEPT. The SELECTs must return union-compatible tables. The first SELECT retrieves a list of all things (in this example, all books); the second retrieves the things that *are* (in the example, all the books that have been ordered). The EXCEPT operator then removes all rows from the first table that appear in the second.

The second syntax retrieves all columns from both source tables but uses the CORRESPONDING BY clause to restrict the columns and make the two tables union compatible.

> *Conformance note: EXCEPT and CORRESPONDING BY are re-quired for intermediate level SQL-92 conformance but not for entry level.*

Intersect

Another of the "not necessary but nice to have" relational algebra operations is INTERSECT, which returns all the rows that two tables have in common.

The Relational Algebra Intersect Operation

The relational algebra intersect operation, which returns all rows two source tables have in common, is actually an inner join over all the columns of two union compatible tables. For example, assume that you have the two customer tables in Figure 14-2. Notice that they share the rows for Jane Jones and Peter Smith.

```
store1_customers

customer_first_name    customer_last_name    customer_phone

John                   Doe                   555-1111
Jane                   Jones                 555-2222
Peter                  Smith                 555-3333
Penny                  Johnson               555-4444

store2_customers

customer_first_name    customer_last_name    customer_phone

Jane                   Jones                 555-2222
Peter                  Smith                 555-3333
Paul                   Watson                555-5555
Emily                  Williams              555-6666
```

Figure 14-2: Two union-compatible tables

The expression

```
store1_customers JOIN store2_customers ON (customer_first_name,
    customer_last_name, customer_phone)
```

is equivalent to

```
store1_customers INTERSECT store2_customers
```

In either case, the result table will contain the two rows that appear in both source tables.

Keep in mind that an intersect looks for rows that are completely identical, character for character. Although you can join two tables that have only one column in common, intersect requires that the tables have *all* columns in common.

Performing Queries with Intersect

As with UNION and EXCEPT, you use the INTERSECT operator to combine the result tables produced by two independent SELECTs. For example, you could use INTERSECT to find out which customers have purchased two specific books:

```
SELECT customer_numb, customer_first_name, customer_last_name
FROM order_lines JOIN orders JOIN books
WHERE isbn = '0-127-3948-2'
INTERSECT
SELECT customer_numb, customer_first_name, customer_last_name
FROM order_lines JOIN orders JOIN books
WHERE isbn = '0-133-5935-2'
```

Note that INTERSECT works in this case only because the two component SELECTs produce union compatible result tables.

As with UNION and EXCEPT, there is an alternative syntax for INTERSECT that involves the CORRESPONDING BY clause:

```
SELECT *
FROM order_lines JOIN orders JOIN books
WHERE isbn = '0-127-3948-2'
INTERSECT CORRESPONDING BY (customer_numb, customer_first_name,
customer_last_name)
SELECT *
FROM order_lines JOIN orders JOIN books
WHERE isbn = '0-133-5935-2'
```

Conformance note: The INTERSECT operator is required for intermediate level SQL-92 conformance but not for entry level.

Additional Predicate Operators

The SQL-92 standard adds new operators that can be used in WHERE clause predicates: UNIQUE, OVERLAPS, and MATCH.

UNIQUE

The UNIQUE operator looks at the result of a subquery and determines whether there are any duplicate rows in the subquery. If there are, the operator returns false. If all rows in the subquery's result table are unique, the operator returns true.

For example, suppose an employee of the online bookstore wants to see information about books that have unique titles (in other words, books whose titles aren't duplicated by that of any other book). The following query, containing a correlated subquery and using the UNIQUE operator, would do the trick:

```
SELECT author, title
FROM books t1
WHERE UNIQUE (SELECT title
    FROM books
    WHERE t1.isbn = books.title)
```

The SQL command processor will perform the subquery for each row in the BOOKS table. In this particular case, only books for which the subquery returns one row will be included in the result table.

OVERLAPS

OVERLAPS is a specialized operator that determines whether two DATETIME intervals overlap one another. The operator requires two sets of DATETIME information, as in

first_interval OVERLAPS *second_interval*

If the two intervals overlap in time, the predicate is true; if the two intervals do not overlap, or merely have a boundary in common (for example, a matching starting and ending time), the predicate is false.

The intervals that you compare must be expressed in one of two formats:

(*start_time_and/or_date*, *duration*)

or

(*start_time_and/or_date*, *end_time_and/or_date*)

Although both intervals in the predicate do not need to use the same format, the starting and ending times must be of the same data type (either DATE, TIME, or DATETIME).

For example, assume that the online bookstore wants to see data about customers who have placed orders within the past week. The query might be written

```
SELECT customer_first_name, customer_last_name
FROM customers JOIN orders
WHERE (order_date, INTERVAL '7' DAYS) OVERLAPS
    (CURRENT_DATE - 7, CURRENT_DATE)
```

The predicate in this query examines the contents of the ORDER_DATE column to determine whether the interval of the order date plus seven days falls within the interval seven days prior to the current date through the current date. Notice that the first expression uses the starting date/duration format while the second uses the starting date/ending date format. Nonetheless, all three dates are of data type, DATE.

MATCH

The MATCH predicate is designed to allow you to test referential integrity before actually storing data in tables. When included in an application program, it can help identify potential data modification errors.

For example, assume that the online bookstore wanted to verify that a book requested by a customer was in the BOOKS table before attempting to add it to an order by placing a row in the ORDER_LINES table. An application program might therefore include the following query:

```
EXEC SQL SELECT isbn
FROM books
WHERE (:entered_author, :entered_title) MATCH (SELECT author, title
                                                      FROM books);
```

The subquery selects all the rows in the BOOKS table and then matches the author and title columns against the values entered by the customer, both of which are stored in host language variables. If the preceding query returns one or more rows, then the author and title pair entered by the customer exist in the BOOKS relation. However, if the result table has no rows, then inserting the book into ORDER_LINES would produce a referential integrity violation and the insert should not be performed.

If the online bookstore wanted to verify a primary key constraint, it could use a variation of the MATCH predicate that requires unique values in the result table. For example, to determine whether a book is already in the BOOKS table, the online bookstore could use

```
EXEC SQL SELECT isbn
FROM books
WHERE UNIQUE (:entered_author, :entered_title)
MATCH (SELECT author, title
       FROM books);
```

By default, MATCH returns true if *any* value being tested is null or, when there are no nulls in the value being tested, a row exists in the result table that matches the values being tested. You can, however, change the behavior of MATCH when nulls are present:

> ◆ MATCH FULL is true if *every* value being tested is null or, when there are no nulls in the values being tested, a row exists in the result table that matches the values being tested.

◆ MATCH PARTIAL is true if *every* value being tested is null or a row exists in the result table that matches all nonnull values being tested.

Note that you can combine UNIQUE with both MATCH FULL and MATCH PARTIAL.

Table Constructors in Queries

SQL-92 specifies that the table on which a SELECT is performed can be a virtual table, rather than just a base table. This means that a DBMS should allow a complete SELECT (in other words, a subquery) to be used in a FROM clause to prepare the table on which the remainder of the query will operate. Expressions that create tables for use in SQL statements in this way are known as *table constructors*.

> *Note: When you join tables in the FROM clause you are actually generating a source table for a query on the fly. What is described in this section is just an extension of that principle.*

For example, the following query lists all books that were either ordered on the current date or have a price of more than $29.95:

```
SELECT DISTINCT isbn, author, title
FROM books JOIN (SELECT isbn
                 FROM order_lines JOIN orders
                 WHERE order_date = CURRENT_DATE
UNION
SELECT isbn
FROM order_lines JOIN orders
WHERE retail_price > 29.95)
```

Notice that the row selection is being performed in the subquery that is part of the FROM clause. This forces the SQL command processor to perform the subquery, including its union, prior to performing the join. Although this query could certainly be written in another way, using the subquery in the FROM clause gives the programmer additional control over the order in which relational algebra operations are performed.

Additional Foreign Key Options

The SQL-92 standard introduces additional flexibility in the definition of foreign keys, including the following:

◆ Rules for determining what occurs when all or part of a foreign key is null. By default, if any part of a foreign key is null, then the DBMS will accept it. If you add MATCH PARTIAL to the foreign key definition and part of a foreign key is null, then the nonnull portions of the foreign key must match parts of an existing foreign key. If you add MATCH FULL, a foreign key must either be completely null or match an existing primary key completely.

◆ Rules for determining the action to take when a primary key referenced by the foreign key is updated. If you specify ON UPDATE CASCADE, then the DBMS will automatically update the foreign key values when the primary key values they reference are modified. (In most cases, this will be the desired option because it maintains the consistency of cross-references throughout the database.) In addition, you can choose to ON UPDATE SET NULL (set the foreign key values to NULL), ON UPDATE SET DEFAULT (set the foreign key values to their columns' default values), ON UPDATE NO ACTION (do nothing).

Note: In a well-designed DBMS, primary key values should never be modified. However, given that people persist in using meaningful primary keys, you may want to be certain that cross-references are maintained.

◆ Rules for determining the action to take when a primary key referenced by the foreign key is deleted. If you specify ON DELETE CASCADE, all matching foreign key rows will be deleted when the referenced primary key row is deleted. If you specify ON DELETE SET NULL, the foreign key rows will be left in the table and the values of the foreign key columns set to null. The option ON DELETE SET DEFAULT replaces the values of the foreign key columns with the columns' default values. The final option—ON DELETE NO ACTION—leaves foreign key rows untouched when the row containing the primary key they reference is deleted. This will, of course, leave the database with violations of referential integrity.

Assertions

An *assertion* is a constraint that is applied to any or all tables in a schema, rather than to a specific table. It therefore can be based on more than one table or be used to verify that a table is not empty. Assertions exist as independent database objects that can be created and dropped as needed.

To create an assertion, you use the CREATE ASSERTION command:

```
CREATE ASSERTION assertion_name
CHECK (logical_expression_for_validation)
```

For example, to ensure that the AUTHORS table has at least one row, the online bookstore could define the following assertion:

```
CREATE ASSERTION validate_authors
CHECK (SELECT COUNT (*) FROM authors > 0)
```

Because an assertion is a database object, you remove one from a schema just as you would any other database object:

```
DROP ASSERTION assertion_name
```

Determining When Constraints Are Checked

Most of today's DBMSs check constraints whenever any modification is made to the contents of a table. The SQL-92 standard, however, gives users the ability to determine when constraints are checked. Constraints may be *not deferrable* (the default), in which case they are checked after each SQL statement. If constraints are *deferrable*, they are checked at the end of a transaction.

> *Note: If you are working in an interactive environment where each statement is a distinct transaction, then deferring constraints essentially has no effect.*

There are several places where you can specify when constraints are checked:

- ◆ When constraints are defined within a table definition. In this case, you can set constraints to INITIALLY DEFERRED or INITIALLY IMMEDIATE to determine the initial setting of constraint checking. If you want to prevent anyone from deferring constraints at a later time, you can also specify that the constraints are NOT DEFERRABLE. To allow constraints to be deferred at a later time, you can specify them as DEFERRABLE.
- ◆ When you create a domain using CREATE DOMAIN, you can indicate that domain checking should be INITIALLY IMMEDIATE or INITIALLY DEFERRED. In addition, you can prevent domain checking from ever being deferred by adding NOT DEFERRABLE. To allow deferring of domain checking at a later time, specify DEFERRABLE.
- ◆ When you create an assertion using CREATE ASSERTION, you can indicate that assertion checking should be INITIALLY IMMEDIATE or INITIALLY DEFERRED. In addition, you can prevent assertion checking from ever being deferred by adding NOT DEFERRABLE. To allow deferring of assertion checking at a later time, specify DEFERRABLE.

Changing the Constraint Mode

The time at which constraints defined as database objects are checked can be altered with the SET CONSTRAINTS MODE statement:

```
SET CONSTRAINTS MODE constraint_name DEFERRED
```

or

```
SET CONSTRAINTS MODE constraint_name IMMEDIATE
```

Of course, this assumes that the named constraint is deferrable.

> *Note: If you want to affect all the named constraints in the current schema, use the keyword ALL instead of one or more constraint names.*

Because the SET CONSTRAINTS MODE statement requires a named constraint, it cannot be applied to constraints created within a CREATE TABLE statement unless those constraints have been named. This means that if you want to have control over when the checking of such constraints occurs, you need to add a CONSTRAINT clause to the table declaration so you have somewhere to name a constraint.

As an example, consider the following table declaration:

```
CREATE TABLE employee
(int id_numb,
vchar first_name 20,
vchar last_name 20,
vchar department_name 20,
CONSTRAINT employee_pk
PRIMARY KEY (id_numb)
    INITIALLY IMMEDIATE NOT DEFERRABLE,
    CONSTRAINT employee2dept
FOREIGN KEY (department_name)
    REFERENCES departments (department_name)
    INITIALLY IMMEDIATE DEFERRABLE)
```

The addition of the CONSTRAINT clause allows both the primary key and the foreign key to be named, making them accessible to a SET CONSTRAINTS MODE statement (although the primary key has been specified as not deferrable).

15

Object-Oriented Features of the SQL:1999 Standard

As mentioned in Chapter 3, the SQL:1999 standard adds support for many parts of the object-oriented paradigm to SQL. This chapter will introduce you to the two major ways in which the standard indicates that objects should be integrated into a relational DBMS.

> *Note: A complete description of the object-oriented features of SQL:1999 requires an entire book in and of itself. This chapter therefore can serve only as an overview of what is found in the standard. For details, see Advanced SQL:1999: Understanding Object-Relational and Other Advanced Features by Jim Melton (Morgan Kaufmann, 2002).*

To get the most out of this material, you will need an understanding of the object-oriented paradigm. The first major section of this chapter therefore introduces basic object-oriented concepts. If you are familiar with concepts such as classes, objects, and inheritance, then you can skip to the second major section, *SQL:1999 versus Pure Object Orientation* on page 286.

The Basics of Object Orientation

The object-oriented paradigm was the brainchild of Dr. Kristen Nygarrd, a Norwegian who was attempting to write a computer program to model the behavior of ships, tides, and fjords. He found that the interactions were extremely complex and realized that it would be easier to write the program if he separated the three types of program elements and let each one model its own behavior against each of the others.

The object-oriented programming languages in use today (most notably C++, SmallTalk, and Java) are a direct outgrowth of Nygarrd's early work. The way in which objects are used in relational databases today is an extension of object-oriented programming.

> *Note: This is in direct contrast to the relational data model, which was designed specifically to model data relationships, although much of its theoretical foundations are found in mathematical set theory.*

To understand the role of objects in relational databases, you therefore must first understand the object-oriented paradigm as it is used in object-oriented programming. In this chapter, you will read about the fundamental concepts of that paradigm. Do not worry if you cannot program: You *do not* need to be a programmer to understand this material. If you *are* fluent in an object-oriented programming language, however, you can skip the portion of this chapter that deals with object-oriented concepts and just read the section titled *Integrating Objects into a Relational Database* at the end of the chapter.

The easiest way to understand what object-oriented programming is all about is to begin with an example that has absolutely nothing to do with programming at all.

Writing Instructions

Assume that you have a 16-year-old daughter (or sister, whichever is more appropriate) named Jane and that your family is going to take a long car trip. Like most 16-year-olds, Jane is less than thrilled about a trip with the family and in particular with spending so much time with her 12-year-old brother. In self-defense, Jane needs something to keep her 12-year-old brother busy so he won't bother her as she reads while her parents are driving. She therefore decides to write up some instructions for playing solitaire card games for him.

The first set of instructions is for the most common solitaire game, Klondike. As you can see in Figure 15-1, the deal involves seven piles of cards of increasing depth, with the top card turned over. The rest of the deck remains in the draw pile. Jane decides to break the written instructions into two main parts: information about the game and questions her brother might ask. She therefore produces instructions that look something like Figure 15-2. She also attaches the illustration of the game's deal.

The next game she tackles is Canfield. Like Klondike, it is played with one deck, but the deal and play are slightly different (see Figure 15-3). Jane uses the same pattern for the instructions as she did for Klondike because it cuts down the amount of writing she has to do (see Figure 15-4).

And finally, just to make sure her brother doesn't get too bored, Jane prepares instructions for Forty Thieves (see Figure 15-5). This game uses two decks of cards and plays in a very different way from the other two games (see Figure 15-6). Nonetheless, preparing the instructions for the third game is fairly easy, because she has the template for the instructions down pat.

After completing three sets of instructions, it becomes clear to Jane that having the template for the instructions makes the process extremely easy. Jane can use the template to organize any number of sets of instructions for playing solitaire. All she has to do is photocopy the template and fill in the values for the information about the game.

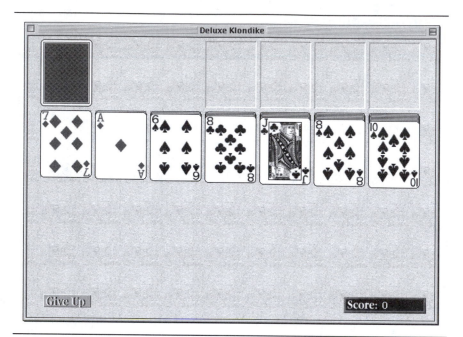

Figure 15-1: The initial deal for Klondike

Objects

If someone were writing an object-oriented computer program to manage the instructions for playing solitaire, each game would be known as an *object*. It is a self-contained element used by the program. It has things that it knows about itself: its name, an illustration of its layout, the number of decks needed to play, how to deal, how to play, and how to determine when the game is won. In object-oriented terms, the values that an object stores about itself are known as *attributes* or *variables* or occasionally, *properties*.

The solitaire game object also has some things it knows how to do: explain how to deal, explain how to play, explain how to identify a win, and so on. In object-oriented programming terminology, actions that objects know how to perform are called *methods*, *services*, *functions*, *procedures*, or *operations*.

```
Information about the Game
    Name: Klondike
    Illustration: See next page
    Decks: One
    Dealing: Deal from left to right.
        First pass: First card face up, six cards down.
        Second pass: First card face up on top of card #2, five cards down.
        Third pass: First card face up on top of card #3, four cards down.
        ... repeat pattern for total of seven passes ...
    Playing: One or three cards can be turned at a time.
        As encountered, put aces on top. Build up in suits.
        Build down from deal, opposite suit colors.
        Can move cards from the middle of a stack, moving card and all cards
    built below it.
        Move kings only into empty spots.
        If turning one card, make only one pass through the deck.
        If turning three cards, make as many passes as you like through the
    deck.
    Winning: All cards built on top of their aces.
Questions to Ask
    What is the name of the game?
        Read Name section.
    How many decks do I need?
        Read Decks section.
    What does the layout look like?
        Read Illustration section.
    How do I deal the game?
        Read the Dealing section.
    How do I play the game?
        Read the Playing section.
    How do I know when I've won?
        Read the Winning section.
```

Figure 15-2:   Instructions for playing Klondike

Note: It is unfortunate, but there is no single accepted terminology for the object-oriented paradigm. Each programming language or DBMS chooses which terms it will use. You therefore need to recognize all of the terms that might be used to describe the same thing.

An object is very security minded. It typically keeps the things it knows about itself private and releases that information only through a method whose purpose is to share data values. For example, a user or program using the Klondike game object cannot access the contents of the Dealing variable directly. Instead, the user

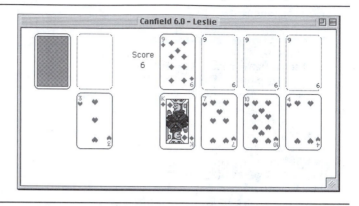

Figure 15-3:   The initial Canfield deal

Information about the Game
   Name: Canfield
   Illustration: See next page
   Decks: One
   Dealing: Deal four cards face up.
      Place an additional card face up above the first four as the starting card for building suits.
      The remaining cards stay in the draw pile.
   Playing: Turn one card at a time, going through the deck as many times as desired.
      Build down from deal, opposite suit colors.
      Can move cards from the middle of a stack, moving card and all cards built below it.
      Place cards of the same value as the initial foundation card above the deal as encountered.
      Build up in suits from the foundation cards.
      Any card can be placed in an empty slot.
   Winning: All cards built on top of the foundation cards.
Questions to Ask
   What is the name of the game?
      Read **Name** section.
   How many decks do I need?
      Read **Decks** section.
   What does the layout look like?
      Read **Illustration** section.
   How do I deal the game?
      Read the **Dealing** section.
   How do I play the game?
      Read the **Playing** section.
   How do I know when I've won?
      Read the **Winning** section.

Figure 15-4:   The instructions for playing Canfield

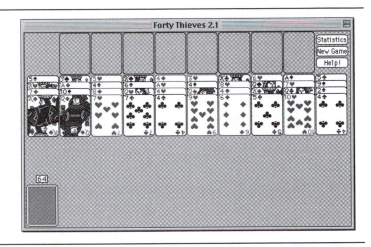

Figure 15-5: The initial deal for Forty Thieves

Information about the Game
    Name: Forty Thieves
    Illustration: See next page
    Decks: Two
    Dealing: Make ten piles of four cards, all face up.
        Jog cards so that the values of all cards can be seen.
        Remaining cards stay in the deck.
    Playing: Turn one card at a time. Make only one pass through the deck.
        Build down in suits.
        Only the top card of a stack can be moved.
        As aces are encountered, place at top of deal and build up in suits
    from the aces.
        Any card can be moved into any open space in the deal.
    Winning: All cards built on top of their aces.
Questions to Ask
    What is the name of the game?
        Read **Name** section.
    How many decks do I need?
        Read **Decks** section.
    What does the layout look like?
        Read **Illustration** section.
    How do I deal the game?
        Read the **Dealing** section.
    How do I play the game?
        Read the **Playing** section.
    How do I know when I've won?
        Read the **Winning** section.

Figure 15-6:   The instructions for playing Forty Thieves

or program must execute the How Do I Deal the Game? method to see those data.

Objects also keep private the details of the procedures for the things they know how to do, but they make it easy for someone to ask them to perform those actions. Users or programs cannot see what is inside any of the methods. They see only the result of executing the method. This characteristic of objects is known as *information hiding* or *data encapsulation*.

An object presents a public interface to other objects that might use it. This provides other objects with a way to ask for data values or for actions to be performed. In the example of the solitaire games, the questions that Jane's little brother can ask are the game's public interface. The instructions below each question represent the procedure to be used to answer the question. A major benefit of data encapsulation is that as long as the object's public interface remains the same, you can change the details of the object's methods without needing to inform any other objects that might be using those methods. For example, the card game objects currently tell the user to "read" the contents of an attribute. However, there is no reason that the methods couldn't be changed to tell the user to "print" the contents of an attribute. The user would still access the method in the same way, but the way in which the method operates would be slightly different.

An object requests data or an action by sending a *message* to another object. For example, if you were writing a computer program to manage the instructions for solitaire games, the program (an object in its own right) could send a message to the game object asking the game object to display the instructions for dealing the game. Because the actual procedures of the method are hidden, your program would ask for the instruction display and then you would see the instructions on the screen. However, you would not need to worry about the details of how the screen display was produced. That is the job of the game object rather than the object that is asking the game to do something.

An object-oriented program is made up of a collection of objects, each of which has attributes and methods. The objects interact by sending messages to one another. The trick, of course, is figuring out exactly which objects a program needs and the attributes and methods those objects should have.

Classes

The template on which the solitaire game instructions are based is the same for each game. Without data, it might be represented as in Figure 15-7. The nice thing about this template is that it provides a consistent way of organizing all the characteristics of a game. When you want to create the instructions for another game, you make a copy of the template and "fill in the blanks": You write the data values for the attributes. The procedures that make up the answers to the questions someone might ask about the game have already been completed.

```
Information about the Game (Variables)
    Name:
    Illustration:
    Decks:
    Dealing:
    Playing:
    Winning:
Questions to Ask (Methods)
    What is the name of the game?
        Read Name section.
    How many decks do I need?
        Read Decks section.
    What does the layout look like?
        Read Illustration section.
    How do I deal the game?
        Read the Dealing section.
    How do I play the game?
        Read the Playing section.
    How do I know when I've won?
        Read the Winning section.
```

Figure 15-7:   The solitaire game instruction template

In object-oriented terminology, the template on which similar objects like the solitaire game instructions are based is known as a *class*. When a program creates an object from a class, it provides data for the object's variables. The object can then use the methods that have been written for its class. All of the objects created from the same class share the same procedures for their methods. They also have the same types of data, but the values for the data may differ, for example, just as the names of the solitaire games are different.

A class is also a data type. In fact, a class is an implementation of what is known as an *abstract data type*, which is just another term for a user-defined data type. The implication of a class being a data type is that you can use a class as the data type of an attribute.

Suppose, for example, you were developing a class to handle data about the employees in your organization. The attributes of the class might include the employee ID, the first name, the last name, and the address. The address itself is made up of a street, city, state, and zip. Therefore, you would probably create an address class with those attributes and then, rather than duplicating those attributes in the employee class, simply indicate that an object of the employee class will include an object created from the address class to contain the employee's address.

Types of Classes

There are three major types of classes used in an object-oriented program:

♦ *Control classes:* Control classes neither manage data nor have visible output. Instead, they control the operational flow of a program. For example, *application classes* represent the program itself. In most cases, each program creates only one object from an application class. The application class's job includes starting the execution of the program, detecting menu selections, and executing the correct program code to satisfy the user's requests.

♦ *Entity classes:* Entity classes are used to create objects that manage data. The solitaire game class, for example, is an entity class. Classes for people, tangible objects, and events (for example, business meetings) are entity classes. Most object-oriented programs have at least one entity class from which many objects are created. In fact, in its simplest sense, the object-oriented data model is built from the representation of relationships between objects created from entity objects.

♦ *Interface classes:* Interface classes handle the input and output of information. For example, if you are working with a graphic user interface, then each window and menu used by the program is an object created from an interface class.

In an object-oriented program, entity classes do not do their own input and output (I/O). Keyboard input is handled by interface objects that collect data and send them to entity objects for storage and processing. Screen and printed output is formatted by interface objects that get data for display from entity objects. When entity objects become part of a database, the DBMS takes care of file I/O; the rest of the I/O is handled by application programs or DBMS utilities.

Why is it so important to keep data manipulation separate from I/O? Wouldn't it be simpler to let the entity object manage its own I/O? It might be simpler, but if you decided to change a screen layout, you would need to modify the entity class. If you keep them separate, then data manipulation procedures are independent of data display. You can change one without affecting the other. In a large program, this can not only save you a lot of time but also help you avoid programming errors. In a database environment, the separation of I/O and data storage becomes especially critical, because you do not want to modify data storage each time you decide to modify the look and feel of an application program.

Many object-oriented programs also use a fourth type of class: a *container class*. Container classes exist to "contain," or manage, multiple objects created from the same type of class. Because they gather objects together, they are also known as *aggregations*. For example, if you had a program that handled the instructions for playing solitaire, then that program would probably have a container class that organized all the individual card game objects. The container class would keep the objects in some order, list them for you, and probably search through them as well. As you will see, many pure object-oriented DBMSs require container classes, known as *extents*, to provide access to all objects created from the same class.

Types of Methods

Several types of methods are common to most classes, including the following:

- ◆ *Constructors:* A constructor is a method that has the same name as the class. It is executed whenever an object is created from a class. A constructor therefore usually contains instructions to initialize an object's variables in some way.
- ◆ *Destructors:* A destructor is a method that is executed when an object is destroyed. Not all object-oriented languages support destructors, which are usually used to release system resources (for example, main memory) allocated by the object.
- ◆ *Accessors:* An accessor, also known as a *get method*, returns the value of a private attribute to another object. This is the typical way in which external objects gain access to encapsulated data.
- ◆ *Mutators:* A mutator, or *set method*, stores a new value in an attribute. This is the typical way in which external objects can modify encapsulated data.

The remaining methods defined for a class depend on the specific type of class and the specific behaviors it needs to perform.

Method Overloading

One of the characteristics of a class is its ability to contain *overloaded* methods, methods that have the same name but require different data to operate. Because the data are different, the public interfaces of the methods are distinct.

As an example, assume that a human relations program has a container class named AllEmployees that aggregates all objects created from the Employees class. Programs that use the AllEmployees class create one object from the class and then relate all employee objects to the container using some form of program data structure (for example, an array, linked list, or binary tree).

To make the container class useful, there must be some way to locate specific employee objects. You might want to search by the employee ID number, by first and last name, or by telephone number. The AllEmployees class therefore contains three methods named FIND. One of the three requires an integer (the employee number) as input, the second requires two strings (the first and last name), and the third requires a single string (the phone number). Although the methods have the same name, their public interfaces are different because the combination of the name and the required input data is distinct.

Many classes have overloaded constructors. One might accept interactive input, another might read input from a file, and a third might get its data by copying the data in another object (a *copy constructor*). For example, most object-oriented environments have a Date class that supports initializing a date object with a string, three integers (day, month, year), the current system date, another Date object, and so on.

The benefit of method overloading is that the methods present a consistent interface to the programmer. Whenever a programmer wants to locate an employee, he or she knows to use a method named FIND. Then, the programmer just uses whichever of the three types of data he or she happens to have. The object-oriented program locates the correct method by using its entire public interface (its *signature*), made up of the name and the required input data.

Naming Classes, Attributes, and Methods

There are a few naming conventions used throughout the object-oriented world. Although there is absolutely nothing that says you have to name your classes, attributes, and methods in this way, you will be consistent with other programmers and database designers if you do so.

- ◆ Class names start with uppercase letters, followed by lowercase letters. If a class name is more than one word, it either uses an underscore (_) to separate the words — as in Merchandise_item—or uses embedded uppercase letters, as in MerchandiseItem.
- ◆ Attribute and method names start with lowercase letters and contain uppercase letters, lowercase letters, and numbers. If an attribute or method name is more than one word, it either uses an underscore to separate the words (for example, product_numb or display_label) or uses embedded uppercase letters, as in productNumb or displayLabel.
- ◆ Accessor method names begin with the word *get* followed by the name of the attribute whose value is to be retrieved. For example, a method to retrieve a product number would be *getProductNumb*.
- ◆ Mutator method names begin with the word *set* followed by the name of the attribute whose value is to be modified, as in *setProductNumb*.

Class Relationships

The classes in an object-oriented environment aren't always independent. The basic object-oriented paradigm has two major ways to relate objects, distinct from any logical data relationships that might be included in a pure object-oriented database: inheritance and composition.

Inheritance

As you are developing an object-oriented program or an object-oriented database, you will run into situations where you need to use similar—but not identical—classes. If these classes are related in general to specific relationships, then you can take advantage of one of the major features of the object-oriented paradigm known as *inheritance*.

Inheriting Attributes. To see how inheritance works, assume that you are writing a program to manage a pet shop. One of the entity classes you will use is ANIMAL, which will describe the living creatures sold by the shop. The data that describe objects created from the ANIMAL class include the English and Latin names of the animal, the animal's age, and the animal's gender. However, the rest of the data depend on what type of animal is being represented. For example, for reptiles, you want to know the length of the animal, but for mammals, you want to know the weight. And for fish, you don't care about the weight or length, but you do want to know the color. All the animals sold by the pet shop share some data, yet have pieces of data that are specific to certain subgroups.

You could diagram the relationship as in Figure 15-8. The ANIMAL class provides the data common to all types of animals. The subgroups—MAMMALS, REPTILES, and FISH—*add* the data specific to themselves. They don't need to repeat the common data because they *inherit* them from ANIMALS. In other words, MAMMALS, REPTILES, and FISH all include the four pieces of data that are part of ANIMAL.

If you look closely at Figure 15-8, you'll notice that the lines on the arrows go from the subgroups up to ANIMAL. This is actually contrary to what is happening: The data from ANIMAL are flowing down the lines into the subgroups. Unfortunately, the direction of the arrows is dictated by convention, even though it may seem counterintuitive.

In object-oriented terminology, the subgroups are known as *subclasses* or *derived* classes. The ANIMAL class is a *superclass* or *base* class.

The trick to understanding inheritance is to remember that subclasses represent a more specific occurrence of their superclass. The relationships between a base class and its derived classes therefore can be expressed using the phrase "is a":

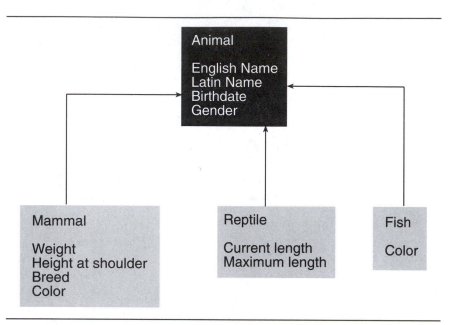

Figure 15-8:   **The relationship of classes for a program for a pet shop**

- ◆ A mammal is an animal.
- ◆ A reptile is an animal.
- ◆ A fish is an animal.

If the "is a" phrasing does not make sense in a given situation, then you are not looking at inheritance. As an example, assume that you are writing a program to handle the rentals of equipment at a ski shop. You create a class for a generic merchandise item and then subclasses for the specific types of items being rented, as in the top four rectangles in Figure 15-9. Inheritance works properly here because skis are a specific type of merchandise item, as well as boots and poles.

However, you run into trouble when you begin to consider the specific items being rented and the customer doing the renting (the renter). Although there is a logical database-style relationship between a renter and an item being rented, inheritance does not work because the "is a" test fails. A rented item is not a renter!

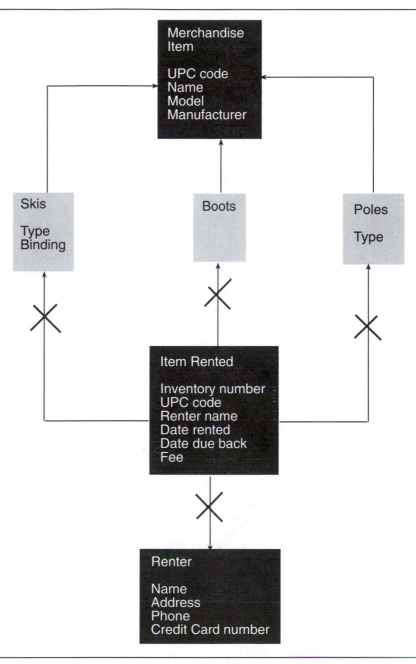

Figure 15-9: Inheritance and no inheritance in a program for a ski shop

The situation with merchandise items and rental inventory is more complex. The MERCHANDISE ITEM, SKIS, BOOTS, and POLES classes represent descriptions of types of merchandise but not physical inventory. For example, the ski shop may have many pairs of one type of ski in inventory and many pairs of boots of the same type, size, and width. Therefore, what are being rented are individual inventory items, represented by the ITEM RENTED class. A given inventory item is either skis, boots, or poles. It can only be *one*, not all three as shown in Figure 15-9. Therefore, an item rented is not a pair of skis, a pair of boots, and a set of poles. (You also have the problem of having no class that can store the size or length of an item.)

One solution to the problem is to create a separate rented item class for each type of merchandise, as in Figure 15-10. When you are looking at this diagram, be sure to pay attention to the direction of the arrows. The physical layout of the diagram does not correspond to the direction of the inheritance. Remember that by convention, the arrows point from the derived class to the base class.

The SKI ITEM class inherits information about the type of item it is from the SKIS class. It also inherits information about an item being rented from the ITEM RENTED class. A ski item "is a" pair of skis; a ski item "is a" rented item as well. Now the design of the classes passes the "is a" test for appropriate inheritance. (Note that this also gives you a class that can contain information such as the length and size of a specific inventory item.) The RENTER class does not participate in the inheritance hierarchy at all.

Multiple Inheritance. When a class inherits from more than one base class, you have *multiple inheritance*. The extent to which multiple inheritance is supported in programming languages and by DBMSs varies considerably from one product to another. You will read much more about this concept throughout this book.

Not every class in an inheritance hierarchy is necessarily used to create objects. For example, in Figure 15-10 it is unlikely that any objects are ever created from the MERCHANDISE ITEM or ITEM RENTED classes. These classes are present simply to provide the common attributes and methods that their derived classes share.

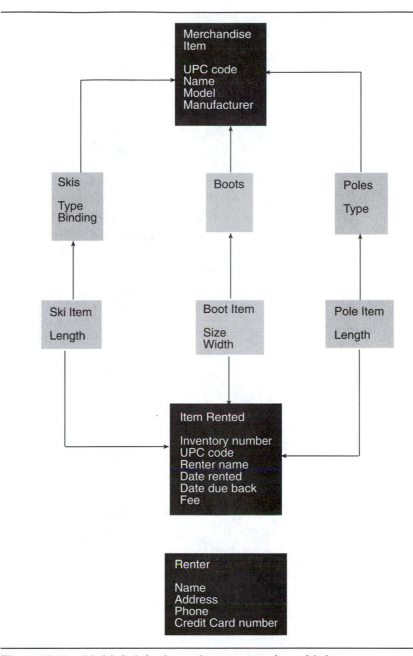

Figure 15-10:   Multiple inheritance in a program for a ski shop

Such classes are known as *abstract*, or *virtual*, classes. In contrast, classes from which objects are created are known as *concrete* classes.

> *Note: Many computer scientists use the verb "instantiate" to mean "creating an object from a class." For example, you could say that abstract classes are never instantiated. However, this author finds that term rather contrived (although not quite as bad as saying "we now will motivate the code" to mean "we will now explain the code") and prefers to use the more direct "create an object from a class."*

Inheriting Methods: Polymorphism. In general, methods are inherited by subclasses from their superclass. A subclass can use its base class's methods as its own. However, in some cases it may not be possible to write a generic method that can be used by all subclasses. For example, assume that the ski rental shop's MERCHANDISE ITEM class has a method named PRINTCATALOGENTRY, the intent of which is to print a properly formatted catalog entry for each distinct type of merchandise item. The subclasses of MERCHANDISE ITEM, however, have attributes not shared by all subclasses, and the PRINTCATALOG-ENTRY method therefore must work somewhat differently for each subclass.

To solve the problem, the ski rental shop can take advantage of *polymorphism*, the ability to write different bodies for methods of the same name that belong to classes in the same inheritance hierarchy. The MERCHANDISE ITEM class includes a *prototype* for the PRINT-CATALOGENTRY method, indicating just the method's public interface. There is no body for the method, no specifications of how the method is to perform its work (a *virtual method*). Each subclass then redefines the method, adding the program instructions necessary to execute the method.

The beauty of polymorphism is that a programmer can expect methods of the same name and same type of output for all the subclasses of the same base class. However, each subclass can perform the method according to its own needs. Encapsulation hides the details from all objects outside the class hierarchy.

> *Note: It is very easy to confuse polymorphism and overloading. Just keep in mind that overloading applies to methods of the same class that have the same name but different signatures, whereas polymorphism applies to several subclasses of the same base class that have methods with the same signature but different implementations.*

Composition

Inheritance can be described as a general–specific relationship. In contrast, *composition* is a whole-part relationship. It specifies that one class is a component of another and is often read as "has a."

To help you understand how composition can be used, let's look at another version of the ski shop classes (see Figure 15-11). Notice that the diagram is considerably simpler. Not only has the multiple inheritance been eliminated, but there are only three classes

The RENTER class continues to stand alone. However, the inheritance hierarchy for the types of merchandise and items that are rented is now made up of two classes, each of which contains an object of another class. A merchandise item has an object of the MERCHANDISE TYPE class to classify it as either a ski, boot, or pole. By the same token, an item rented has an object of the RENTAL ITEM class to contain descriptive information (size, width, and length, as appropriate).

Some pure object-oriented DBMSs take composition to the extreme. They provide simple data types such as integers, real numbers, characters, and Booleans. Everything else in the database—even strings—is built by creating classes from those simple data types and using those classes to build more complex classes, and so on.

Benefits of Object Orientation

There are several reasons why the object-oriented paradigm has become so pervasive in programming. Among the perceived benefits are the following:

◆ An object-oriented program consists of modular units that are independent of one another. These units can therefore be reused in multiple programs, saving development time. For example, if you have a well-debugged employee class, you can use it in any of your business programs that require data about employees.

◆ As long as a class's public interface remains unchanged, the internals of the class can be modified as needed without requiring any changes to the programs that use the class. This can significantly speed up program modification. It can also make program modification more reliable, as it cuts down on many unexpected side effects of program changes.

◆ An object-oriented program separates the user interface from data handling, making it possible to modify one independent of the other.

◆ Inheritance adds logical structure to a program by relating classes in a general to specific manner, making the program easier to understand and therefore easier to maintain.

However, the object-oriented paradigm merely provides a framework for organizing the elements in a database. It does not eliminate the need to perform a good database design that identifies entities and the relationship between entities..

SQL:1999 versus Pure Object Orientation

Now that you have a feeling for the object-oriented paradigm, you can understand the major difference between a pure object-oriented database and a relational database that uses the object-oriented capabilities of SQL:1999: the lack of unique object identifiers.

In an object-oriented database, the DBMS gives each object a unique internal identifier that is not visible to the user or application programmer. Relationships between objects are represented as collections of these object identifiers. However, SQL:1999 makes no

Figure 15-11: Composition

provision for such internal identifiers and requires an additional column in a table storing objects as an object identifier (a *self-referencing column*). One-to-many relationships can be defined to use these reference values as pointers between objects (directly violating the principles of a relational database). However, foreign key–primary key references can also be used to represent data relationships and referential integrity can be enforced.

The SQL:1999 standard supports only single inheritance.

SQL:1999 supports classes as *structured user-defined data types* (UDTs). They can then be used as column data types (for object-relational support) or as objects (for simulating an object-oriented database).

Object-Relational Support

In the pure object-oriented data model, a class is an entity, the element that is involved in data relationships. However, in what is known as the *object-relational data model*, a class takes on an entirely different role. As mentioned at the beginning of this chapter, it becomes a domain, acting as the data type for a column.

> *Note: While domains haven't been specifically deprecated in the SQL:1999 standard, they won't be enhanced any further. The alternative is to use a class as a domain, which is actually more flexible than the DOMAIN facility.*

There are two very important implications of using a class as a domain:

♦ It becomes possible to store multiple values in the same column in the same row because an object usually contains multiple values. However, if a class is a domain assigned to a column, then any given intersection of a column and row can contain only one object created from that class. The relation therefore still conforms to the relational constraint of there being no multivalued attributes.

♦ It becomes possible to store procedures in a relation, because an object is linked to the program code for the processes that it knows how to do.

Note: Oracle and DB2 supported classes as domains for some time prior to the adoption of the SQL:1999 standard. However, their support did not include inheritance nor did it necessarily match the syntax that was ultimately adopted as part of the new standard.

Typed Tables

The SQL:1999 standard goes beyond the object-relational model to allow the use of tables to hold collections of objects (*typed tables*). In this case, an entire row is an object and the table has one column for every variable defined for the class.

In addition, a typed table has the *self-referencing column* mentioned earlier. This column holds a value that uniquely identifies each row in the table, but it is not the same as a primary key. Although primary key values must be unique throughout a table at any given time, the self-referencing column must be unique throughout the life of the table in the database. To ensure this property, the DBMS should be generating values for the self-referencing column. There is no way to be certain that application-supplied values can be unique in this way.

Typed tables can be arranged in an inheritance hierarchy. However, the SQL:1999 standard does not specify how the inheritance is to be implemented. Should a derived table include all the columns (i.e., variables) that it inherits from its base class, or should there be a row in a base class table that is logically linked to a derived class table by a self-referencing column? There are indeed a number of ways in which a DBMS might implement this capability, none of which appears to be preferred over another at this time.

Creating Classes

The complete syntax for declaring a class—for use either as a column data type or a typed table—is as follows:

```
CREATE TYPE [UNDER supertype_name] type name
    [ <external Java type clause> ]
    [ AS representation ]
    [ [ NOT ] INSTANTIABLE ]
    [ NOT ] FINAL
    [ reference-type-specification ]
    [ <reference cast option> ]
    [ cast option ]
    [ method specification list ]
```

In its simplest form, the syntax requires the first, third, and fourth lines just shown. For example, a telephone number could be represented as:

```
CREATE TYPE phone_number
AS (
area_code char (3),
exchange char (3),
site_number char (4),
extension char (5),
number_type varchar (15))
NOT FINAL;
```

The NOT FINAL syntax is required as is. It means that subclasses can be derived from that class. The SQL:1999 standard does not provide for a FINAL option to prevent the derivation of subclasses.

By default, a class is *instantiable*: Objects can be created from it. If you want a class to be abstract—to prevent objects from being created from it—add the NOT INSTANTIABLE clause.

When creating a class for a typed table, the syntax must indicate from where the value for the self-referencing column will come. If you want the DBMS to generate the value, add

```
REF IS SYSTEM GENERATED
```

as the reference type specification clause. If you want an application program to generate the reference values, use

```
REF USING data type
```

where the data type is some type, either SQL standard or user defined, that has already been defined. You can also ask the DBMS to derive the reference value from data stored in the table:

```
REF FROM list of attributes
```

In most cases, you will want to allow the DBMS to generate the references, since this is the only way to guarantee that the reference values will never duplicate.

A SQL implementation that supports classes provides accessor and mutator methods (methods to retrieve and modify data) for each attribute in the class. It also provides a default *constructor*, an initialization method that is executed when an object is created from the class, setting the value of all attributes to NULL. Therefore, you need only add methods that perform additional data manipulation.

Creating and Using Classes for Domains

As mentioned earlier, the online bookstore could use a class as a domain to store customer addresses. First, you would define the address class:

```
CREATE TYPE address
AS (
street CHAR 30,
city CHAR 25,
state CHAR (2),
zip CHAR (5))
NOT FINAL;
```

Then you would create the table using the standard CREATE TABLE syntax:

```
CREATE TABLE customers
    (customer_numb integer,
    customer_first_name varchar (15) NOT NULL,
    customer_last_name varchar (15) NOT NULL,
    customer_address address,
    customer_phone phone_number NOT NULL,
    customer_email varchar (40),
    PRIMARY KEY (customer_number));
```

As you can see, the preceding statement uses both the ADDRESS and PHONE_NUMBER classes as if they were any other column data type.

A database gains two benefits from using classes in this way, even if the classes contain no user-defined methods:

- ♦ The structure of the multivalued attribute is the same throughout the entire database, simplifying both querying and the writing of application programs.
- ♦ The table declarations are shorter and simpler.

Creating Typed Tables

The basic syntax for creating a typed table is

```
CREATE TABLE table name
OF type name
[ subtable clause ]
[ table element list ]
```

Assuming that you wanted to create a typed table to hold the customer data, you would first need a class for the customers:

```
CREATE TYPE customer_type
AS (
customer_numb integer,
customer_first_name varchar (15) NOT NULL,
customer_last_name varchar (15) NOT NULL,
customer_address address,
customer_phone phone_number NOT NULL,
customer_email varchar (40))
NOT FINAL;
```

Notice that this new type is virtually identical to the customer table created earlier. As you will see, however, it is used in a rather different way.

Once the type exists, it can be used to create a typed table:

```
CREATE TABLE customers OF customer_type
(REF IS customer_id SYSTEM GENERATED,
PRIMARY KEY (customer_numb));
```

The source of the self-referencing column must be repeated in the declaration (SYSTEM GENERATED, USER GENERATED, or DERIVED). Notice in the preceding example that the repetition serves to give the reference column a name.

One way to relate typed tables is to explicitly include a column in a table for a reference to another object. For example, if the online bookstore wanted to relate an order to a customer, it could include the reference value of a customer object in an order object. The order type would be created as

```
CREATE TYPE orders
AS (
order_numb integer,
ordering_customer REF (customer),
order_date date,
credit_card_numb varchar,
credit_card_expiration_date char (5),
order_filled boolean)
NOT FINAL
REF IS SYSTEM GENERATED;
```

The declaration of a reference to a customer is indicated by

```
column name REF (reference table name)
```

When you want to insert data into this column, you can retrieve the value from the CUSTOMER table, using the name given to the reference column when the CUSTOMER table was created.

Typed tables can contain foreign key specifications and column constraints, just as ordinary tables. However, if a typed table is a subtable (i.e., it is part of an inheritance hierarchy), it cannot be given a primary key; only the top supertable in an inheritance hierarchy can have a primary key. If the inherited primary key columns aren't sufficient to uniquely identify a subclass object, you can simulate a primary key by using the UNIQUE constraint on any necessary columns.

Note: The specification and implementation of methods requires programming knowledge and is therefore beyond the scope of this book. If you have a programming background and are interested in learning to write SQL:1999 methods, I would again refer you to Jim Melton's book.

SQL:1999 Inheritance

One of the drawbacks to current implementations of object-oriented structures within relational databases is that they don't support inheritance. The SQL:1999 standard, however, does provide for single inheritance.

Suppose that the online bookstore wanted to sell electronic books as well as print books. Because electronic books can be provided in several formats, a class to represent electronic books will need at least one extra attribute beyond those already in the BOOKS table. The simplest way to do this is to create a subclass of BOOKS for the electronic items:

```
CREATE TYPE book
AS (
isbn char (12),
author_name varchar (40),
title varchar (60),
publisher_name varchar (40),
publication_year char (4),
binding char (2),
source_numb integer,
retail price numeric (6,2),
number_on_hand integer)
INSTANTIABLE
NOT FINAL
REF IS SYSTEM GENERATED;
```

```
CREATE TYPE electronic_book UNDER book
AS (
format char (12))
INSTANTIABLE
NOT FINAL;

CREATE TABLE books OF book
(PRIMARY KEY (isbn),
REF IS book_id SYSTEM GENERATED);

CREATE TABLE electronic_books OF electronic_book
UNDER books;
```

As mentioned earlier, a primary key can be declared only for the highest superclass in an inheritance hierarchy (in this case, the BOOKS table).

Querying with Classes

For the most part, you query a table that uses classes in the same way you query any other table. However, the presence of multiple values in a single column means that you need to have some way of referencing the individual attributes within an object.

We're already familiar with using dot notation to separate a schema name from a table name from a column name. It would therefore seem logical to allow an extension of that same syntax to include the names of attributes within complex data types. For example,

```
customers.address.street
```

would refer to the street address attribute within the ADDRESS column of the CUSTOMERS table. Unfortunately, there is a slight chance that the

```
table.column.attribute
```

syntax could be confused with

```
schema.table.column
```

should matches exist within the same database file. SQL:1999 there-fore requires that you use correlation names for tables. To retrieve the customer address in a query, you might use something like

```
SELECT customer_numb, t1.address.street, t1.address.city,
    t1.address.state, t1.address.zip
FROM customers t1
...
```

One interesting twist to SQL's behavior appears when you are re-trieving data from a typed table that is a superclass. Unless you state otherwise, SQL will retrieve data from the table specified in the query and all of its subclasses. Then it will perform a union be-fore returning the final result. For example, if you were to issue the following query to the online bookstore database, you would get re-sults from both the BOOKS and ELECTRONIC_BOOKS tables:

```
SELECT author_name, title, retail_price
FROM books
WHERE publication_year = '2005';
```

If you want to restrict the query to just the supertable, you can in-clude the keyword ONLY in the FROM clause:

```
SELECT author_name, title, retail_price
FROM ONLY (books)
WHERE publication_year = '2005';
```

The final modification to the SELECT statement involves using refer-ence values. When you want to retrieve an attribute value from an object pointed to by a reference value column, you use arrow nota-tion (the same notation used by C++ programmers to invoke meth-ods when working with a pointer to an object):

```
SELECT ordering_customer -> first_name, order_customer -> last-name,
    title, author_name
FROM orders
WHERE order_date = '10/27/04';
```

In the preceding query, the name of the column containing the ref-erence is followed by the arrow (a dash and a greater than symbol) and the name of the column from the referenced table.

Modifying Data for Classes as Domains

When you use a class as a domain, you must create an object of the class to store it in the database using the NEW operator. In an object-oriented programming language such as C++ or Java, NEW sets aside storage for a new object and the class's constructor. It behaves in a similar way under the SQL:1999 standard.

For example, to insert a new customer into the online bookstore database, you might use

```
INSERT INTO customers VALUES (
    57930,
    'Frederik',
    'Michaels',
    NEW address (
        '156 Maple Grove',
        'Alternate Highway',
        'This Town',
        'NY',
        '12345'),
    NEW phone_number (
        '555',
        '123',
        '1234',
        ' ',
        'home'),
    'fredm@isp.net');
```

To update data, you use the standard SQL UPDATE command. Attributes need to be qualified by column names only when there is more than one column in the table that has the same name. For example, if you create a table with more than one phone number column (e.g., HOME_PHONE and WORK_PHONE), then you would need to qualify the phone number attributes with the specific column name using dot notation (e.g., HOME_PHONE.AREA_CODE and WORK_PHONE.AREA_CODE.

Part Six

Appendices

A

The Online Bookstore Database

This appendix contains the design and test data for the online book-store database used for examples throughout this book.

author_name
Twain, Mark
Stevenson, Robert Louis
Scott, Sir Walter
Bronte, Emily
Bronte, Charlotte
Burroughs, Edgar Rice
Ludlum, Robert
Barth, John
McCaffrey, Anne
Rice, Anne
Clavell, James
Butler, Octavia
Cherryh, C. J.
Lee, Tanith
Dumas, Alexandre

Figure A-1: Authors

```
publisher_name

Grosset & Dunlap
World Pub. Co.
Harper
Platt & Munk
P. F. Collier & Son
Methuen
Atheneum
Delacorte
Knopf
Ballantine Books
James R. Osgood and Co.
American Publishing Co.
Scribner
J. W. Lovell Co.
University of Nebraska Press
Dodd, Mead
Clarendon Press
D. Appleton & Co.
Hart Publishing Co.
St. Martin's Press
Columbia University Press
Random House
E. R. Burroughs, Inc.
Tandem
New English Library
Gregg Press
R. Marek Publishers
Dial Press
Putnam
Franklin Library
Deutsch
Anchor Press
Doubleday
Macmillan
Overlook Press
Warner Books
```

Figure A-2: Publishers

isbn	author_name	title	publisher_name	publication_year	binding	source#	retail_price	numb_on_hand
0-123-1233-0	Dumas, Alexandre	Three Musketeers, The	Grosset & Dunlap	1953	hc	1	15.95	10
0-124-5544-X	Dumas, Alexandre	Titans, The	Harper	1957	hc	1	18.95	4
0-126-3367-2	Dumas, Alexandre	Count of Monte Cristo, The	Platt & Munk	1968	hc	1	21.95	12
0-125-3344-1	Dumas, Alexandre	Black Tulip, The	P. F. Collier & Son	1902	hc	1	18.95	3
0-127-3948-2	Dumas, Alexandre	Corsican Brothers, The	Metheun	1970	hc	1	15.95	5
0-128-4321-1	Clavell, James	Tai-Pan	Delacorte	1966	hc	1	22.95	12
0-129-9876-5	Clavell, James	Shogun	Atheneum	1975	hc	1	24.95	12
0-128-3939-X	Clavell, James	Noble House	Delacorte	1981	hc	1	22.95	6
0-128-3939-2	Clavell, James	Gai-Jin	Delacorte	1993	hc	1	25.95	15
0-129-4567-1	McCaffrey, Anne	Dragonsong	Atheneum	1976	hc	2	18.95	12
0-129-4912-0	McCaffrey, Anne	Dragonsinger	Atheneum	1977	hc	2	19.95	13
0-130-2939-4	McCaffrey, Anne	White Dragon, The	Ballantine Books	1978	hc	2	21.95	8
0-124-7989-1	Twain, Mark	Dog's Tale, A	Harper	1904	hc	1	19.95	5
0-133-2956-6	Twain, Mark	Innocents Abroad, The	American Books	1869	hc	3	19.95	6
0-133-5935-2	Twain, Mark	Pudd'nhead Wilson	American Books	1894	hc	3	17.95	8
0-134-3945-7	Stevenson, Robert Louis	Child's Garden of Verses, A	Scribner	1905	hc	4	21.95	12
0-135-2222-2	Stevenson, Robert Louis	Treasure Island	J. W. Lovell Co.	1886	hc	4	24.95	8
0-137-1293-9	Scott, Sir Walter	Rob Roy	D. Appleton & Co.	1898	hc	4	21.95	22
0-136-3956-1	Stevenson, Robert	Kidnapped	Dodd, Mead	1949	hc	2	22.95	12
0-136-3966-7	Stevenson, Robert Louis	Strange Case of Dr. Jekyll and Mr. Hyde	Dodd, Mead	1964	hc	2	23.95	18
0-138-1379-8	Scott, Sir Walter	Ivanhoe	Hart Publishing	1977	hc	1	22.95	6
0-140-3877-0	Scott, Sir Walter	Waverly Novels	University of Nebraska Press	1978	hc	4	27.95	3
0-142-3867-8	Bronte, Emily	Wuthering Heights	St. Martin's Press	1968	hc	3	21.95	8
0-141-9876-X	Bronte, Emily	Complete Poems of Emily Bronte, The	Columbia University Press	1941	hc	4	21.95	5
0-150-5948-9	Bronte, Charlotte	Jane Eyre	Random House	1943	hc	3	19.95	15
0-151-9876-2	Bronte, Charlotte	Vilette	Clarendon Press	1984	hc	3	21.95	15
0-155-2346-5	Burroughs, Edgar Rice	Tarzan and the Forbidden City	Tandem, Inc.	1938	hc	2	18.95	12
0-157-3849-X	Burroughs, Edgar Rice	People That Time Forgot, The	Tandem, Inc.	1975	hc	3	19.95	8
0-158-0493-2	Burroughs, Edgar Rice	Tarzan the Magnificent	New English Library	1974	hc	4	21.95	3
0-158-8374-3	Burroughs, Edgar Rice	Tarzan of the Apes	New English Library	1975	hc	4	21.95	3

Figure A-3: Books

ISBN	Author	Title	Publisher	Year				
0-157-9876-2	Burroughs, Edgar Rice	Out of Time's Abyss	Tandem	1973	hc	3	21.95	4
0-159-5839-3	Burroughs, Edgar Rice	Apache Devil	Gregg Press	1933	hc	2	19.95	4
0-159-3845-3	Burroughs, Edgar Rice	Bandit of Hell's Bend, The	Gregg Press	1925	hc	2	19.95	12
0-159-2948-2	Burroughs, Edgar Rice	War Chief, The	Gregg Press	1927	hc	2	19.95	6
0-150-3765-2	Ludlum, Robert	Aquitaine Progression, The	Random House	1984	hc	3	25.95	6
0-161-0123-9	Ludlum, Robert	Bourne Identity, The	Random House	1980	hc	3	23.95	10
0-150-3949-9	Ludlum, Robert	Parsifal Mosaic, The	Random House	1982	hc	1	24.95	14
0-161-8478-1	Ludlum, Robert	Holcroft Covenant, The	R. Marek Publishers	1978	hc	2	24.95	16
0-160-8325-7	Ludlum, Robert	Chancellor Manuscript, The	Dial Press	1977	hc	3	23.95	18
0-160-3456-7	Ludlum, Robert	Gemini Contenders, The	Dial Press	1976	hc	3	24.95	22
0-162-3948-0	Barth, John	Chimera	Deutsch	1974	hc	3	17.95	6
0-164-4857-2	Barth, John	Sabbatical: A Romance	Putnam	1982	hc	4	24.95	7
0-164-5968-0	Barth, John	Letters: A Novel	Putnam	1979	hc	3	27.95	5
0-166-8394-3	Barth, John	Sot-Weed Factor, The	Franklin Library	1980	hc	3	27.95	6
0-167-1945-1	Barth, John	Floating Opera and The End of the Road, The	Anchor Press	1988	hc	4	24.95	9
0-167-3965-2	Barth, John	Giles Goat-Boy	Anchor Press	1987	hc	3	24.95	8
0-142-0084-2	Butler, Octavia	Clay's Ark	St. Martin's Press	1984	hc	2	21.95	12
0-180-8644-2	Butler, Octavia	Wild Seed	Doubleday	1980	hc	3	19.95	9
0-180-8655-0	Butler, Octavia	Kindred	Doubleday	1979	hc	3	18.95	8
0-180-4567-3	Butler, Octavia	Survivor	Doubleday	1978	hc	3	15.95	8
0-180-4712-X	Butler, Octavia	Mind of My Mind	Doubleday	1977	hc	1	19.95	4
0-180-3948-2	Butler, Octavia	Patternmaster	Doubleday	1976	hc	4	18.95	19
0-185-8776-2	Lee, Tanith	Castle of Dark, The	Macmillan	1978	hc	4	21.95	19
0-180-2945-9	Lee, Tanith	Electric Forest, The	Doubleday	1979	hc	2	19.95	6
0-185-9855-2	Lee, Tanith	Winter Players, The	Macmillan	1977	hc	2	15.95	21
0-142-3988-2	Lee, Tanith	East of Midnight	St. Martin's Press	1978	hc	2	19.95	12
0-180-6464-4	Cherryh, C. J.	Serpent's Reach	Doubleday	1980	hc	3	19.95	15
0-180-7388-1	Cherryh, C. J.	Faded Sun, Kesrith, The	Doubleday	1978	hc	3	21.95	8
0-180-7400-X	Cherryh, C. J.	Faded Sun, Shon'jir, The	Doubleday	1978	hc	3	21.95	9
0-180-4921-4	Cherryh, C. J.	Hunter of Worlds	Doubleday	1977	hc	3	21.95	18
0-180-4977-5	Cherryh, C. J.	Brothers of Earth	Doubleday	1976	hc	3	23.95	12
0-129-9293-2	Lee, Tanith	Black Unicorn	Atheneum	1991	hc	3	21.95	6
0-190-3967-5	Lee, Tanith	Book of the Dead, The	Overlook Press	1991	hc	4	22.95	3
0-190-3956-1	Lee, Tanith	Book of the Beast, The	Overlook Press	1991	hc	4	22.95	8
0-190-2345-2	Lee, Tanith	Book of the Damned, The	Overlook Press	1990	hc	4	21.95	5
0-191-8654-3	Cherryh, C. J.	Hellburner	Warner Books	1992	hc	4	23.95	10
0-191-4934-8	Cherryh, C. J.	Heavy Time	Warner Books	1991	hc	2	23.95	7
0-191-4893-0	Cherryh, C. J.	Rimrunners	Warner Books	1989	hc	2	19.95	2
0-191-4959-2	Cherryh, C. J.	Cyteen	Warner Books	1988	hc	2	18.95	5
0-200-3939-2	Bronte, Emily	My Very Best Work	Harper	1810	hc	2	18.95	6

Figure A-3: (Continued) Books

custo-mer_numb	customer_first_name	customer_last_name	customer_street	customer_city	customer_state	custo-mer_zip	customer_phone	customer_email
1	Jane	Jones	125 W. 88th Blvd.	Anytown	ST	01011	552-555-1234	jane_jones@anywhere.net
2	Tom	Smith	4592 Maple Lane	Some City	SU	12345	555-555-4321	tom_smith@this.net
3	Mary	Johnson	98 Elm St.	Little Town	SM	23456	551-555-4567	mary_johnson@somewhere.net
4	John	Smith	867 Apple Tree Road	Anytown	ST	01011	552-555-9876	john_smith@somewhere.net
5	Emily	Jones	7921 Fir Road	Anytown	SU	12344	555-555-7654	emily_jones@somewhere.net
6	Peter	Johnson	709 Hemlock St.	Some City	SU	12345	555-555-3456	peter_johnson@anywhere.net
7	Edna	Hayes	158 Oak Road	Some City	SM	23458	551-555-1234	edna_hayes@this.net
8	Franklin	Hayes	1990 Pine St.	Little Town	SM	23456	551-555-3939	franklin_hayes@this.net
9	Mary	Collins	RR1 Box 297	Rural Area	SO	45678	553-555-1234	mary_collins@rural.net
10	Peter	Collins	170 Dogwood Lane	Little Town	SM	23456	551-555-8484	peter_collins@anywhere.net
11	Anne	Smith	RR 2 Box 9	Rural Area	SO	45678	553-555-9090	anne_smith@rural.net
12	Peter	Smith	21 Elm St.	Anytown	ST	01011	552-555-3459	peter_smith@somewhere.net
13	Jerry	Brown	9745 Main Street	Anytown	ST	01011	552-555-9876	jerry_brown@somewhere.net
14	Helen	Brown	2588 North Road	Some City	SU	01255	555-552-3939	helen_brown@somewhere.net

Figure A-4: Customers

source_numb	source_name	source_street	source_city	source_state	source_zip	source_phone
1	Ingram	123 West 99th	Philadelphia	PA	19112	555-555-1111
2	Baker and Taylor	99 256th Ave.	Minneapolis	MN	68112	551-555-2222
3	Jostens	19594 Highway 28	Seattle	WA	98333	552-555-3333
4	Brodart	1944 Bayview Blvd.	Los Angeles	CA	96111	553-555-4444

Figure A-5: Sources

order_ numb	customer_ numb	order_date	credit_card_ numb	credit_card exp_date	order_filled
1	1	12/5/04	123 123 123 123	07/01	Y
2	1	7/6/05	123 123 123 123	07/01	N
3	2	11/12/04	234 234 234 234	11/05	Y
4	2	3/18/05	234 234 234 234	11/05	N
5	2	7/6/05	234 234 234 234	11/05	N
6	3	8/15/04	345 345 345 345	01/02	Y
7	3	12/2/04	345 345 345 345	01/02	Y
8	4	11/22/04	456 456 456 456	04/01	Y
9	4	1/6/05	456 456 456 456	04/01	N
10	5	3/12/05	567 567 567 567	05/05	N
11	6	9/19/04	678 678 678 678	12/05	Y
12	6	3/12/05	678 678 678 678	12/05	N
13	6	7/21/05	678 678 678 678	12/05	N
14	7	12/13/04	789 789 789 789	12/02	Y
15	7	1/9/05	789 789 789 789	12/02	N
16	8	10/12/04	890 890 890 890	11/02	Y
17	8	2/22/05	890 890 890 890	11/02	N
18	8	5/13/05	890 890 890 890	11/02	N
19	9	7/15/04	901 901 901 901	12/04	Y
20	10	11/15/04	1000 1000 1000	10/02	Y
21	10	3/4/05	1000 1000 1000	10/02	N
22	11	9/19/04	1100 1100 1100	02/05	Y
23	11	2/21/05	1100 1100 1100	02/05	N
24	11	5/14/05	1100 1100 1100	02/05	N
25	12	10/10/04	1200 1200 1200	09/01	Y
26	1	11/14/97	123 123 123 123	11/97	Y

Figure A-6: Orders

order_numb	isbn	quantity	cost_each	cost_line	shipped
1	0-136-3966-7	1	23.95	23.95	Y
1	0-129-4912-0	1	19.95	19.95	Y
1	0-123-1233-0	1	15.95	15.95	Y
4	0-140-3877-0	1	27.95	27.95	N
3	0-131-4966-9	1	23.95	23.95	Y
3	0-191-4934-8	1	23.95	23.95	Y
3	0-180-4712-X	2	19.95	39.90	Y
3	0-150-5948-9	1	19.95	19.95	Y
2	0-159-3845-3	2	19.95	39.95	N
2	0-131-4912-X	1	24.95	24.95	N
8	0-127-3948-2	1	15.95	15.95	Y
8	0-133-5935-2	1	17.95	17.95	Y
8	0-161-0123-9	1	21.95	21.95	Y
8	0-167-1945-1	1	24.95	24.95	Y
8	0-190-3967-5	1	22.95	22.95	Y
7	0-191-4934-8	1	23.95	23.95	Y
7	0-141-9876-4	5	21.95	109.75	Y
7	0-135-2222-2	5	24.95	124.75	Y
6	0-151-9876-2	1	21.95	21.95	Y
6	0-132-3949-2	2	15.95	31.90	Y
6	0-180-7400-X	1	21.95	21.95	Y
6	0-191-4934-8	1	23.95	23.95	Y
6	0-142-0084-2	1	21.95	21.95	Y
5	0-180-7388-1	1	21.95	21.95	N
5	0-124-2999-9	1	18.95	18.95	N
5	0-140-3877-0	1	27.95	27.95	N
12	0-142-0084-2	1	21.95	21.95	N
12	0-130-2939-4	1	21.95	21.95	N
12	0-157-3849-X	1	19.95	19.95	N
12	0-161-8478-1	1	24.95	24.95	N
11	0-166-8394-3	1	27.95	27.95	Y
11	0-134-3945-7	1	21.95	21.95	Y
11	0-127-3948-2	1	15.95	15.95	Y
10	0-136-3956-1	1	22.95	22.95	Y
10	0-155-2346-5	1	18.95	18.95	Y
10	0-132-3949-2	1	19.95	19.95	N
10	0-142-0084-2	1	21.95	21.95	N
9	0-140-3877-0	1	27.95	27.95	N
9	0-159-5839-3	1	19.95	19.95	N
8	0-180-4712-X	1	19.95	19.95	Y
8	0-131-4912-X	1	24.95	24.95	Y
8	0-130-2939-4	1	21.95	21.95	Y
16	0-157-9876-2	1	21.95	21.95	Y
16	0-134-3945-7	1	21.95	21.95	Y
16	0-132-9876-4	2	19.95	39.90	Y

Figure A-7: Order_lines

16	0-131-3021-2	1	24.95	24.95	Y
16	0-128-4321-1	1	22.95	22.95	Y
15	0-123-1233-0	1	15.95	15.95	N
14	0-130-3941-7	1	24.95	24.95	Y
14	0-159-5839-3	1	19.95	19.95	Y
14	0-157-3849-X	1	19.95	19.95	Y
14	0-137-1293-9	1	21.95	21.95	Y
14	0-131-4912-X	1	24.95	24.95	Y
13	0-142-0084-2	1	21.95	21.95	N
13	0-160-3456-7	1	24.95	24.95	Y
13	0-180-8655-0	1	18.95	18.95	Y
13	0-191-4959-2	1	18.95	18.95	Y
23	0-129-9293-2	1	21.95	21.95	N
23	0-164-5968-0	1	27.95	27.95	N
23	0-166-8394-3	1	27.95	27.95	N
23	0-157-3849-X	1	19.95	19.95	N
23	0-135-2222-2	1	24.95	24.95	N
23	0-128-3939-2	1	25.95	25.95	N
23	0-131-4966-9	1	23.95	23.95	N
22	0-130-2943-2	2	15.95	31.90	Y
21	0-126-3367-2	1	21.95	21.95	N
21	0-131-4966-9	1	23.95	23.95	N
21	0-134-3945-7	1	21.95	21.95	N
20	0-142-3988-2	1	19.95	19.95	Y
20	0-191-8654-3	1	23.95	23.95	Y
19	0-150-3765-2	1	25.95	25.95	Y
19	0-150-5948-9	1	19.95	19.95	Y
19	0-131-3021-2	1	24.95	24.95	Y
19	0-161-8478-1	1	24.95	24.95	Y
19	0-191-4893-0	1	19.95	19.95	Y
18	0-190-3967-5	1	22.95	22.95	N
18	0-180-4567-3	1	15.95	15.95	N
18	0-134-3945-7	1	21.95	21.95	N
18	0-128-4321-1	1	22.95	22.95	N
17	0-131-3021-2	1	24.95	24.95	N
17	0-190-3956-1	1	22.95	22.95	Y
17	0-161-0123-9	1	23.95	23.95	Y
25	0-129-9293-2	1	21.95	21.95	Y
25	0-159-5839-3	1	19.95	19.95	Y
24	0-131-4966-9	1	23.95	23.95	N
24	0-164-5968-0	1	27.95	27.95	N
24	0-191-8654-3	1	23.95	23.95	N

Figure A-7:   (Continued) Order_lines

B

SQLSTATE Return Codes

This appendix contains a numeric listing of the SQLSTATE return codes specified in the SQL-92 standard. SQLSTATE is a five-character string. The leftmost two characters represent the error class; the rightmost three characters identify the subclass. Because SQLSTATE is a string, an embedded SQL program will need to use a substring function if it needs to separate the two parts of the code.

The standard classes and subclasses begin with the digits 0 through 4 and the letters A through H. The digits 5 through 9 and the letters I through Z are reserved for implementation-defined classes and subclasses. (Keep in mind that these codes are strings of characters.)

Class	Class definition	Subclass	Subclass definition
00	Successful completion	000	*none*
01	Warning	000	*none*
		001	Cursor operation conflict
		002	Disconnect error
		003	Null value eliminated in set function
		004	String data, right truncation
		005	Insufficient item descriptor areas
		006	Privilege not revoked
		007	Privilege not granted
		008	Implicit zero-bit padding
		009	Search expression too long for information schema
		00A	Query expression too long for information schema
02	No data	000	*none*
07	Dynamic SQL error	000	*none*
		001	Using clause does not match dynamic parameters
		002	Using clause does not match target specifications
		003	Cursor specification cannot be executed
		004	Using clause required for dynamic parameters

Table B-1: SQLSTATE return codes

Class	Class definition	Subclass	Subclass definition
		005	Prepared statement not a cursor specification
		006	Restricted data type attribute violation
		007	Using clause required for result fields
		008	Invalid descriptor count
		009	Invalid descriptor index
08	Connection exception	000	*none*
		001	SQL client unable to establish SQL connection
		002	Connection name in use
		003	Connection does not exist
		004	SQL server rejected establishment of SQL connection
		006	Connection failure
		007	Transaction resolution unknown
0A	Feature not supported	000	*none*
		001	Multiple server transactions
21	Cardinality violation	000	*none*
22	Data exception	000	*none*
		001	String data, right truncation
		002	Null value, no indicator
		003	Numeric value out of range

Table B-1: (Continued) SQLSTATE return codes

Class	Class definition	Subclass	Subclass definition
		005	Error in assignment
		007	Invalid datetime format
		008	Datetime field overflow
		009	Invalid time zone displacement value
		011	Substring error
		012	Division by zero
		015	Interval field overflow
		018	Invalid character value for cast
		018	Invalid escape character
		021	Character not in repertoire
		022	Indicator overflow
		023	Invalid parameter value
		024	Unterminated C string
		025	Invalid escape sequence
		026	String data, length mismatch
		027	Trim error
23	Integrity contraints validation	000	*none*
24	Invalid cursor state	000	*none*
25	Invalid transaction state	000	*none*
26	Invalid SQL statement name	000	*none*
27	Triggered data change violation	000	*none*

Table B-1: (Continued) SQLSTATE return codes

Class	Class definition	Subclass	Subclass definition
28	Invalid authorization specification	000	*none*
2A	Syntax error or access rule violation in direct SQL statement	000	*none*
2B	Dependent privilege descriptors still exist	000	*none*
2C	Invalid character set name	000	*none*
2D	Invalid transaction termination	000	*none*
2E	Invalid connection name	000	*none*
33	Invalid SQL descriptor name	000	*none*
34	Invalid cursor name	000	*none*
35	Invalid condition number	000	*none*
37	Syntax error or access rule violation in dynamic SQL statement	000	*none*
3C	Ambiguous cursor name	000	*none*
3F	Invalid schema name	000	*none*
40	Transaction rollback	000	*none*
		001	Serialization failure
		002	Integrity constraint violation
		003	Statement completion unknown
42	Syntax error of access rule violation	000	*none*
44	With check option violation	000	*none*

Table B-1: (Continued) SQLSTATE return codes

C

SQL Syntax Summary

This appendix contains a summary of the SQL syntax used throughout this book, arranged alphabetically by command. The notation is as follows:

- ◆ Keywords that must be typed exactly as they appear are in uppercase characters, such as REFERENCES.
- ◆ Parts of commands that are determined by the user appear in italics and name the item that must be supplied, such as table_name.
- ◆ Optional portions of a command are surrounded by brackets ([and]).
- ◆ Portions of commands that form a single clause are grouped within braces ({ and }).
- ◆ Sets of options from which you choose one or more are separated by vertical lines (|).
- ◆ Portions of commands that may be repeated as needed are followed by an ellipsis (…).

Allocate space for a descriptor area for a dynamic SQL statement

```
ALLOCATE DESCRIPTOR descriptor_name
   [ WITH MAX maximum_number_of_parameters ]
```

Change the specifications of a domain

```
ALTER DOMAIN domain_name
   { SET DEFAULT default_value }
   | { DROP DEFAULT }
   | { ADD constraint_definition_clause }
   | { DROP CONSTRAINT constraint_name }
```

Change the specifications of a table

```
ALTER TABLE table_name
   { ADD [COLUMN] column_definition }
   | { ALTER [COLUMN]
      { SET DEFAULT default_value}
      | { DROP DEFAULT } }
      | { DROP [COLUMN] column_name
         RESTRICT | CASCADE }
   | { ADD table_constraint_definition_clause }
   | { DROP CONSTRAINT constraint_name
         RESTRICT | CASCADE }
```

Close an embedded SQL cursor

```
CLOSE cursor_name
```

Commit a transaction, making its changes permanent

```
COMMIT [WORK]
```

Connect to a database, specifying its cluster, catalog, and schema if necessary

```
CONNECT TO { cluster.catalog.schema.database_name
   [ AS connection_name }
   [ USER user_name ] }
      | DEFAULT
```

Create an assertion, a constraint that is not attached to a specific table

```
CREATE ASSERTION assertion_name
    CHECK ( check_predicate )
        [ { INITIALLY DEFERRED } | { INITIALLY IMMEDIATE } ]
        [ DEFERRABLE | { NOT DEFERRABLE } ]
```

Create a domain

```
CREATE DOMAIN domain_name
    [ AS ] data_type
        [ DEFAULT default_value ]
        CHECK ( check_predicate )
[        { INITIALLY DEFERRED } | { INITIALLY IMMEDIATE }]
        [ DEFERRABLE | { NOT DEFERRABLE } ]
```

Create a schema

```
CREATE SCHEMA { schema_name
    | AUTHORIZATION authorization_ID
    | schema_name AUTHORIZATION authorization_ID }
```

> *Note: A CREATE SCHEMA statement may also include CREATE statements for any database elements that are to be part of the schema.*

Create a table

```
CREATE [ [ GLOBAL | LOCAL ] TEMPORARY ] TABLE table_name
    ( { column_name { data_type | domain_name } [column_size]
    [ column_constraint …] } , …
    [ DEFAULT default_value]
    [ table_constraint ], …
    [ ON COMMIT DELETE | PRESERVE ROWS ] )
```

Create a view

```
CREATE VIEW view_name [ (column_list) ]
    AS (complete_SELECT_statement
    [ WITH [ CASCADED | LOCAL ] CHECK OPTION ])
```

Remove a dynamic SQL descriptor area from main memory

```
DEALLOCATE DESCRIPTOR descriptor_name
```

Remove a prepared dynamic SQL statement from main memory

```
DEALLOCATE PREPARE prepared_dynamic_SQL_statement_name
```

Declare a cursor for processing an embedded SQL SELECT that returns multiple rows

```
DECLARE CURSOR cursor_name [ INSENSITIVE ] [ SCROLL ] CURSOR
    FOR { (complete_SELECT_statement)
      [ FOR { READ ONLY | UPDATE [ OF column_name, … ] } ]
  | prepared_dynamic_SQL_statement_name
```

Delete rows from a table

```
DELETE FROM table_name
   [ { WHERE row_selection_predicate }
   | { WHERE CURRENT OF cursor_name } ]
```

Describe the dynamic parameters in a prepared dynamic SQL statement for a descriptor area

```
DESCRIBE [ INPUT | OUTPUT ]
   prepared_dynamic_SQL_statement_name
   USING SQL DESCRIPTOR descriptor_name
```

Disconnect from a database

```
DISCONNECT connection_name | ALL | CURRENT
```

Remove an assertion from a schema

```
DROP ASSERTION assertion_name
```

Remove a domain from a schema

```
DROP DOMAIN domain_name CASCADE | RESTRICT
```

Remove a schema from a catalog

```
DROP SCHEMA schema_name CASCADE | RESTRICT
```

Remove a table from a schema

```
DROP TABLE table_name CASCADE | RESTRICT
```

Remove a view from a schema

```
DROP VIEW view_name CASCADE | RESTRICT
```

Execute a prepared dynamic SQL statement

```
EXECUTE [ GLOBAL | LOCAL ] prepared_dynamic_SQL_statement
    [ INTO { parameter, … }
    | { SQL DESCRIPTOR [ GLOBAL | LOCAL ] descriptor_name } ]
    [ USING { parameter, … }
    | { SQL DESCRIPTOR [ GLOBAL | LOCAL ] descriptor_name } ]
```

Execute a dynamic SQL statement immediately, without a separate preparation step

```
EXECUTE IMMEDIATE SQL_statement_text_literal_or_variable
```

Retrieve a row from an open cursor's result table

```
FETCH [ [ NEXT | PRIOR | FIRST | LAST |
    { ABSOLUTE | RELATIVE row_number } ]
    FROM cursor_name
    INTO host_language_variable, …
```

Retrieve information from a dynamic SQL descriptor area

```
GET DESCRIPTOR descriptor_name
        { host_language_variable = COUNT }
    | { VALUE descriptor_number
        { host_language_variable = descriptor_field } , …
```

> *Note: Descriptor fields most commonly used are TYPE (data type of parameter), DATA (actual value of parameter), and IN-DICATOR (value of indicator variable associated with parameter).*

Grant access rights to other users

```
GRANT { ALL PRIVILEGES }
    | SELECT
    | DELETE
    | INSERT [ (column_name, …) ]
    | UPDATE [ (column_name, …) ]
    | REFERENCES [ (column_name, …) ]
    | USAGE
        ON [ TABLE ] table_name
    | DOMAIN domain_name
        TO { user_ID, … } | PUBLIC
    [ WITH GRANT OPTION ]
```

Insert new rows into a table

```
INSERT INTO table_name
    [ (column_name, …) }
    complete_SELECT_statement | (value1, value2, …)
    | DEFAULT VALUES
```

Open a cursor, executing the SELECT and positioning the cursor at the first row

```
OPEN cursor_name
    [ { USING host_language_variable_or_literal, … }
    | { SQL DESCRIPTOR descriptor_name } ]
```

Prepare a dynamic SQL statement for execution

```
PREPARE [ GLOBAL | LOCAL ]
    prepared_dynamic_SQL_statement_name
    FROM SQL_statement_text_literal_or_variable
```

Remove access rights from a user

```
REVOKE [ GRANT OPTION FOR ]
    { { ALL PRIVILEGES }
    | SELECT | DELETE
    | INSERT
    | UPDATE
    | REFERENCES
    | USAGE }
    ON [ TABLE ] table_name
    | DOMAIN domain_name
    FROM PUBLIC | { user_ID. … }
    CASCADE | RESTRICT
```

Roll back a transaction

```
ROLLBACK [ WORK ]
```

Retrieve rows from a table

```
SELECT [ DISTINCT ]
    { { summary_function, … }
    | { data_manipulation_expression, … }
    | { column_name, … } }
FROM
    { { table_name [ AS ] [ correlation_name ]}
    | complete_SELECT_statement
| joined_tables }
    [ WHERE row_selection_predicate ]
[ GROUP BY column_name, …
    [ HAVING group_selection_predicate ] ]
[ UNION | INTERSECT | EXCEPT
    [ CORRESPONDING BY (column_name, … ) ]
    complete_SELECT_statement ]
[ ORDER BY (column_name [ ASC | DESC ], … ) ]
```

Choose the current schema catalog

```
SET CATALOG catalog_name
```

Choose an active connection
```
SET CONNECTION connection_name | DEFAULT
```

Choose when constraints are checked

```
SET CONSTRAINTS MODE { constraint_name, … | ALL }
    DEFERRED | IMMEDIATE
```

Store values in a SQL descriptor area

```
SET DESCRIPTOR [ GLOBAL | LOCAL ] descriptor_name
        { COUNT = integer_value }
    | { VALUE descriptor_number
          { descriptor_field = value, …}, … }
```

Choose the current schema

```
SET SCHEMA schema_name
```

Choose the characteristics of the next transaction

```
SET TRANSACTION
    { ISOLATION LEVEL
        { READ UNCOMMITTED
        | READ COMMITTED
        | REPEATABLE READ
        | SERIALIZABLE } }
    | { READ ONLY | READ WRITE }
```

Change data in a table

```
UPDATE table_name
    SET { column_name = {value
                        | NULL
                        | DEFAULT }, … }
      [ { WHERE row_selection_predicate }
    | { WHERE CURRENT OF cursor_name } ]
```

D

SQL:1999 Core Features

The SQL characteristics listed in this appendix are required for Core compliance to the SQL:1999 standard. Subfeatures are indented beneath the more inclusive feature. Note that the feature IDs are not necessarily contiguous; gaps in numbering occur in several places. These IDs were used when the standard was being developed and at this time have no meaning other than as identifiers.

ID	Description
B011	Embedded Ada
B012	Embedded C
B013	Embedded COBOL
B014	Embedded Fortran
B015	Embedded MUMPS

ID		Description
B016		Embedded Pascal
B017		Embedded PL/1[a]
E011		Numeric data types
	E011-01	INTEGER and SMALLINT data types (and all variations thereof)
	E011-02	REAL, DOUBLE PRECISION, and FLOAT data types
	E011-03	DECIMAL and NUMERIC data types
	E011-04	Arithmetic operators
	E011-05	Numeric comparison
	E011-06	Implicit casting among the data types
E021		Character data types
	E021-01	CHARACTER data type (and all variations thereof)
	E021-02	CHARACTER VARYING data type (and all variations thereof)
	E021-03	Character literals
	E021-04	CHARATER_LENGTH function
	E021-07	OCTET_LENGTH function
	E021-08	UPPER and LOWER functions
	E021-09	TRIM function
	E021-10	Implicit casting among the character data types
	E021-11	POSITION function
	E021-12	Character comparison
E031		Identifiers
	E031-01	Delimited identifiers

ID		Description
	E031-02	Lowercase identifiers
	E031-03	Trailing underscore
E051		Basic query specification
	E051-01	SELECT DISTINCT
	E051-02	GROUP BY clause
	E051-04	GROUP BY can contain columns not in SELECT list
	E051-05	SELECT list items can be renamed
	E051-06	HAVING clause
	E051-07	Qualified * in SELECT list
	E051-08	Correlation names in the FROM clause
	E051-09	Rename columns in the FROM clause
E061		Basic predicates and search conditions
	E061-01	Comparison predicate
	E061-02	BETWEEN predicate
	E061-03	IN predicate with list of values
	E061-04	LIKE predicate
	E061-05	LIKE predicate: ESCAPE clause
	E061-06	NULL predicate
	E061-07	Quantified comparison predicate
	E061-08	EXISTS predicate
	E061-09	Subqueries in comparison predicate
	E061-11	Subqueries in IN predicate
	E061-12	Subqueries in quantified comparison predicate

ID		Description
	E061-13	Correlated subqueries
	E061-14	Search condition
E071		Basic query expressions
	E071-01	`UNION DISTINCT` query operator
	E071-02	`UNION ALL` table operator
	E071-03	`EXCEPT DISTINCT` table operator
	E071-05	Columns combined via table operators need not have exactly the same data type. For example, `CHAR` and `CHAR VAR` are considered union compatible.
	E071-06	Table operators in subqueries
E081		Basic privileges
	E081-01	`SELECT` privilege
	E081-02	`DELETE` privilege
	E081-03	`INSERT` privilege at the table level
	E081-04	`UPDATE` privilege at the table level
	E081-05	`UPDATE` privilege at the column level
	E081-06	`REFERENCES` privilege at the table level
	E081-07	`REFERENCES` privilege at the column level
	E081-08	`WITH GRANT OPTION`
E091		Set functions
	E091-01	`AVG`
	E091-02	`COUNT`
	E091-03	`MAX`

ID		Description
	E091-04	MIN
	E091-05	SUM
	E091-06	ALL quantifier
	E091-07	DISTINCT quantifier
E101		Basic data manipulation
	E101-01	INSERT statement
	E101-03	Searched UPDATE statement
	E101-04	Searched DELETE statement
E111		Single-row SELECT statement
E121		Basic cursor support
	E121-01	DECLARE CURSOR
	E121-02	ORDER BY columns need not be in SELECT list
	E121-03	Value expressions in ORDER BY clause
	E121-04	OPEN statement
	E121-06	Positioned UPDATE statement
	E121-07	Positioned DELETE statement
	E121-08	CLOSE statement
	E121-10	FETCH statement: implicit NEXT
	E121-17	WITH HOLD cursors
E131		Null value support
E141		Basic integrity constraints
	E141-01	NOT NULL constraints
	E141-02	UNIQUE constraints of NOT null columns

ID		Description
	E141-03	PRIMARY KEY constraints
	E141-04	Basic FOREIGN KEY constraints with NO ACTION as the default for both referential updates and deletes
	E141-06	CHECK constraints
	E141-07	Column defaults
	E141-08	NOT NULL inferred for PRIMARY KEY
	E141-10	Names in a foreign key can be specified in any order
E151		Transaction support
	E151-01	COMMIT statement
	E151-02	ROLLBACK statement
E152		Basic SET TRANSACTION statement
	E152-01	SET TRANSACTION statement: ISOLATION LEVEL SERIALIZABLE clause
	E152-02	SET TRANSACTION statement: READ ONLY and READ WRITE clauses
E153		Updatable queries with subqueries
E161		SQL comments using leading double minus
E171		SQLSTATE support
E182		Module language
F021		Basic information schema
	F021-01	COLUMNS view
	F021-02	TABLES view
	F021-03	VIEWS view

ID		Description
	F021-04	TABLE_CONSTRAINTS view
	F021-05	REFERENTIAL_CONSTRAINTS view
	F021-06	CHECK_CONSTRAINTS view
F031		Basic schema manipulation
	F031-01	CREATE TABLE statement to create persistent base tables
	F031-02	CREATE VIEW statement
	F031-03	GRANT statement
	F031-04	ALTER TABLE statement: ADD COLUMN clause
	F031-13	DROP TABLE statement: RESTRICT clause
	F031-16	DROP VIEW statement: RESTRICT clause
	F031-19	REVOKE statement: RESTRICT clause
F041		Basic joined table
	F041-01	INNER JOIN (but not necessarily the INNER keyword)
	F041-02	INNER keyword
	F041-03	LEFT OUTER JOIN
	F041-04	RIGHT OUTER JOIN
	F041-05	Nested outer joins
	F041-07	The inner table in a left or right outer join can also be used in an inner join
	F041-08	Support for joins based on all comparison operators
F051		Basic date and time
	F051-01	DATE data type (including support of DATE literal)

ID		Description
	F051-02	TIME data type (including support of TIME literal) with fractional seconds prescision of at least 0
	F051-03	TIMESTAMP data type (including support of TIMESTAMP literal) with fractional seconds precision of at least 0 and 6
	F051-04	Comparison predicate for DATE, TIME, and TIMESTAMP data types
	F051-05	Explicit CAST between datetime types and character types
	F051-06	CURRENT_DATE
	F051-07	LOCALTIME
	F051-08	LOCALTIMESTAMP
F081		UNION and EXCEPT in views
F131		Grouped operations
	F131-01	WHERE, GROUP BY, and HAVING clauses supported in queries with grouped views
	F131-02	Multiple tables supported in queries with grouped views
	F131-03	Set functions supported in queries with grouped views
	F131-04	Subqueries with GROUP BY and HAVING clauses and grouped views
	F131-05	Single-row SELECT with GROUP BY and HAVING clauses and grouped views
F181		Multiple module support
F201		CAST function
F221		Explicit defaults

ID		Description
F261		CASE expression
	F261-01	Simple `CASE`
	F261-02	Search `CASE`
	F261-03	`NULLIF`
	F261-04	`COALESCE`
F311		Schema definition statement
	F311-01	`CREATE SCHEMA`
	F311-02	`CREATE TABLE` for persistent base tables
	F311-03	`CREATE VIEW`
	F311-04	`CREATE VIEW: WITH CHECK OPTION`
	F311-05	`GRANT` statement
F471		Scalar subquery values
F481		Expanded `NULL` predicate
F501		Features and conformance views
	F501-01	`SQL_FEATURES` view
	F501-02	`SQL_SIZING` view
	F501-03	`SQL_LANGUAGES` view
F812		Basic flagging
S011		Distinct data types
	S011-01	`USER_DEFINED_TYPES` view
T321		Basic SQL-invoked routines
	T321-01	User-defined functions with no overloading

ID	Description
T321-02	User-defined stored procedures with no overloading
T321-03	Function invocation
T321-04	CALL statement
T321-05	RETURN statement
T321-06	ROUTINES view
T321-07	PARAMETERS view

a. It is interesting to note that the languages required for Core compliance don't include the two most popular application programming languages at this time—C++ and Java. Given the selection of languages for which embedded SQL support is required, it seems to me that it would be impossible for any DBMS to be completely Core SQL:1999 compliant.

Glossary

Assertion: A constraint that is not attached to a table but is instead a distinct database object. It can therefore be used to enforce rules that apply to multiple tables or to verify that tables are not empty.

Attribute: A column in a relation.

Base table: A relation whose contents are physically and permanently stored in a database.

Before-image file: A file that contains images of every action taken by a transaction and is used to undo actions when a transaction is rolled back.

Case sensitive: Aware of the difference between upper- and lower-case characters.

Catalog: A group of schemas, usually composed of all schemas handled by a single DBMS.

Cluster: A group of catalogs. Catalog definition is specific to a given DBMS.

Commit (a transaction): End a transaction, making any changes that it made permanent. A committed transaction is never rolled back.

Concatenated primary key: A primary key made up of the combination of two or more columns.

Concurrent execution: The simultaneous handling of multiple transactions by a single database.

Connect (to a database): Establish a user session with a database.

Constraint (on a relation): A rule to which data stored in a relation must adhere.

Correlated subquery: A subquery that a DBMS cannot process completely before turning to the outer query. The DBMS must execute the subquery repeatedly for every row in the outer query.

Correlation name: An alias for a table used in a SQL query.

Cursor: A pointer to a row in the result table generated when an embedded SQL SELECT returns multiple rows.

Data dictionary: In the broadest sense, documentation of the logical structure of a database. In relational database terms, a collection of tables that store data about the database.

Data dictionary driven: A property of a relational database that all access to data begins with a check of the data dictionary to determine whether the requested database elements are present in the database and whether the user has the necessary access rights to perform the requested action.

Difference: A relational algebra operation that returns the rows found in one table but not another.

Dirty read: The problem that arises when a transaction reads the same data more than once, including data modified by concurrent transactions that are later rolled back.

Disconnect: Terminate a user session with a database.

Domain: An expression of the values from which the values stored in a column of a relation are taken.

Drop: Delete an element of database structure from a database.

Dynamic embedded SQL: Embedded SQL in which the entire SQL statement cannot be assembled prior to running the program. The SQL statement is therefore completed and processed during the program run.

Dynamic parameter: A value given to an embedded SQL statement at runtime rather than when the program in which the statement is contained is compiled.

Embedded SQL: SQL statements placed within a host language, allowing SQL to be executed by application programs.

Equi-join: A join that combines two tables based on matching data in rows in the two tables.

Escape character: A character, usually \, that removes the special meaning of whatever follows it in a literal string.

Exclusive lock: A lock on a database element that prevents other transactions from updating or viewing the database element while the lock is held.

Foreign key: A column or combination of columns that is the same as the primary key of another relation.

Grant: Give access rights to database elements to users. The user that creates a database element has all rights to that element. Other users have no access unless they are specifically granted access rights.

Granularity (of a lock): The size of database element on which a lock is placed (usually, a table or a row within a table).

Grouping query: A query that groups rows of data based on common values in one or more columns and that optionally computes summary values from each group.

Host language: A programming language in which SQL statements are embedded.

Indeterminate cursor: A cursor in which the effects of updates by the same transaction on the result table are left up to each individual DBMS.

Index: A data structure that provides a fast-access path to one or more columns in a relation.

Indicator variable: A variable that accompanies an embedded SQL dynamic parameter to indicate the presence of nulls in the parameter.

Inner join: A join that excludes rows for which there is no match between the tables being joined.

Input parameter: A value sent by an embedded SQL statement to the DBMS.

Insensitive cursor: A cursor for which the contents of the result table to which it points are fixed.

Instance (of a relation): A relation containing one or more rows of data.

Interactive SQL: Individual SQL statements entered from the keyboard and processed immediately.

Interleaved execution: A sequence of executing concurrent transactions in which the actions of two or more transactions alternate.

Intersect: A relational algebra operation that returns all rows common to two tables.

Isolation level: The degree to which a transaction can view data modified by other transactions running concurrently.

Join: A relational algebra operation that combines two tables by making new rows that are combinations of one row from each of the two source tables.

Locking: The processing of giving a transaction exclusive rights to view and/or update a database element to prevent problems that arise with interleaved transaction execution.

Lost update: An error condition that occurs when the interleaved execution of a transaction wipes out an update of another transaction.

Natural equi-join: An equi-join.

Nonprocedural: A process that specifies "what" but not "how," leaving the manner in which the result is obtained up to the DBMS.

Nonrepeatable read: The difference in result tables that occurs when a nonserialized transaction reads the same data twice and retrieves different values but the same rows as the result of the actions of other interleaved transactions.

Null: A value, distinct from 0 or a blank, that means "unknown."

Outer join: A join that preserves all rows from both source tables. Where a new row cannot be formed by combining rows, the outer join places nulls in empty columns.

Output parameter: A value returned by an embedded SQL statement to the host language program.

Phantom: The difference in result tables that occurs when a nonserialized transaction reads the same data twice and different rows are retrieved as a result of the actions of other interleaved transactions.

Precedence: The order in which a DBMS evaluates operators in a predicate when multiple operators are present.

Precision: In a floating-point number, the number of digits to the right of the decimal point.

Precompiler: A program processor that examines a source code file for SQL statements and translates them into calls to routines in external program libraries. The result is another source code file that can be compiled by a normal programming language compiler.

Predicate: A logical expression used to qualify the rows that are affected by a data manipulation request.

Primary key: One or more columns whose values uniquely identify every row in a relation.

Procedural: A process that is expressed in a step-by-step manner. It specifies "how" as well as "what."

Product: A relational algebra operation that forms all possible combinations of rows from two source tables.

Project: A relational algebra operation that takes a vertical subset of a table by extracting specific columns.

Query optimizer: A part of a DBMS that examines a nonprocedural data manipulation request and makes a determination of the most efficient way to process that request.

Read lock: A lock on a database element that prevents other transactions from updating the database element while the lock is held.

Referential integrity: A constraint on a relation that states that every nonnull foreign key must reference an existing primary key.

Relation: The definition of the structure of a two-dimensional table with columns and rows.

Relational algebra: A set of procedural operations used to manipulate relations.

Relational calculus: A set of nonprocedural operations used to manipulate relations.

Restrict: A relational algebra operation that takes a horizontal subset of the rows in a table, usually choosing the rows that meet the logical criteria specified in a predicate.

Revoke: Remove previously granted access rights from a user.

Roll back (a transaction): End a transaction, undoing any changes made by the transaction and restoring the database to the state it was in before the transaction began.

Schema: The overall logical design of a database.

Scope (of a temporary table): The visibility of a temporary table. Local temporary tables can be seen only by the program module that created them. Global temporary tables can be seen by the entire database session.

Scrollable cursor: A cursor that can move to the first, last, or prior row in a table rather than just to the next row.

Serial execution: A sequence of executing concurrent transactions in which one transaction runs from start to finish before a second transaction begins.

Serializable: A property of interleaved transaction execution such that the result of the interleaved execution is the same as the result of serial execution.

Session: A block of time during which a user interacts with a database.

Shared lock: A lock on a database element that prevents other transactions from updating the database element while the lock is held.

Static embedded SQL: Embedded SQL in which the entire SQL statement can be specified when the program is written, allowing the statement to be precompiled before the program is executed.

Subquery: A complete SELECT statement that is part of another SELECT.

Subselect: A subquery.

System tables: The tables that make up the data dictionary in a relational database.

Temporary table: A relation whose contents are not stored in the database but that exists only during the database session in which it was created.

Three-valued logic: A system of logic in which logical expressions can be evaluated to true, false, or maybe. It is the result of the presence of nulls in relations.

Transaction: A unit of work presented to a database. The transaction may be committed, in which case any changes it made to the database are permanent, or it may be rolled back, in which case any changes it made to the database are rolled back.

Tuple: A row in a relation.

Two-phase locking: A locking scheme in which a transaction is given a shared lock on a database element when it retrieves a value. The shared lock is upgraded to an exclusive lock when the transaction attempts to modify the value.

Uncorrelated subquery: A subquery that a DBMS can process completely before processing the query in which the subquery is contained.

Union: A relational algebra operation that combines two tables by merging their rows into the same structure.

Union compatible: A property of two tables that all columns in both tables are drawn from the same logical domains.

Updatability: A property of a view that indicates whether it can be used to perform updates that can then be propagated to the base table from which it was derived.

View: A stored SQL query from which a virtual table is created for use each time the name of the view is used.

Virtual table: A table that exists only in main memory. It may be created by the end user as a temporary table or it may be created by a DBMS to hold the results of a query.

Wait state: A hold placed by a DBMS on the execution of a transaction because the transaction is unable to obtain a needed lock on a database element, usually because the element is locked by another transaction. The transaction must wait until the lock can be placed.

Write lock: A lock on a database element that prevents other transactions from updating or viewing the database element while the lock is held.

Index

LIMITED WARRANTY AND DISCLAIMER OF LIABILITY